Naked Angels

NAKED ANGELS

*The Lives and Literature
of the Beat Generation*

by John Tytell

Grove Press, Inc./New York

for ten years of love,
to MELLON

Portions of "The Broken Circuit," copyright ©1973 by John Tytell, were published in a somewhat different form in *The American Scholar.*

First Evergreen Edition 1986
First Printing 1986
ISBN: 0-394-62179-4
Library of Congress Catalog Card Number: 86-45400

Library of Congress Cataloging-in-Publishing Data
Tytell, John
  Naked Angels.
  Bibliography: p.
  Includes index.
  1. Burroughs, William S., 1914-   2. Ginsberg, Allen, 1926-   3. Kerouac, John, 1922-1969.
4. Bohemianism-United States.   I. Title.
PS228.B6T9   813.5'409   86-45400
ISBN 0-394-62179-4 (pbk.)

Printed in the United States of America

Grove Press, Inc., 196 West Houston Street, New York, N.Y. 10014

5 4 3 2 1

Contents

Photographs following page 108

The Broken Circuit

PART I

Society everywhere is in conspiracy against the manhood of everyone of its members.

—Ralph Waldo Emerson
"Self-Reliance"

JACK KEROUAC, ALLEN GINSBERG, WILLIAM BURROUGHS, and a group of other writers, artists, and mavericks of inspiration like Neal Cassady, formed a "movement" which began near the end of the Second World War, found its voice during the fifties, and became especially influential in the sixties. Though the movement lacked any shared platform such as the Imagist or Surrealist manifestoes, it cohered as a literary group. While the work of one informed the approach and style of another—in the way that Kerouac's prose line and aesthetic of spontaneity affected Ginsberg's poetic—the mutuality among these men developed more as a result of a mythic outlook on their own lives and interactions.

In 1952, Jack Kerouac listed the chief members of the movement in a letter to Ginsberg, explaining that the crucial motivation for their union was the ability to honestly confess each other their deepest feelings. Such open revelation of private matters contradicted the spirit of the age, but led to aesthetic and intellectual discoveries. The Beat movement was a crystallization of a sweeping discontent with American "virtues" of progress and power. What began with an exploration of the bowels and entrails of the city—criminality, drugs, mental hospitals—evolved into an expression of the visionary sensibility. The romantic militancy of the Beats found its roots in American transcendentalism. Their spiritual ancestors were men like Thoreau with his aggressive idealism, his essentially conservative distrust of machines and industry, his desire to return to the origins of man's relations to the land; or Melville, with his adventurous tolerance of different tribal codes; or Whitman, optimistically proclaiming with egalitarian gusto the raw newness and velocity of self-renewing change in America while joyously admiring the potential of the common man.

Beginning in despair, the Beat vision was elevated through the shocks of experience to a realization of what was most perilous about American life. One of the images that best captures the motivating energy of this search is the nakedness that was expressed aesthetically in Jack Kerouac's idea of the writer committing himself irrevocably to the original impulses of his imagination, in Ginsberg's relentless self-exposure in a poem like "Kaddish," in Burroughs' refusal in *Naked Lunch* to disguise the demonic aspects of his addiction. But for the Beats nakedness did not exist simply as an aesthetic standard, it was to become a symbolic public and private stance, making art and action inseparable: thus Allen Ginsberg disrobed at poetry readings, and Kerouac once wrote that he wanted to be like the medieval Tibetan scholar-monk Milarepa who lived naked in caves—and as a supreme final statement Neal Cassady was found naked and dead near a railroad track in Mexico. This emphasis on baring the body and exposing the soul was an intuitive reaction to a betrayal the Beats felt because of mass acceptance of demeaning changes in the American idea of self-determination. Nakedness signified rebirth, the recovery of identity.

The Beats saw themselves as outcasts, exiles within a hostile culture, freaky progenitors of new attitudes toward sanity and ethics, rejected artists writing anonymously for themselves. Seeking illumination and a transvaluation of values, they deified Rimbaud who had exclaimed in *Une Saison en Enfer:* "Moi! moi qui me suis dit mage ou ange, dispense de toute morale . . . " Messengers of imminent apocalypse, the Beats believed that they were the angels of holocaust—like Kerouac's portrayal of his friend Neal Cassady as a "burning, frightful, shuddering angel, palpitating across the road." The angel image reappears in Kerouac's writing as it does so frequently in the work of all the Beats. In one of Gregory Corso's letters to Allen Ginsberg, there is a drawing of an angelic Virgin cradling William Burroughs in her arms while Ginsberg and Kerouac hover like desolate cherubim—the picture a brooding reminder of the messianic and reformist impulses of a movement that was steeped in sorrow while yearning for beatitude.

Foundlings of the fifties, the Beats were like a slowly burning fuse in a silent vacuum. The postwar era was a time of extraordinary insecurity, of profound powerlessness as far as individual effort was concerned, when personal responsibility was being abdicated in favor of corporate largeness, when the catchwords were coordination and adjustment, as if we had defeated Germany only to become "good Germans" ourselves. The nuclear blasts in Japan had created new sources of terror, and the ideology of technology became paramount; science was seen as capable of totally dominating man and his environment. And the prospects of total annihilation through nuclear explosion, of mass conditioning through the media, only increased the awesome respect for scientific powers.

Few periods in our history have presented as much of an ordeal for artists and intellectuals. In *The Prisoner of Sex*, Norman Mailer has wondered how he survived those years without losing his mind. What Allen Ginsberg has called the Syndrome of Shutdown began in the late forties: the move toward a closed society where all decisions would be secret; the bureaucratic disease that Hannah Arendt has characterized as rule by Nobody where ultimately, as in Watergate, there is no final authority or responsibility; the paralysis caused by the use of technological devices that invade privacy; the increasing power of the Pentagon with its military bases designed to contain a new enemy supposedly (and suddenly) more threatening than the Nazis. The hysteria of rabid anticommunism was far more damaging, as Thomas Mann told the House Un-American Activities Committee, than any native communism; the patriotic blood-boiling became a convenient veil assuring a continued blindness to domestic social conditions that desperately needed attention. An internal freeze gripped America, an irrational hatred that created intense fear and repression, and since any repression feeds on oppression as its necessary rationalization, the red witch-hunts, the censorship of artists and filmmakers, the regimentation of the average man, began with unparalleled momentum and design. The contamination caused by this psychic and moral rigidity has been discussed by Allen Ginsberg in his *Paris Review* interview:

> The Cold War is the imposition of a vast mental barrier on everybody, a vast anti-natural psyche. A hardening, a shutting off of the perception of desire and tenderness which everybody *knows* . . . [creating] a self-consciousness which is a substitute for communication with the outside. This consciousness pushed back into the self and thinking of how it will hold its face and eyes and hands in order to make a mask to hide the flow that is going on. Which it's aware of, which everybody is aware of really! So let's say shyness. Fear. Fear of total feeling, really, total being is what it is.

With the exception of the Civil War period, never before had the sense of hopefulness usually associated with the American experience been so damaged.

In the late forties and early fifties, the axioms of the upright in America were belief in God, family, and the manifestly benevolent international ambitions of the nation. Americans still conceived of themselves as innocent democratic warriors, protectors of a holy chalice that contained a magic elixir of progress in technology, cleanliness, and order. The middle-class American had become Kipling's white man burdened by a tank that he kept confusing with a tractor. Yet the national consciousness and the face of the land had been inevitably altered by the war effort. Fascism, as Susan Sontag has observed, was not a monstrously sudden growth excised by the war, it is the normal condition of the modern industrial state. As Herbert Marcuse demonstrated in *One Dimensional Man*, productive apparatus tends to become totalitarian to the extent that it determines individual needs and aspirations, and results in a "comfortable, smooth, and reasonable democratic unfreedom." The social goal becomes efficiency; the toll, privacy and freedom. As the war machine of industry became insatiable, the inevitable result was the convenient fiction of the Cold War and the cost of perpetual rearmament. Henry Miller realized the ensuing paradox:

> Never has there been a world so avid for security, and never has life been more insecure. To protect ourselves, we invent the most fantastic instruments of destruction, which prove to be boomerangs. No one seems to believe in the power of love, the only dependable power. No one believes in his neighbor, or in himself, let alone a supreme being. Fear, envy, suspicion are rampant everywhere.

The "war on communism" created an atmosphere of coercion and conspiracy. The nation's legacy of individuality had been changed to a more standardized expectation of what constituted "Americanism." Traditional tolerance of ideological difference had been subverted to a passion for organization and political similitude. It was a bitter and ironic distortion of our history: the character of the country had always been as various as its topography, and the lack of homogeneity meant that Americans had to work to develop a national consciousness resilient enough to embrace the aspirations of multitudes. Suddenly, there was an alleged contagion of treasonous spies, a mania for internal security, a repression that fostered anxiety and discouraged dissent. Some vital ingredient of the "American Dream" was warped and out of control.

What was the effect on a generation of such a politics of infidelity, such a time of false securities and mistrust? C. Wright Mills saw the emergence of a "mass society" composed of isolated units, formed by media, encouraged only to consume, never to decide. Other social critics noted the development of a mentality that refused to question authority. *Death of a Salesman* dramatized, in the passive victimization of Willy Loman, the immolation of the American soul in the impersonal abstractions of money for its own sake. Even worse, the psychology of the McCarthy era made truth itself suspect; it became something manipulated by "credible" authorities. As Yale chaplain William Sloan Coffin, Jr. observed, students in the fifties agreed their way through life. Education was a means of earning an income, no longer a way of stimulating critical inquiry or deepening sensibility. Novelist Philip Roth has admitted that he belonged to the most patriotic generation of American schoolchildren, the one most willingly and easily propagandized. For those who had reached their majority during the war, the indignity was greater. William Styron claimed that his generation was "not only not intact, it had been cut to pieces." While the end of the war brought with it an enormous sense of relief and a dull weariness, Styron wrote:

> We were traumatized not only by what we had been through and by the almost unimaginable presence of the bomb, but by the realization that the entire mess was not finished after all: there was now the Cold War to face, and its clammy presence oozed into our nights and days.

The cosmos seemed unhinged to Styron's generation as it confronted the "ruthless power and the loony fanaticism of the military mind."

The Beats were part of this beseiged generation. At first, political consciousness was dormant: politics, Blake had maintained long before, was an objectification of "mental war." The violence, tyranny, and corruption of world leaders, as the Buddhist notion of karma explained, was only the realization of every individual's carelessness, deliberate ignorance, and uninvolvement. But young men like Kerouac were sensitively aware of the disappearing landmarks of regional diversity, the end of that special adaptability that had for so long invigorated the American character. The Beats could still nostalgically recall the time when one could bargain for an article purchased in a general store, when one bought land rather than paper shares in huge corporations, when radio and the airplane represented occasions of tremendous excitement. Kerouac's friend, novelist John Clellon Holmes, reflecting on the late thirties and early forties, saw that it was then—both because of the Depression and the anticipations of the war—that a great fissure had occurred in the American psyche, an uprooting of family relationships, of the sense of place and community that was compounded by a fear of imminent devastation. It was a shared premonition that the entire society was going to be changed in a major way, and that young men were to be particularly sacrificed. In a dream that he recorded, Kerouac noted that somewhere during the war he lost his way and took the wrong path. Holmes offered the image of a broken circuit to suggest the lack of connection to the immediate present felt by the members of his generation. It was as dangerous a condition as a hot electrical wire discharging energy randomly into the universe without a proper destination. The philosophical cause was not so much the horrible fact of the war, as it had been for the Lost Generation of the twenties, but the emergence of the new postwar values that accepted man as the victim of circumstances, and no longer granted him the agency of his own destiny: the illusion of free will, the buoyantly igniting spark in the American character, had been suddenly extinguished.

Simultaneously in Europe, a similar merger of bitterness and idealism resulted in Existentialism. Like the Beats, the Existentialists began by negation, refusing to accept the social given. While the Beats agreed with the Existentialist argument that man defines himself through his actions, they also shared a Spenglerian expectation of the total breakdown of Western culture. The Beats danced to the music of the absurdity they saw around them. When Ginsberg's friend Carl Solomon sent him an unsigned postcard reading simply: "VANISHED!" it was a token of an irrepressible anarchic gaiety, but also an ominous warning of the totalitarian potentials of the age—a writer could hobo on the road or be kidnapped to the mental wards, the new concentration camps.

It is now clear that during the forties and fifties the Beats were operating on a definition of sanity that defied the expectations of their time, but proved potently prophetic. In other words, it was not only their writing that was important, but the way they chose to live. As Longfellow once remarked about the transcendentalist utopians, it was a "divine insanity of noble minds." In a culture that suspected mere difference in appearance as deviant behavior, or regarded homosexuality as criminal perversion, Allen Ginsberg maintained that "my measure at the time was the sense of personal genius and acceptance of all strangeness in people as their nobility." In the face of the asphyxiating apathy of the fifties, the Beats enacted their desires, seeking a restoration of innocence by purging guilt and shame. The model was Blakean, but it was never a path of easy irresponsibility. Gary Snyder, keeping a journal while working as a fire lookout on Sourdough Mountain in 1953, wrote:

> Discipline of self-restraint is an easy one; being clear-cut, negative, and usually based on some accepted cultural values. Discipline of following desires, *always* doing what you want to do, is hardest. It presupposes self-knowledge of motives, a careful balance of free action and sense of where the cultural taboos lay.

In the terms of their time, the Beats were regarded as madmen, and they suffered the consequences of the reformatory, the insane asylum, public ridicule, censorship, even prison. But what would seem defeat in the eye of ordinary experience simply instigated them to further adventures. The Beats were attracted to "madness" as a sustained presence; a lucid, singular, and obsessive way to illuminate the shadows of the day. Was William Blake, for example, acting madly when he read *Paradise Lost* with his wife while both sat naked in their garden? Melville had once perceived that the difference between sanity and insanity was analagous to the points in the rainbow where one color begins and another ends. As the eye could not distinguish any demarcation, a subjective value judgment was necessary. In the nineteenth century, madness became interpreted as unusual behavior, an affront to agreed social codes—so as long as Blake remained naked in the privacy of his garden, he was merely eccentric. But like the European Surrealists, the Beats wanted their Blake to dance naked in the public garden, and this was interpreted as a threat to public dignity. In the fifties, the Beats were still not quite as overtly political as the Surrealists had been, but they certainly paid for whatever self-assertions they managed with great psychic costs. There is no accident in the lament of the first line of "Howl": "I saw the best minds of my generation destroyed by madness." The Christian mystic Thomas Merton understood the spirit of revolt that inspired the Beat redefinition of sanity:

> We equate sanity with a sense of justice, with humaneness, with prudence, with the capacity to love and understand other people. We rely on the sane people of the world to preserve it from barbarism, madness, destruction. And now it begins to dawn on us that it is precisely the *sane* ones who are the most dangerous.

Recognizing that madness was a kind of retreat for those who wanted to stay privately sane, the Beats induced their madness with drugs, with criminal excess, and the pursuits of ecstasy. They used "madness"—which they regarded as naturalness—as a breakthrough to clarity, as a proper perspective from which to see. At times temporarily broken by the world for their disobedience, they developed, as Hemingway put it in *A Farewell To Arms*, a new strength "at the broken places." As Edmund Wilson argues in "The Wound and the Bow," there exists an inextricable relationship between genius and disease in modern artists who have so precisely predicted and reflected the general insanity surrounding them. The acting out of repressed inhibitions and taboos relieves binding public pressures to conform, and the artist as scapegoat/shaman creates an alternative with his very being.

In three works particularly, *Naked Lunch*, "Howl," and *On the*

Road, the Beats reacted to the embalming insecurities that had quelled the spirit of a generation. Each of these works represented a major departure in literary form as well as a courageous response to the dominating passivity of the age. In retrospect, these books can be seen as the confirmation that America was suffering a collective nervous breakdown in the fifties, and that a new nervous system was a prerequisite to perception. In these three works, then, we will find the key to the cultural disorder of an era.

Nowhere was the fear of institutional power more pronounced than in the nightmarish collage of *Naked Lunch*. Burroughs pictured a future possibility far more dismal and terrifying then Orwell's *1984* or Huxley's *Brave New World*, a dystopia where technology strangles all vestiges of freedom, a police state where the human attributes of love and community are stripped away and defiled. *Naked Lunch* is a hallucinatory vision of the very worst expectations of the fifties. Burroughs' central figure is the junkie, the weakest, most despised and vulnerable of citizens, a Western version of India's untouchable caste. Ginsberg has written that to be a drug addict in America is like having been a Jew in Nazi Germany, and Burroughs reflects this idea of fascist control, magnifying its horror through the distorted lens of the junkie. Burroughs' image of the faceless addict counterpoints his view of a society that controls all its parts while remaining invisibly undetectable. The view of the drug experience is harshly antiromantic. Clinical, detached, almost scientifically cinematic, *Naked Lunch* is an educative warning against the horrors of addiction. It relentlessly parodies our institutional life, and at the same time makes apparent the deconditioning effects of drugs, which, like Dr. Benway's cures, are an end in themselves. Rarely has any novelist managed so explosive a struggle between the demands of total control and the nihilistic impulse to defeat those in control. The ensuing combat is so ferocious that the voice of the novelist, ordering experience, seems distant and lost, especially to the reader already distracted by Burroughs' experimental bias.

If there is an intellectual center in *Naked Lunch*, it will be found in a pervasive suspicion of the dangers inherent in technological organization:

> The end result of complete cellular representation is cancer. Democracy is cancerous, and bureaus are its cancer. A bureau takes root anywhere in the state, turns malignant like the Narcotics Bureau, and grows and grows, always reproducing more of its own kind, until it chokes the host if not controlled or excised. Bureaus cannot live without a host, being true parasitic organisms. (A cooperative on the other hand can live without the state. That is the road to follow. The building up of independent units to meet the needs of the people who participate in the functioning of the unit. A bureau operates on opposite principles of *inventing needs* to justify its existence.) Bureaucracy is wrong as a cancer, a turning away from the human evolutionary direction of infinite potentials and differentiation and independent spontaneous action to the complete parasitism of a virus.

This passage—anticipating the cancer metaphor in Mailer's *An American Dream*—exaggerates a social awareness into a political ideology. It is important because it is one of Burroughs' rare projections of anything that might resemble an ideal, for his usual mood is a disgust so intense, so voluptuously vicious as to make any ideal seem false and impossible, and American ideals, especially, precariously incompatible with the realities of world power.

Burroughs' disdain for future possibilities and his staunch antiromantic bitterness make him an exception among Beat writers. He represents a logical fulfillment of the despair of T. S. Eliot's "The Waste Land." Curiously enough, the backgrounds of the two writers are similar: both were born in St. Louis, both were descendants of old American families, and both attended Harvard. Both writers, especially in "The Waste Land" and *Naked Lunch*, share a destructive attitude toward form and structure. Conrad Aiken was the first to notice that the critics who took such great pains to discover the links and continuities of "The Waste Land" were misreading a poem that intended to reveal dissonance and kaleidoscopic confusion through violently contrasting fragments; Burroughs' discontinuity—his microcosmic focus on what frequently appear to be unrelatable experiences—is part of a similar attempt to deny the organic unities of nineteenth-century structure in poetry and fiction. Burroughs' use of the "cut-up" method—an arbitrary juxtaposition of randomly selected words and phrases—is part of an attempt to restructure the grammar of perception; the new linguistic order that Burroughs invents initiates the Beats' assault on the conditioning influences of language.

Burroughs takes the motif of the unreal city from "The Waste Land" and compounds it with a nauseating imagery of hideous physical disintegration and degradation that promises a state of future plague. His hanged-men episodes in *Naked Lunch* are grotesque parodies of the talismanic material Eliot himself parodied with the grail legend in "The Waste Land." Burroughs presents these horrors with an unsettling calm, a cold earnestness reminiscent of Swift, a view of the psychological transformations latent in fantasy close to Kafka, and a picture of man as helpless victim that reminds us of Sartre, Beckett, and Genêt. Entering the absolute nadir of existence, Burroughs' fiction defines a purgatory of endless suffering—Beat in the sense of beaten, oppressed, and dehumanized. Yet Ginsberg's and Kerouac's pathway to beatitude stemmed from Burroughs' nightmare of devastation.

Burroughs' affinity with Eliot's objectivity and impersonality raises an aesthetic issue that is crucial for the Beats; because of this affinity, Burroughs once denied belonging to the Beat movement, and emphasized the differences in form among writers he considered more as friends than as literary compatriots. The effect of Burroughs' vision on Ginsberg and Kerouac—who both frequented Burroughs' apartment near Columbia University in 1944–45—cannot be denied; Kerouac, for example, makes Burroughs an oracular source of the wisdom of experience as Bull Lee in *On The Road*. But Burroughs' fiction, while capable of diagnosing what the Beats saw as threatening about American values—especially the worship of technology—did not project a sense of self strong enough to counter the debilitating apathy of the culture. Burroughs clarified his aesthetic of narrative near the end of *Naked Lunch*:

> There is only one thing a writer can write about: *what is in front of his senses at the moment of writing.* . . . I am a recording instrument . . . I do not presume to impose 'story' 'plot' 'continuity.' . . . Insofaras [sic] I succeed in *Direct* recording of certain areas of psychic process I may have limited function . . . . I am not an entertainer . . . .

In this respect, Burroughs is in accord with Eliot's notion that the artist's progress is measured by how well he transcends personality and private emotion.

While it is tempting to see this suppression of self as a classical imperative, it is partly an oversimplification to do so. As romantic a figure as Keats declared, in his letters, that the poet had no identity since he was constantly filling in for some other body. Keats was thinking of the poetic persona, the mask, which is the logical direction of artistic development in British poetry from Donne to Browning, and realized almost to perfection in Eliot. Ginsberg and Kerouac felt that the time had come to challenge this concept, as Whitman had previously, by making personality the center and subject of their work. Now this is a rather delicate and relative issue; it is really the *degree* of self allowed by the artist, and the extent to which an artistic mask subsumes the priorities of self. Henry James, reviewing Whitman's *Drumtaps* shortly after the Civil War, created a touchstone for the classical standard when he criticized Whitman and argued that "art requires above all things the suppression of oneself to an idea." Whitman's idea, which James to his credit later realized, was this expansive and cosmic sense of self: "what I give I give of myself," Whitman proclaimed in "Song of Myself." The classical temper will argue, however, that Whitman enters the atmosphere of emotion, not the terrain of idea. The tradition of Eliot and Pound suspected the manner in which feeling had been rendered in poetry, and attempted its subordination to ideas—thus,

Eliot's theory of "objective correlative," a group of images standing in place of the direct expression of emotion. Partly as a result of this fear of statement, Pound and Eliot created a poetry that veered closer and closer to arcane scholarship, as both men, dependent on literary allusion, on other languages, fashioned poetry that became increasingly remote, intellectual, unintelligible, cryptically withdrawn. The seer/poet seemed extinct.

It would be wrong to suggest that the Beats rejected the legacy of Eliot or Pound. Ginsberg, in "Death to Van Gogh's Ear," makes Pound his secretary of economics, and "Howl" is a poem in the tradition of "The Waste Land." Pound, with his attacks on banking (Ginsberg: "Moloch whose soul is electricity and banks"), on the credit system to which most of the Western world is now in bondage, and with his devotion to the poetry of the East, is regarded with considerable admiration by the Beats. No, what was rejected was the tendency toward abstraction (which is ironic when we recall the original impulse of Pound's Imagism), and the abnegation of self that is suggested by the footnotes to "The Waste Land."

In the fifties, when the voice of personality seemed so endangered by an anonymity of sameness, the Beats discovered a natural counter for the silence of the day in a new sense of self, a renaissance of the romantic impulse to combat unbelievably superior forces. The Beats crashed through the restraining mask of the removed artist—the Flaubertian tradition that saw the artist as God, omnipresent but invisible—in a search for what Ginsberg termed "Unified Being." The objective camera eye of "The Waste Land" would be replaced by the "I" of the personal "Howl"; the difference can be felt simply by listening to the sound of Eliot reading his work—dry, unemotional, ironic, distant—and comparing that to Ginsberg's impassioned, arousing rhapsody of voice.

The Beats' denial of the artistic mask had extraordinary implications for the nature of language in literary art and the quality of experience to be expressed. Prematurely conscious of the potentials for lying on a national scale, the Beats raised the standard of honesty no matter what the artistic consequences. Art is created by the polar tensions of spontaneity and artifice, improvisation and contrivance, and the Beats passionately embraced the extreme of uncontained release and denounced superimposed and confining forms. Kerouac, in "The Essentials of Spontaneous Prose," attacked the concept of revision sacred to most writers as a kind of secondary moral censorship imposed by the unconscious, and compared the writer to the jazz saxophonist in a search for language as an undisturbed flow from the mind. In a sense, the nitrous oxide experiments of William James and Gertrude Stein at Harvard, which resulted in automatic writing, anticipated Kerouac's denial of the artist's traditional selectivity.

In *Sunday After the War*, Henry Miller had argued that art was only the path to reality, and that "man's task is to make of himself a work of art." In *Plexus*, he had anticipated the significance of natural speech, remembering that "some of my more honest friends, brutally candid as they often were, would occasionally remind me that in talking to them I was always myself but that in writing I was not. 'Why don't you write like you talk?' they would say." The desire to remove the literary superego was a sign of how the Beats would struggle with the conditioning influences of language; in many ways it represented a fulfillment of the romantic credo as formulated in the preface to the *Lyrical Ballads* in which Coleridge and Wordsworth promised to use the language of ordinary men.

Ginsberg has addressed this question in his *Paris Review* interview with great clarity:

> . . . what happens if you make a distinction between what you tell your friends and what you tell your Muse? The problem is to break down that distinction: when you approach the Muse to talk as frankly as you would talk with yourself or with your friends. So I began finding, in conversations with Burroughs and Kerouac and Gregory Corso, in conversations with people whom I knew well, whose souls I respected, that the things we were telling each other for real were different from what was already in literature. And that was Kerouac's great discovery in *On The Road*. The kind of things that he and Neal Cassady were talking about, he

finally discovered were *the* subject matter for what he wanted to write down. That meant, at that minute, a complete revision of what literature was supposed to be, in *his* mind, and actually in the minds of the people that first read the book. . . . In other words, there's no distinction, there should be no distinction between what we write down, and what we really know to begin with. As we know it every day, with each other. And the hypocrisy of literature has been—you know like there's supposed to be a formal literature, which is supposed to be different from . . . in subject, in diction and even in organization, from our quotidian inspired lives.

The goal of complete self-revelation, of nakedness as Ginsberg has put it, was based on a fusion of bohemianism, psychoanalytic probing, and Dadaist fantasy in "Howl" that dragged the self through the slime of degradation to the sublime of exaltation. While the idea of self is the Beat focal point, it represents only a beginning, an involvement to be transcended. The movement in Ginsberg's poetry is from an intense assertion of personal identity to a merger with larger forces in the universe. The ensuing tension between the proclamation of self—evident in a poem like "America"—and an insistence upon man's eternal place in time creates a central dialectical opposition in Ginsberg's poetry. Believing that consciousness is infinite, and that modern man has been taught to suppress much of his potential awareness, Ginsberg has attempted to exorcise the shame, guilt, and fear that he sees as barriers to self-realization and total being. Ginsberg's work, generally, is an outgrowth of the tradition begun by Coleridge: to search for the source of dream, to release the unconscious in its pure state (avoiding literary simulation), to free the restraints on imagination and seek (as Blake did) for the potency and power of the visionary impulse.

Ginsberg sees his poetry as transmitting a sacred trust in human potentials, and he speaks in his *Paris Review* interview of how his mystical encounter with the spirit of Blake in 1948 revealed to him the nature and direction of his own search as a poet, making him see that his role would be to widen the area of consciousness, to open the doors of perception, to continue to transmit messages through time that could reach the enlightened and receptive.

Ginsberg's poetry is characteristic of the Beat desire *to be*, affirming existence as a positive value in a time of apathy. The quest for experience is as obsessive and all-consuming in "Howl" as in *On The Road*. Whether these experiences are destructive or not is of less importance than the fact of contact, especially the kind of experience that allows an individual to discover his own vulnerability, his humanness, without cowering. As Gary Snyder has argued in his essay "Why Tribe," to follow the grain of natural being "it is necessary to look exhaustively into the negative and demonic powers of the Unconscious, and by recognizing these powers—symbolically acting them out—one releases himself from these forces." This statement suggests the shamanistic implications of Beat literature; "Howl," like *Naked Lunch*, is an attempt to exorcise through release. While Burroughs' novel futuristically projects into fantasy, "Howl" naturalistically records the suffering and magnanimity of a hipster avant-garde, a group refusing to accept standard American values as permanent. The experiences in "Howl," certainly in the opening part of the poem, are hysterically excessive and frantically active. It is the sheer momentum of nightmare that unifies these accounts of jumping off bridges, of slashing wrists, of ecstatic copulations, of purgatorial subway rides and longer journeys, a momentum rendered by the propelling, torrential quality of Ginsberg's long line, a cumulative rhythm, dependent on parallelism and the repetition of initial sounds, that is biblical in origin.

While the pace and the autobiographical content of "Howl" shocked the sensibilities of Ginsberg's readers, the deeper significance of the poem was in its formal breakthrough. His long line was like a trip to the sun in the fifties: inconceivable, shattering prior expectations of what a poem could be like. Whitman had predicted that "the cleanest expression is that which finds no sphere worthy of itself and makes one." Rimbaud, discussing Baudelaire's poems, remarked that unknown discoveries demanded new form, and

Kerouac had taught Ginsberg that "something that you feel will find its own form." In "Howl," Ginsberg proved that the organic basis of his prosody was neither the result of preconceived expectation nor imposed formal limitation, but an ability to flow with the natural: if "mind is shapely, art is shapely," he asserted.

Ginsberg's poetry ranges in tone from ecstatic joy to utter despair, soaring and plunging from one line to the next, confident, paranoid, always seeking ways to retain the ability to feel in numbing times, always insisting on a social vision that stresses transcendence and the need for spirit in the face of a materialistic culture. No wonder Bob Dylan has remarked that Ginsberg's poetry was for him the first sign of a new consciousness, of an awareness of regenerative possibilities in America. That Dylan shares Ginsberg's surrealistic imagination is evident in early recordings like "Subterranean Homesick Blues," but even more, Dylan participates in the Beat affinity for the road, the symbol of an attitude toward experience that braves anything as long as movement is encouraged.

The first account of this sensibility is found in Norman Mailer's essay "The White Negro." Mailer announced the appearance of a new man, whom he termed the "hipster," who found an existential model in the danger felt by the black man every time he walked down an American street. Seeking, sometimes psychopathically, the "rebellious imperatives of the Self," the hipster rejected the conformity of American life, and spread a "disbelief in the words of men who had too much money and controlled too many things." The hipster sought an apocalyptic answer to the demands of adjustment in the American pattern; he would become, Mailer promised, the thorn in an emerging totalitarian society. The hipster, in a constant attempt to change his nervous system, would always express forbidden impulses and actively violate social taboos; like Elvis Presley, Lenny Bruce, even Rojack in Mailer's *American Dream*, he would release primitive energies before a repressive society. Responding to a "burning consciousness of the present," the hipster stressed the energy of movement and magnified Hemingway's concentrated formula of "grace under pressure" to confront a state of perpetual crisis. Mailer's essay, besides defining the code hero of the Beat movement, was prophetic. He claimed that the hip consciousness would spread in proportion to our recognition of the Negro (the fruit of the civil-rights struggle in the sixties), and that as a result of the new forces caused by hip values, the complacent conformity of the fifties would be shattered by a time of violence, confusion, and rebellion.

The "angelheaded hipster," in the nomenclature of "Howl," staggered on the night journey of the Beat soul, answering a mysterious call from the dark, dragging "through the negro streets at dawn looking for an angry fix." The tortures of his damnation were like Orphic ordeals, sending him into an ecstatic song of destruction which ended in the radiance of secret knowledge. The hipster— affecting a looseness in body movement that was reflected in his judgment—was the connection between black and white cultures, the man whose being throbbed to the beat of bop music's variable rhythmic base. Ginsberg realized that Charlie Parker, the great saxophonist, had announced a new rhythm of thought, an extended breathing of the body in music and speech which led to the new awareness: when the mode of the music changes, the walls of the city shake, as Plato observed long ago. Since the hipster perceived differently, he presented himself in a new light, wearing strange combinations of clothing arranged in odd colors, pinks, purples, oranges. In the early fifties, Kerouac described the funeral of Al Sublette, a shipmate on a merchant freighter who had tutored him on the saxophone. Sublette was a one-eyed Negro who had once played drums with Jimmy Forest. He wore jackets without lapels, checkered pants, and wide-brimmed hats. He also snorted cocaine and had needle marks on his arms. What most impressed Kerouac about the funeral, however, was the black speech rhythms, the open rolling vowel sounds that seemed to follow a musical pattern in stark contrast to the clipped nasality of the white speech Kerouac was accustomed to hearing. Jive was a private code language that caricatured white power with hidden resentment and an incisive sense of the ridiculous. Jive was the ordinary black man's equivalent of the jazz musician's extraordinary improvisatory skills, the ability—resulting from years of practice and control of the medium—to invent endless variations on themes, countless combinations and new permutations of sound which signaled a return to the unconscious, the irrational and intuitive without any goal of permanence. As John Clellon Holmes maintained, jazz was a call from the dark to his generation. It was a euphoria of joy, dance let loose, the expression of an exuberance, an energy and untrammeled swinging style that blacks had developed, partially as a defense, partially as a continuation of a heritage that began in Africa and continued in the cotton fields of the South. The Beats eagerly responded to black music Holmes has stated because they "felt like blacks caught in a square world that wasn't enough for us," a world that was neither immediate, nor pleasurable, nor exciting enough.

Hip sensibility was in a process of constant mutation, Burroughs noted. Its language was subject to rapid change and new inflection; the very vocabulary was a register of fugitive intentions. The hipster, black or white, inhabited the world of the city street. His ideal was knowledge of how the regular world functioned so as to circumvent it. In one sense, he was the intellectual of the streets, but instead of the grounding of the academy, he would improvise his facts, confuse his cultural sources and levels by mixing languages of totally distinct kinds of experience. This "jive" was deliberate, part of a necessary disguise. Living in close contact with criminals, prostitutes, knowing the brutality of the police, the hipster acted as if he wanted to laugh the sadness of his world out of existence, always illuminating his despair or ecstasy with music and drugs. Searching for other modalities and inner pleasures, the hipster's secret initiation into consciousness was through marijuana, cocaine, opiates, Benzedrine, anything that would depress or elevate, bring him to a "high" on a tingling continuum of significance to quicken the precious inner presence no matter how drab, routine, or oppressive the outer environment. Kerouac defined the hipster by his ability to procure drugs at any time. The lore of drugs ensured the hipster's position as the marginal man who nevertheless had to know how to penetrate the cosmopolitan center, with a ken for its rules and an instinct for self-preservation. The hipster was a case of the extreme—the man who steps so far out of the legal and civilized sphere as to depend exclusively on his own wits and resources, a survival lesson in an alien environment. The pursuit of drugs—what Ginsberg called the "ancient heavenly connection"—was as complex as it could be perilous, but it set a model of a life free from conventional expectations, and encouraged insidious attitudes to morality which were to have enormous social consequence. In 1953, Kerouac wrote Ginsberg that nearly every jazz genius had been jailed because of drugs, and he warned his friend that in the future writers would have to follow a similar route to prison or madhouse. The hip mentality became integral to Beat consciousness, and its seeds were to surprise the sixties, evident in the transformed values of American youth who actively challenged the socially accepted until change was sought as an end itself.

The new forces released by the discovery of the hipster consciousness form Kerouac's ideological focus in *On The Road*, a novel that seems characteristically American in its search for a fluid, unshaped life, free of preimposed patterns, fearing most the horrors of stasis, of staying in the same place without the possibility of change. The reviewers misread the novel almost without exception, finding it incoherent, unstructured, unsound as art, and unhappy as prophecy. Instead of seeing Dean Moriarty (in real life, Neal Cassady) as a genuine picaresque center, and thereby a source of unity in a novel about turbulence, the reviewers attacked the sensibility of nihilism. It is, perhaps, easier to see Dean today as a remarkable fusion of desperation and glee, as the "ragged and ecstatic joy of pure being" to borrow Kerouac's description, an utterly rootless individual who careens from coast to coast on sudden impulse, a man whose incredible energy makes a mockery of the false idol of security. Dean is drawn in the tradition of Huckleberry Finn but is untainted by Miss Watson's puritanism; as a result he is without guile or guilt. The sign of Dean's freedom is his infectious laughter. In the novel, laughter—even in the presence of despair—

becomes a kind of life-force, a token of spirit; merely to laugh at the world, like the existentialist ability to say no, becomes a valuable source of inspiration for Kerouac. Dean has been in jail and reads Proust; but his defining quality is speed—in conversation, in a car, in his lifestyle. Kerouac, depicting Dean as a function of speed, has saliently tapped the distinguishing strain of American life in the second half of the twentieth century. This speed is reflected in an extraordinary hyperactivity that determines the atmosphere of the novel:

> the only people for me are the mad ones, the ones who are mad to live, mad to talk, mad to be saved, desirous of everything at the same time, the ones who never yawn or say a commonplace thing but burn, burn, burn like fabulous yellow roman candles exploding like spiders across the stars.

But Kerouac himself, through the figure of his narrator, Sal Paradise, tries to offer a check on Dean's exuberant anarchism; indeed, one of the bases for scenic organization in the novel is the way in which other characters find fault with Dean after an episode. And Sal is inevitably drained by the momentum of experience, always aware of growing older and saddened by this; like Kerouac, he is an outsider, an imperfect man in an alien world, brooding, lonely, seized by moments of self-hatred. The refrain in *On The Road* of "everything is collapsing" is a reminder of the effects of disorder, of Kerouac's own vision of uncontained release, on himself. Clearly the endless celebrations, the pell-mell rushing from one scene to the next, create a hysteria that makes Sal want to withdraw from the world. This conflict between the demands of Self as expressed by Dean, and the need to extinguish Self as expressed by Sal, becomes the pivot of Kerouac's fiction; with *The Dharma Bums*, his next published novel, and the influence of Gary Snyder, the movement toward a union with nature is described.

In *The Dharma Bums*, Kerouac dramatized a crucial shift in the Beat sensibility; instead of continuing to seek escape from boredom and the spiritually corrupting emphasis on materialism and careers through desperate activity, Kerouac began an inward search for new roots. *The Dharma Bums* replaces the hysteria of *On The Road* with a quietly contemplative retreat toward meditation. Like *On The Road*, it is a very personal novel based on Kerouac's experiences; in this case living with Allen Ginsberg (Alvah Goldbook in the novel) in Berkeley during the early fifties, and meeting Gary Snyder (Jaffe Ryder in the novel). Kerouac, not always generous when depicting his friends, offers an enthusiastic account of Snyder studying Chinese and Japanese, reading Pound, exploring the tenets of Zen Buddhism, emulating the ascetic Buddhist poet Han Shan; taking Kerouac into the mountains on camping trips, teaching him a new independence, a new pride in the body; acting with charity, giving gifts spontaneously in contrast to Western acquisitiveness; generally preparing Kerouac for a transformation of his values by isolating him in nature, creating in Kerouac a more profound sense of his own vulnerability than hitchhiking ever provided.

For many of the Beat writers, Buddhism became a form of psychic ballast, and their study of various schools of Eastern thought became both a means of deconditioning themselves from Western habits of mind and feeling, and a way out of the morass of Self into which they had so angrily plunged. As Gautama Buddha is reputed to have said: "The house of the self is on fire; get out of it." The Buddhist emphasis on sympathy and compassion for all sentient beings served to balance the Beats' vitriolic condemnation of American materialism. Impressed by the Buddhist concept of the insubstantiality of all apparent sensory phenomena, they learned how to simplify conditioned cravings and desires as Thoreau had a century earlier. Buddhism became a reinforcement of Einsteinian relativity stressing man's insignificance as a dot in space—moving on one planet out of nine circling the sun, which itself was a member of a galaxy of some two hundred and fifty billion stars, which in turn might be one of billions of galaxies. Buddhist scholars saw the changeability of a universe that moved like a whirlwind. Instead of the Western view of separate identity, they were uninterested in ego or soul, claiming that nothing was stationary or permanent, with everything analagous to the dream state. Emphasizing intuition (or "buddhi," to know where once one only knew about), discouraging rational exposition, Buddhist scripture depended on parable, image, and paradox: "If all returns to the One, to what does the One return?" The Buddhists believed that *all* distinctions were falsely imagined, that instead an unimpeded interdiffusion of all things constituted reality—later, Ginsberg would try to achieve what he called "undifferentiated consciousness" in his poetry.

The Beats, antihierarchical, antielitist, were concerned with removing artificial barriers between their lives and art, so they naturally were ready to accept an ethic without an orthodoxy, without dogma, and one whose goal was the discovery of a state in which all differences and separations (from man to man or man to nature) were dissolved. But they wanted a practical accommodation of Buddhist tenets to their existence, and as a result their use of Buddhism was eccentric, inconsistent, and most of all eclectic: Mahayana Buddhism reduced ethical absolutes to relative values; Tantric practices encouraged the kind of free sexual consort that the Beats admired like the *yabyum* position Kerouac described in *The Dharma Bums*; Zen provided them with something like Surrealist antilogic which perfectly suited their notion of what was sane behavior. The point of meditation, for example, was not simply to bathe in the bliss of the great void until one's conflicting ambitions ceased their selfish clamoring, but also a way of affecting one's behavior toward the world, other people, and oneself. One very tangible instruction was the breathing exercises used as a preparation for meditation where a rapid, repeated deep breathing hammers into a vital body center—"kundalini" or the energy in the base of the spine—releasing a reservoir of energy, a flood of electricity in the nervous system. Such breathing exercises, when practiced long enough, could result in the annihilation of thought processes so that all would appear as a flow of indistinguishable parts that would carry with it the suppression of accumulated experience. The result was a weightless catharsis beyond madness which particularly affected

Kerouac's aesthetic intentions, and had an immediate impact on Ginsberg's long line.

The Beats were uninspired by the wordy, speculative, and metaphysical interpretations of some Buddhist scholars, but tended to accept the tougher dialectics of Zen ("If you see the Buddha, kill him!"), a doctrine that originated in the Buddha's remark that the ultimate was unimaginable. In Rinzai Zen meditation, a paradoxical koan or problem released the mind from the limits of logic. Thomas Merton, in *Zen and the Birds of Appetite*, defined Zen's undifferentiated consciousness as the absence of all social or cultural categories, the refusal to believe in any artificially preconceived structures (such as the form of a poem or painting), or to judge beauty and ugliness according to canons of taste. The Beats responded to the Zen principle of final authority in the individual's spontaneous and intuitive insights and actions, as well as Zen's sanctification of every moment of existence. Wittgenstein taught: "Don't think—Look!" and in this fashion Zen transcends communication through words by dramatizing a potential awareness through an action, a gesture, a facial expression. Zen Buddhist "mindfulness" consists of bare attention to details—seeing what is there without commentary, interpretation, judgment, or conclusion, and this appealed to the Beats as they were intent on transgressing standard acceptable morality and convention. So the Zen appeal was in the denial of all value judgment: nothing was more sacred or less holy than anything else, as Ginsberg felt in the conclusion to "Howl." Even Art could not be expected to differ from life itself, and would have to include its accidents, chances, variety, and disorder, and this influenced Kerouac's rejection of the idea of revision as much as it inspired John Cage to create a new music.

The happy lunacy of the Zen mountain poets like Han-Shan was as important to the Beats as the more sacred scripture. They imbibed deeply in the Surrealist spirit of improvised outrageousness, combining it with Gide's idea of the gratuitous act which would encourage the abandonment of reason and a return to the "native truth" of impulse. "We really only live by our fantasies when we give free rein to them," André Breton once declared, and the Beats intuitively understood that literature need not be an exclusively solemn and formal experience, but could induce levity and surprise:

> Milk my mind &
> make it cream
> drink me when you're ready

Kerouac wrote in a poem, and it exemplifies the playfulness with which the Beats responded to the crabbed stuffiness of postwar verse with its emphasis on a futility and despair that may have been sublime with Eliot, but was often mawkish in his imitators.

Perhaps the best illustration of Beat absurdist comedy occurs in *Pull My Daisy*, the film that Robert Frank and Alfred Leslie made at the end of the fifties that focused on the spontaneous antics of Ginsberg, Gregory Corso, Peter Orlovsky, the painter Larry Rivers, and David Amram, the composer. *Pull My Daisy*, filmed in Leslie's loft on the Bowery, is about a railway worker, his wife who is a painter, and three poet friends who toast each other as Hart Crane, talk portentously about the doom of bridges, and play childishly on a couch while waiting for a visit from a bishop from California. The white-suited bishop makes a very formal entrance with his mother and sister. But the poets pester him with questions about Buddhism, asking him whether baseball and alligators are holy, or whether he ever admires women in tight dresses. The absolute incongruity of the scene, the messy kitchen with piles of unwashed dishes, the old wood stove and broken-down furniture, the serious bishop's discomfort and anxiety, the look of baleful condescension on his mother's face as she pouts with an American flag on her lap, results in a hilarious juxtaposition of manners. Although the movie was twenty-nine minutes long, it had been edited from thirty hours of filmscript. In his book *Vibrations*, David Amram described the actual shooting as burlesque madhouse: when things got dull, Ginsberg or Corso would undress and threaten to leap from the window, or would pour water on those present who seemed uninterested. The final version is a classic illustration of the Zen notion of "artless art"—especially because of Kerouac's brilliant and spontaneously improvised narration—and its zaniness only seems meaningless to the uninitiated, like the bishop who declares that the poets act very strangely indeed.

Just as in public the Beats would inevitably offend standard decorum, books like *On The Road*, *Howl*, and *Naked Lunch* were an apparent threat to the established literary as well as cultural order in the fifties. Critics began wondering in print about new barbarians, antiintellectual know-nothings, infidels of babel. The Beats as writers were either ignored, patronized, or condemned as exponents of a new nihilistic illiteracy. Kerouac, who wrote *On The Road* in 1951, could not get it published until 1957 because he resisted the demands of editors and publishers that he change the face of his manuscript; his best book, *Visions of Cody*, completed by 1952, did not appear in its entirety for another two decades. While Kerouac achieved popularity with *On The Road*, it was despite the literary establishment. Randall Jarrell, for example, accepting the National Book Award for poetry in 1960, commented on Kerouac's attempt to record everything that occurred in the action and in the mind of the author while writing. Jarrell argued that this might lead to a successful psychoanalysis, but the aim of art was concentration and the necessary elimination of everything that Kerouac insisted was most significant. Jarrell's analogy of analysis is interesting because many of Ginsberg's early critics felt his poetry was "therapeutic," and therefore valid only as personal exorcism. The literary critics, schooled in the "new criticism" inspired by T. S. Eliot, John Crowe Ransom of *The Kenyon Review*, Cleanth Brooks, and Austin Warren, expected a certain finesse of texture, strict formal adherance to convention, and proper taste in subject matter. They were conditioned to expect irony, self-deprecation, containment, craft; the romantic, especially any overt declaration of feeling, was suspect. The Beats, introducing new literary techniques, were flaunting their own raw personalities and rude vigors as subject matter, using a speech that employed obscenity as well as humor, ideologically responding to forces like Surrealism and Buddhism, and functioning generally on an entirely different idea of sanity than their critics.

"Howl," *On The Road*, and *Naked Lunch* dismayed many of these critics, causing them to respond with a ferocity of attack that resembled the reception of Henry Miller's *Tropics*. Miller is a key predecessor, stressing naturalness and freedom of composition, his aim being not to achieve "art" but an illusion of spontaneity. He saw himself as a literary outlaw, a "gangster author," as he inscribed a photograph in Paris in the early thirties. Miller suffered more from censorship than any American writer since Dreiser who fought in the courts for a decade to have *Sister Carrie* published as contracted. At the end of the fifties, the right to print "Howl" and *Naked Lunch* also had to be established in the courts. Of course, lines like Burroughs' "Gentle reader, we see God through our assholes in the flash bulb of orgasm" were not intended to appeal to readers with conservative tastes, and the resulting charges of editorial degeneracy and obscenity were resolved through judicial procedure. The trials proved to be a testimonial to the potency of the works, even as the resulting publicity enlarged the audience. That audience, small at first, was part of a broad artistic awakening: Jackson Pollock's automatism and his sprawling canvases of poured paint; John Cage's music, which like Kerouac's ideal of natural speech tried to capture every actual sound in the environment; Merce Cunningham in dance; Judith Malina and Julian Beck in the Living Theater performing Brecht and expressing the energy of immediate impulse; Charles Olson and Robert Creeley at Black Mountain College, poets also searching for a new personal voice, aware that the thought process need not be refined out of the poem, that the poet should not shy from his own action, randomness, or whimsy, but should, like the Beats, reach for the center of the subject rather than hover about it intellectually—working in obscurity, ignoring the hostility of the critics, these artists were the creative soul of the fifties.

First Conjunctions

PART II

The mass of men serve the State thus, not as men mainly, but as machines, with their bodies. They are the standing army, and the militia, jailers, constables, *posse comitatus*, & c. In most cases there is no free exercise whatever of the judgment or of the moral sense; but they put themselves on a level with wood and earth and stones; and wooden men can perhaps be manufactured that will serve the purpose as well. Such command no more respect than men of straw, or a lump of dirt. They have the same sort of worth only as horses and dogs. Yet such as these even are commonly esteemed good citizens. Others, as most legislators, politicians, lawyers, ministers, and office-holders serve the State chiefly with their heads; and, as they rarely make any moral distinctions, they are as likely to serve the devil, without intending it, as God. A very few, as heroes, patriots, martyrs, reformers in the great sense, and *men*, serve the State with their consciences also, and so necessarily resist it for the most part; and they are commonly treated by it as enemies.

—Henry David Thoreau
"On the Duty of Civil Disobedience"

Baudelaire's self-conscious exclamation, "I cultivate my own hysteria with joy and terror," offers a clue to the postmodernist sensibility. The prolifigacy of friendship and feud engendered by the French Symbolists historically anticipates the fevered relationships of the Beats as well as their remarkable reciprocity and openness.

The Beats reinvented the confessional mode for our time with an urgency and passion that shocked their contemporaries. They resorted to their lives as suitable literary subject matter with a totemistic reverence qualified by a brutally revealing honesty. They refused to compromise an intuitive quest by acquiescing to dominant ethical mores. Abusing minds and bodies, they discovered a subject in risk. Their defiance of cultural taboos, their concern with homosexual identity and sexual expression, their use of illegal drugs, were all necessary stages in the formation of a new sensibility.

Clearly, they courted danger as a means of deconditioning themselves. Only by denuding personality of its masks could they discover the limits of their own potential and take measure of their surroundings. It was a strenuous process, and the intensity of their experiences was reflected in the confessional impact of their work. More significant than their suffering, however, was their sheer perseverance as writers who were intent on recording the implications of their own changes. Obscurity was irrelevant because their audience was ideal—themselves. In Mexico in the early fifties, despite the havoc of illness, poverty, and wretched working conditions, Kerouac still wrote with prodigious abandon. Burroughs' addiction introduced him to a kind of dislocating invisibility, but at the same time he clinically recorded the process of his disintegration: his fascination with the abominable was peculiarly American in its pragmatically insistent observation. During one attempted drug cure in North Africa, after losing thirty pounds in two weeks, he verged on perpetual hallucination. Trapped in flesh that congealed like fresh dough, appearing like some concentration-camp victim resurrected from the dead, he still recorded "sensations that hit like bullets." Ginsberg believed that Burroughs' free association of visual images at that time was so intense as to place him in "acute psychic danger of uncovering some secret which will destroy him." For such articulation of the unnamable, there could be no guarantee of safe passage. Exposing the recesses of consciousness was like ripping bandages from wounded flesh. The Beats were transgressors, and, in fact, on different occasions Burroughs, Kerouac, and Ginsberg each faced criminal charges. Often defining themselves through impulsive acts, they were all outlaws, libertarians, pursuing the compulsions of private vision in spite of social sanction and law. The Dionysian abandon that seemed like hedonistic barbarism to some staid observers was actually combined with a devotional Apollonian control. The Beats were men of refinement and scholarly discipline, capable of the most ambitious efforts to further their craft, relating Mayan custom, Zen, Cezanne's painting—whatever they learned—to their own aesthetic innovations.

Their common imperative was transformation: "The most dangerous thing to do is to stand still," Burroughs once wrote Ginsberg. Movement had to be spiritual as well as physical, and they expected their art to evolve as old habits were forgotten. While their choices after the war heralded the new freedoms that would later find broad acceptance in the sixties, they had deliberately and sometimes obsessively followed their intuitions as a means of personal redemption. Acting as warning torches for us all, they burned brightly in the shadow of their own anonymity. Out of the anarchic richness of their lives came the vision of the books. Rarely has writing been as integral to action, and few writers have cared to live so incautiously. By the end of the fifties, Burroughs, Kerouac, and Ginsberg had each seen published a major book confirming their own literary aspirations. First Conjunctions *sets the emotional and aesthetic context of their apprenticeship to the word from their beginnings to the point that their respective voices were clearly heard.*

WILLIAM BURROUGHS

WILLIAM SEWARD BURROUGHS remains the least-known figure of the Beat movement, obscuring the details of his past, choosing exile in Mexico, North Africa, and Europe since 1949. Hermetic scholar, eccentric experimenter, and adventurer, he has pursued a cavernous Faustian route, inducing the twists of misfortune out of some sable affinity for the outlawed. His life has been isolated and renegade, his haunted legend has been riddled by rumors of diabolic insinuation. For fifteen years he was painfully addicted to such drugs as morphine and heroin. Making detailed notes, he charted the underground inferno of addiction with casual disregard for his own health and dignity, but emerged from his ordeal with *Naked Lunch*—a book written with the possessed savagery of a man scarred by a trip through hell.

Burroughs has the hauteur of an aristocrat who has known the gutter. His genealogy incorporates classic features of the American ruling class, a lineage both military and industrial: his mother was a direct descendant of Robert E. Lee, and his grandfather perfected the adding machine which bears his name. His childhood was dominated by a mother who could easily have figured in a role created by Tennessee Williams. Proud and poised, Laura Lee Burroughs was a lady of reserve and nineteenth-century refinements who attended to the niceties of Victorian propriety with a fetishistic observance. Her special abhorrence for anything that might pertain to bodily functions was one sign of her removed illusionism—a quality her son would defile with the relentlessly excremental bias of his writing. Mortimer P. Burroughs was a father whose ineffectuality was masked by a curious sense of humor which evidently left its impression on a son who would later express it more mordantly and grotesquely.

In the faceless boredom of his parents' red brick townhouse, Burroughs experienced his first recorded period of delirium at the precocious age of four. Terrible nightmares and hallucinations vexed his youthful nights, leaving him an insomniac for life. Those early dreams were to become the stigmata of his sensibility; his books would later transmogrify them with searing permanence. At the age of fifteen, precariously fragile, Burroughs was sent to an exclusive boarding school for boys in Los Alamos (near the first atomic testing ground) where he was forced to ride horses, exercise, and play outdoors. His refuge was in reading: Anatole France, the stories of de Maupassant, Baudelaire, Remy de Gourmont, Gide, Wilde's *Picture of Dorian Gray.* Incongruously, along with a Jamesian fastidiousness in taste, he developed an obsessive interest in gangsters and crime. The boy whose first literary essay was entitled "The Autobiography of a Wolf" was remote and laconic. A "chronic malingerer" in high school, he kept a journal account of a romantic attachment to one of his classmates which soon nauseated him because of its embarrassing excess of emotion; he was not to attempt to write for another eight years. By the age of sixteen, as Neal Cassady was to describe him, the patrician of magnificent boredom "was as high horse as a Governor in the Colonies, as nasty as an Old Aunt, and as queer as the day is long."

Burroughs studied literature, linguistics, and anthropology at Harvard. Graduating during the Depression, lucky enough to be provided for by a modest trust fund, Burroughs was able to travel in Europe where he spent six months in Vienna studying medicine. That choice anticipated a later emphasis on physiology and the pathology of human decay in his writing. His next strategy was weirdly disconsonant with his future. He tried to join the OSS, the intelligence agency that later evolved into the CIA, but was rejected despite a family connection because he had deliberately sliced off a fingertip with a chicken shears. This was a turning point for Burroughs. His fiction suggests that he might have become a brilliant tactician, the books are suffused with an atmosphere of conspiracy, detection, and game theory. He derived from the right social class, his uncle knew Wild Bill Donovan who organized the agency, but the young man had a perverse inclination for despair and independent thought—he would never fit in.

In 1938, Burroughs returned to Harvard and began graduate work in anthropology, sharing a small frame house with Kells Elvins, an old school-friend. Elvins was studying psychology, and they had many discussions about writing, even starting a detective story in the Dashiell Hammett/Raymond Chandler style. They submitted another story, "Twilight's Last Gleaming," based on the sinking of the *Titanic*, to *Esquire*, but it was not accepted.

The dislocations of the war years distracted Burroughs from his studies and all attempts to write. He began psychoanalysis but felt that the procedure frustrated individual expression. Later, he warned Allen Ginsberg that psychiatrists wanted "some beat clerk who feels with some reason that other people don't like him. In short some one so scared and whipped down he would never venture to do anything that might disturb the analyst." A brief tour in the army ended with a psychological discharge that compounded a sense of aimless despondence.

Like some mote wandering in the void, Burroughs drifted to Chicago responding to its reputation as a city of gangsters. Years afterward, he recalled that "it seemed a romantic extravagance to jeopardize my freedom by some token act of crime." This inclination was a refutation of his origins, a rejection of the elitist aspects of his upbringing. The attraction to crime was gratuitous—Burroughs was drawn by a buried dark need to escape conventional ambitions, to make himself invisible enough so that he could be accepted by his exact opposites in the social spectrum. In Chicago, he worked variously as an exterminator, a bartender, and a private detective. Yet the security of his own private income reminded him of how his social class and conditioning had formed a protective shield that prevented him from perceiving his eventual subject.

In 1943 Burroughs moved to New York City and met Joan Vollner Adams, a pregnant young woman who was studying journalism at Columbia University. After the birth of her daughter, Joan left her husband to share an apartment with Burroughs near the school. Earlier, at Barnard College, Joan's roommate had been a woman named Edie Parker who by 1944 was living with Jack Kerouac. Joan and Edie saw each other occasionally and maintained their friendship. Hearing about Kerouac from Joan Adams, Burroughs was intrigued because Kerouac had been to sea. Curious about obtaining merchant-seaman papers, he visited Kerouac who was mystified by his guest's inscrutability, comparing Burroughs to a shy bank clerk with patrician manners. Returning the call, Kerouac brought his friend Allen Ginsberg to meet Burroughs, and both were enthralled by Burroughs' impromptu reading of Shakespeare. The three men began to meet frequently in Burroughs' apartment to discuss books. While both Kerouac and Ginsberg had been studying literature at Columbia, they knew little about modern or European writers. Their formal literary education ended with the Victorians, and Burroughs was to initiate them into a far more experimental academy which encouraged the discussion of figures like Blake, Rimbaud, Hart Crane, and Auden. Burroughs gave Ginsberg his copies of Yeats' *A Vision* and Eliot's poems and presented Kerouac with Spengler's *Decline of the West*. He introduced his new friends to writers like Kafka and Céline, to Cocteau's writing about opium, to books like *The Cancer Biopathy* by Wilhelm Reich and *Science and Sanity* by Count Korzybski. Soon both Kerouac and Ginsberg were sucked into Burroughs' vortex, and he began to effect subtle changes in their outlook.

It was around this time that Burroughs and his friends met Herbert Huncke, a Times Square hustler and drug user who had a marginal interest in writing. Huncke, who was to appear as Herman in *Junkie*, Burroughs' first book, as Elmo Hassel in *On The Road*, and Huck in *Visions of Cody*, became a Beat Mephisto who, as Ginsberg wrote in "Howl":

> walked all night with shoes full of blood on the
> snowbanks waiting for a door in the East River to
> open to a room full of steamheat and opium

A shady acquaintance had asked Burroughs to dispose of a gun and a supply of morphine Syrettes (part of army first-aid kits during the war) and Huncke was recommended to facilitate matters. Soon afterward, Huncke initiated both Burroughs and Ginsberg into the use of morphine and to aspects of life along the drug route of which they were both previously unaware. Ginsberg probably got the word "beat" from Huncke who used it frequently as part of his hipster argot, referring to his usually hopeless, downtrodden situation. Like Neal Cassady, Huncke became a code figure for the more intellectual Burroughs and Ginsberg, a model of the despair and recklessness that could tempt a man to any excess, thrill, or unexpected pleasure.

Huncke's education had been irregular and unconventional, hitchhiking around the country as a teenager and shipping out on freighters. He had no interest in career, in steady occupation, but instead used his wits to subvert the socially accepted at any opportunity. Burroughs installed him in a fifteen-dollar-a-month slum tenement on the Lower East Side which became a kind of floating den, occupied at intervals by small-time criminals whom Burroughs wanted to meet. One of these men was Bill Garver, notorious then in the Times Square area as a coat thief. Garver's background was similar to Burroughs', causing more than vicarious identification—his father had been an Ohio banker, and Garver was the beneficiary of a trust fund. Later, he lived with Burroughs and Kerouac in Mexico and was described by Burroughs in *Junkie* as Bill Gains, a man who was "positively invisible, a vague respectable presence. . . . [with] a malicious, childlike smile that formed a shocking contrast to his eyes which were pale blue, lifeless and old."

Burroughs left New York City with Joan Adams and her infant daughter in the summer of 1946. His plan was to resettle in the Southwest as a farmer. Though he believed that farming could be a practical route to self-sufficiency, his intentions were not just pastoral. The introduction to the drug underworld had been sudden and overwhelming; Burroughs felt mounting panic and the fear of police prosecution. A quiet retreat from New York City would allow him to assimilate his experiences. Also, the union with Joan had complicated his life. The nervous delicacy of a beautiful woman was not really compatible with his own homosexuality. Their union was too fragile for the tensions of New York City, and life in a remote agricultural community seemed like a situation in which confused emotions could be clarified.

Burroughs bought land in Texas, settling near a town called New Waverly, fifty miles north of Houston. It was bayou country, low, rolling land covered with pines; most of the surrounding weather-beaten farmhouses were owned by poor blacks and sharecroppers. Joan was addicted to Benzedrine and pregnant with William Burroughs, Jr., and Burroughs was injecting heroin three times a day. Perhaps the break from New York had been too drastic. Listless, bored, and uninspired, Burroughs needed a reminder of what he had escaped, so he sent Huncke money for busfare early in the spring of 1947.

That summer, Allen Ginsberg and Neal Cassady, who had been romantically involved in Denver, hitchhiked down to visit Burroughs and Huncke. When they arrived, Burroughs was busy shooting his pistol at the side of a barn—according to Huncke, Burroughs shot his guns so often that neighbors feared a group of gangsters were living on his farm. Huncke relinquished his bedroom for the new guests, and slept on a screened porch where he could hear armadillos and see the moon through trees draped in Spanish moss. Ginsberg and Cassady spent their days swimming, walking in the woods, trying to build a fence, and talking. Burroughs had unsuccessfully attempted to cultivate opium poppies, but had managed to grow marijuana between rows of alfalfa. In the fall, Burroughs, Huncke, with Cassady at the wheel, filled a jeep with mason jars of marijuana which they drove to New York to sell.

Contact with men like Huncke had affected Burroughs' ethical notions. Burroughs advised Ginsberg in a letter that there was considerable semantic confusion about the meaning of crime. He stated that the word *crime* simply referred to behavior outlawed by a given culture. There was no relationship, for example, between lying and legal violation. Burroughs maintained that there was more pretense, dissimulation, and misrepresentation in acceptable business practices like advertising, public relations, and television than in the sale of heroin. Since the Second World War, Burroughs claimed, the line between legitimate and criminal activity had vanished: "Most everyone in business violates the law everyday." He based his argument on the example of the farmers in the Rio Grande Valley who depended entirely on Mexican labor that was illegally imported with government cooperation and assistance. As a respectable farmer, he concluded, his ethical foundation was shakier than when selling heroin. That one act was condoned while the other was condemned was simply relative to power. From such a position, Burroughs developed a broader theory of irresponsibility to institutions which he articulated in another letter to Ginsberg:

> A company because it is depersonalized and guided by no other principle than profit thereby surrenders all claims to ethical consideration. All codes of conduct that have any validity are based on the relations between individuals. An individual entrusts money to me, and I would not steal the money even though I could steal it without danger of consequence. . . . A company never trusts anybody with anything. Therefore a company is fair game, and personally I would not hesitate to defraud a company if I could.

While through such letters Burroughs was able to suggest the theoretical justification for his acts, the risks were still often intolerable. In February of 1948 he voluntarily committed himself to the drug rehabilitation center at Lexington, Kentucky. But by spring he returned to New Waverly. He had been harassed by the local police for using an old car, and when he was arrested for drunken driving, his license suspended, he decided it was time to leave Texas. He moved Joan and the children to Algiers, a town just outside New Orleans where Burroughs purchased less than an acre of land. The city provided easy access to drugs, and Burroughs was beguiled by the ruined grandeur of the French Quarter. In some ways, New Orleans, with its tourists, seamen, gamblers, drifters, whores, and homosexuals existing in a state of unconsummated alertness reminded him of New York, but with a more inverted and contained pressure. But the pressure must soon have begun to intensify unbearably because he wrote Kerouac that he had enough guns to stand off a siege.

In his letters, Burroughs complained of the menace of government control, detesting the officials who determined agricultural quotas, seeing them as a germinal "cancer on the political body of this country which no longer belongs to its citizens." According to Burroughs, the federal government was dominated by a treacherously weak and vindictively petty liberal establishment. He imagined a damnable tyranny of sniveling union leaders, social workers, and psychiatrists, who were conspiring to lead the country into a socialism that meant increasing interference in the business of every citizen. In Kerouac, who was also innately conservative, Burroughs found a more sympathetic audience than in Ginsberg. When Ginsberg advocated the idea of the welfare state in his letters, suggesting that the American labor movement was still progressive, Burroughs retaliated on May 1, 1950, with a libertarian Jeffersonianism that anticipated the analogy between bureaucracy and cancer in *Naked Lunch:*

Increased government control leads to a totalitarian state. Bureaucracy is the worst possible way of doing anything because it is the most inflexible and therefore the deadest of all political instruments. As I see it the only possible solution is the cooperative system. Any move in the direction of cooperatives is blocked by the *manufacturers and* the *unions.* The present day union is simply a branch of government bureaucracy as is the manufacturers.

Ignoring the gun and drug laws with impunity, Burroughs had become a lawless figure who was no longer prepared to pretend allegiance to any institutional authority. In the spring of 1949, his farm at Algiers was illegally entered by police who found a cache of firearms and drugs. This invasion precipitated Burroughs' decision to leave the United States. He had been attracted by the prospect of buying land for two dollars an acre in Mexico. With Joan and the children, Burroughs moved to Mexico City where he attended Mexico City College, studying Aztec history and the Mayan codices, language and archaeology which influenced the use of myth and ritual in *Naked Lunch,* and anticipated a later concern with psychological control systems.

At first Burroughs felt very free in Mexico, unpersecuted by the policeman of his dreams and unharried. Habitually, he walked the streets with a loaded revolver, reporting several incidents to Ginsberg of encounters with police who merely confiscated his gun. He also found his access to drugs much easier, as many could be obtained without prescription. But his view of Mexico began to change rapidly. He had applied to the Mexican Department of Immigration for permanent citizenship, but he found a bureaucratic web far more complex than in the States. Without his papers, Burroughs knew it was futile to farm in Mexico since foreign investment was discouraged. After he had spent nearly a thousand dollars on the relevant documents, the authorities lost his file.

Burroughs had urged Kerouac to visit, and Kerouac was writing extravagantly romantic letters of anticipation. But now Burroughs warned him that Mexico was neither simple, gay, nor idyllic. For every real policeman, there were several self-appointed ones with fabricated or stolen badges and .45s secured in trouser holsters. Several of Burroughs' classmates at Mexico City College had been apprehended in police shakedowns, and Burroughs also had problems with middle-class neighbors who suspected him of using drugs. Writing to Kerouac, he concluded that Mexico was "an Oriental country that reflects 2000 years of disease and poverty and degradation and stupidity and slavery and brutality and psychic and physical terrorism."

The terrifying chaos of flat nightmare became the actual register of Burroughs' existence when, on September 7, 1951, he accidentally shot his wife through the head. Burroughs always carried his pistol, and liked to use it. Although he was nearsighted, he had shot a mouse in a bar called the Bounty frequented by his fellow students. Late at night, at a party in the apartment of John Healy, an American from Milwaukee, Joan had tempted Burroughs into a version of the William Tell game. Firing at close range at a champagne glass balanced on her head, he missed it and killed her. The story made the newspapers. On the next day Burroughs denied it, claiming that his loaded gun had dropped on the kitchen table and misfired.

Writing to Ginsberg, Burroughs commented on the decency of the Mexican police at a preliminary interrogation, surprised that they were helpful and not sadistic. Yet, if Burroughs had experienced difficulties previously with the Immigration Department, he was to become involved now in a far more intricate bureaucratic snare with much higher stakes, as the inquest and judicial proceedings dragged on. Although Burroughs, with his immaculate appearance, his habit of punctuality, his punctilious courtroom decorum, impressed the Mexican authorities, he was finally declared a "pernicious foreigner." On the advice of his lawyer, who had also just shot a man, Burroughs jumped bail and wrote Ginsberg that he did not intend to return: "I get the horrors at the thought of going back to the States to live." The shooting may have had certain unconscious motivations related to the period of self-imposed exile to follow. Joan's brittle nervousness had been a touchy lever in a relationship as full of hate as love; according to Huncke, she had seemed to depend on Burroughs much more than he needed her.

The accident and the consequent loss of his children and his family's financial support freed Burroughs from his own past. His use of drugs, his consort with criminals, and finally his shooting Joan—all were steps to outcasting himself, becoming unacceptable in a society which he had already rejected. The shooting was the ultimate rupture of respectability. Burroughs was now an "untouchable."

The immediate repercussion was that for the first time he was able to describe realistically the underworld that had for so long fascinated him. During the year that followed Joan's death, Burroughs wrote *Queer*, a book about homosexuality that was never printed, and *Junkie*—a graphic geography of the easy betrayals, the casual violence, the hustlers and thieves of the drug world. This remorseless account of the intricacies of addiction, the horrors of dependence and withdrawal, was unprecedented, and Burroughs doubted its commercial feasibility. Nevertheless, he had been sending his manuscript, chapter by chapter, to Ginsberg in New York. Excited about Burroughs' work, Ginsberg showed *Junkie* to his friend Carl Solomon, a nephew of A. A. Wyn who published it under Burroughs' pseudonym, William Lee.

After hearing of the acceptance of *Junkie*, Burroughs left Mexico in the winter of 1952, sequestering himself in a male whorehouse in Tangier that was owned by a gangster. In January of 1953, he returned to South America to journey into the heart of the jungle in search of a drug called yage. Psychologically, the trip was an exercise in exorcism, an attempt to eradicate the memory of Joan and the past, a *rite de passage* through the dark night of the soul. The strangely hallucinatory circumstances of the voyage were to help formulate the new aesthetic perspective of **Naked Lunch**. In that novel he would later mercilessly caricature the Civil Service of the Panama Canal Zone, as well as the university in Bogota. He described the latter in a letter to Ginsberg as an institute whose random illogicality was a modern version of Swift's Academy at Lagado:

> All sciences are lumped in The Institute. This is a red brick building, dusty corridors, unlabeled offices mostly locked. I climbed over crates and stuffed animals and botanical presses. These articles are continually being moved from one room to another for no discernible reason. People rush out of offices and claim some object from the litter in the hall and have it carried back into their offices. The porters sit around on crates smoking and greeting everybody as 'Doctor.'

In Columbia, by bus, truck, and canoe, Burroughs traveled deeper into the interior, pursuing his contacts for yage. There were constant police checks and harassment because of guerrilla revolutionary activities. A provincial governor found an error on Burroughs' tourist card—the consul in Panama had dated it 1952 instead of 1953, a testimonial to bureaucratic inefficiency. Despite the validity of his passport, plane tickets, and other receipts, Burroughs was arrested in Puerto Assis, a town on the Putumayo River with one muddy street, a hotel, a few shops, and a Capuchin mission. After five days, he was escorted by police to another town farther up the river, jailed for a night, then suddenly released the following morning. Meanwhile, he had succumbed to secondary anemia.

This inauspicious beginning was followed by a series of absurd encounters and incongruities. Frequently, Burroughs was bullied by nondescript customs inspectors, and then suddenly received as royalty because of an unfounded rumor that he was the secret representative of an oil company. In a letter to Ginsberg, he described the town of Puerto Leguisomo as one illustration of Conradian miasma:

> The place looks like it was left over from a receding flood. Rusty abandoned machinery scattered here and there. Swamps in the middle of town. Unlighted streets you sink up to your knees in. There are five

whores in town sitting out in front of blue walled cantinas. The young kids of Puerto Leguisomo cluster around the whores with the immobile concentration of tom cats. The whores sit there in the muggy night under one naked electric bulb in the blare of juke box music, waiting.

Burroughs succeeded in finding several Indian shamans who prepared and administered the yage vine, an intense hallucinatory experience which surely left its impact on *Naked Lunch*. In late spring he went to Peru where he again voyaged into the countryside, living with Indians and sampling yage and other local drugs through July.

In the fall of 1953, Burroughs returned to New York City for the first time in six years. He lived with Ginsberg on the Lower East Side, and Ginsberg described him in a letter to Neal Cassady:

> I haven't seen him for six years. Peculiar how my memory served me well—he is really exciting to talk to, more so for me than ever. His new loquaciousness is something I never had the advantage of. I am older now and the emotional relationship & conflict of will & mutual digging are very intense, continuous, exhausting and fertile. He creates small usable literary symbolic psychic fantasies daily. One of the deepest people. He is staying with me, I come home from work at 4:45 and we talk until one AM or later. I hardly get enough sleep, can't think about work seriously, am all hung up in a great psychic marriage with him for the month— amazing also his outwardness and confidence, he is very personal now, and gives me the impression of suffering terribly and continuously. I am persuading him to write a great sincere *novel*. By sincere I mean pour himself forth and use his mind fully & create an enduring story of truth and life.

Burroughs returned to Tangier where he remained—except for another visit to Ginsberg in 1954 in San Francisco in an attempt to form a more binding physical and emotional relationship. Back in Tangier in 1955, Burroughs lived in the Villa Muniria (sometimes known as the Villa Delirium) and began writing the fragments that were later assembled as *Naked Lunch*. He kept writing until 1956 when his addiction became intolerable. For a year he had lived in one room in the native quarter of Tangier without bathing or changing his clothes. His exclusive ambition had been "to stick a needle every hour in the fibrous grey wooden flesh of terminal addiction." Burroughs then heard of a doctor in London who used the drug apomorphine to induce a metabolic balance, and the arduous cure was successful. The long addiction had emancipated Burroughs from the conditioning of his time, but at great cost. His letters to Allen Ginsberg during the fifties describe his frequent illnesses: uremic poisoning in 1951, liver disease in 1952 followed by jaundice, rheumatic fever accompanied by an ankle infection in 1954, several bouts of viral hepatitis, and the constant sickness caused by attempts to withdraw from drugs.

In the summer of 1956, Burroughs resumed work on *Naked Lunch*. Returning to the Villa Muniria in Tangier, he added to his growing manuscript, writing while eating *majoun*, a hashish candy prepared with honey and spices. Kerouac and Ginsberg visited Burroughs in Tangier early in 1957 and helped with the manuscript which was littered all over his little room along with hundreds of empty Eukadol bottles—occasionally, pages would blow out into the garden. One wall of the room was used for target practice and was scarred with holes. Burroughs would reach into the pile of pages and read to anyone who would listen, often convulsing with laughter. Paul Bowles, the American writer who lived in Tangier, remembers that the accompanying laughter would be interrupted when Burroughs would digressively attack whatever social condition had inspired the passage. Ginsberg was Burroughs' intellectual antagonist at this time, and the two would argue aesthetics into the night. Typing portions of the manuscript, Kerouac claimed that it was so vivid and horrifying that his sleep was upset by nightmares. Kerouac compared Burroughs to some furious Dr. Mabuse scribbling changes in his "strange Etruscan script," and felt Burroughs was an aristocratic master of language who would not be published because of his uninhibited frankness. The circumstances of publication were as peculiar as the manner of composition. In 1958, Burroughs moved to a hotel in Paris at 9 Rue Git le Coeur with a suitcase full of manuscript which he showed to Maurice Girodias, publisher of Olympia Press. Girodias became interested after sections of the manuscript caused a censorship controversy in Chicago. Ginsberg had arranged to have excerpts appear in a magazine sponsored by the University of Chicago, but university authorities found the material offensive. Rather than publish an innocuous issue, the editors formed a new magazine called *Big Table* whose first issue featured Burroughs' writing. Girodias gave Burroughs only two weeks to present a final version. Working under considerable pressure, he was assisted by two friends, Sinclair Beiles (one of Girodias' editors) and the painter, Brion Gysin. The individual sections of *Naked Lunch* were selected from a huge collection of material, and piled in a stack on a table. Burroughs planned to reread what he had chosen to determine an appropriate order, but Beiles suggested that the accidental order then on the table might be better than any that Burroughs could invent. Burroughs accepted the advice.

Rimbaud once declared that the real problem for the poet was to make the soul monstrous in the literal sense of the latin root *moneo*—to warn. In *Naked Lunch*, Burroughs juxtaposed the phantasmagoria of drugs with the lucidity of what he had perceived about his culture with an intense ferocity of purpose:

> By plane, car, horse, camel, elephant, tractor, bicycle and steam roller, on foot, skis, sled, crutch and pogo-stick the tourists storm the frontiers, demanding with inflexible authority asylum from the "unspeakable conditions obtaining in Freeland," the Chamber of Commerce striving in vain to stem the debacle: "Please to be restful. It is only a few crazies who have from the crazy place outbroken."

For fifteen years, Burroughs had been an addicted flagellant, torturing his sensibility with inquisitorial relentlessness. As he says in *Naked Lunch*, the untouchables of any society perform a "priestly function in taking on themselves all human vileness." The result of his purgatorial plunge was a book whose terrifying vision of dehumanized control was like the telepathic warning of some awful future.

JACK KEROUAC

JACK KEROUAC was a figure of antithesis and contradiction. While he clearly was the living center of the Beat movement—not only the one who named it but its heart and impetus—he was also withdrawn, often shying from the consequences of friendship, torn between his solitary needs to toil with language and more gregarious inclinations.

Stubbornly true to himself, Kerouac was a man with a firmly defined center and an insistent devotion to his craft. At the same time, he was the most empathetic member of his group, influenced by his friends even as he was intent on encouraging them. His secret strength as an artist was his receptivity. He allowed himself to be lured from his work table into a new world which became his subject—a hip carnival of other writers and artists, intellectuals, nihilists, and underground men. When he met Neal Cassady, he fled west searching for the freedom and innocence of a lost frontier, and then south to Mexico, a country then still emerging from the nineteenth century, a place distant and different enough from the United States to permit a clearer perspective on his own culture. Ultimately, he was to be baffled and hurt by his own country, and his response was escape and isolation.

Kerouac's career is one of the more anomalous in the history of

American letters. During the years when he was devising a new aesthetic and writing his most significant books, he remained unknown and virtually unpublished. Finally, when *On The Road* appeared in 1957, six years after completion, its author was lost in a blur of sensational media distortion and controversy surrounding the novel. Despite the confessional ardor of the book, Kerouac cannot be viewed through the exclusive lens of his fiction since he romanticized, idealized, and shaped his narratives far more consciously than he would ever admit. Essentially an observer, he stood apart from life, only too aware of his own tenuous connections with most people, feeling isolated, lonely, separate even from the family he loved. His friend John Clellon Holmes has remarked that Kerouac seemed almost completely contained within his own consciousness. His writing, his religious adorations, and a few close friendships were all part of a constant effort to crash through the pasteboard mask of things, to reach outside of himself and communicate with the world. It followed that some of his friends were aspiring writers, but what was most remarkable about the relationships Kerouac had with men like Burroughs and Ginsberg was the extent to which he stimulated their literary endeavors. Ginsberg acknowledges that he learned more about poetry from Kerouac than from any other figure. Burroughs stated that Kerouac had been his major source of inspiration, always encouraging without admonishment, repeatedly predicting with calm assurance that he would one day write a book to be called *Naked Lunch*. Both Burroughs and Ginsberg admired Kerouac's facility with words, the seriousness of his commitment, the faithful manner in which he recorded his experiences and then wove them into an artistic texture. The journal entries, the habitual articulation of adventures with Cassady, Ginsberg, and others, became the stuff of future books. This mythologizing imagination was to become an integral element of Beat writing.

The present in the light of the past was always a disturbing and confusing phenomenon for Kerouac. His roots were small town, and he would struggle with a provincial heritage despite the powers of an imagination that was sufficiently comprehensive to embrace the spirit of a generation.

There was a coherence to Kerouac's early years which he was never to find again. His family lived in Pawtucketville, a French-Canadian community in Lowell, Massachusetts, where there was a large circle of relatives and friends with frequent gatherings for holidays, weddings, and funerals. French, the tongue of his parents, was Kerouac's first language. He only began speaking English in grade school, and for the rest of his life would often translate from the French in his head. French became a linguistic reinforcement of his sense of himself as an outsider as well as a means by which he could treat English with an otherwise unavailable freedom.

Kerouac's father, Leo Kerouac, was well known in Lowell. An excitable, generous, even extravagant man, he had a fondness for the barroom and a love of horse racing. He was proud of his independence and of the small printing business which supported the roomy old house in which his two sons, Gerard and Jack, and his daughter Caroline were born. In 1936, when Kerouac was fourteen, the Merrimack River overflowed and swamped his father's plant. What the Depression started, natural catastrophe completed, and Leo Kerouac's confidence was never to be restored. He was forced to sell the house, move into a tenement, and find work as a journeyman printer when and where he could, often having to leave his family. As the paternal prestige in the household declined, the mother's influence became all the more powerful.

Gabrielle Ange Kerouac was the center of the family. Far more traditional than her husband, intensely devout in her Catholicism, she was practical and domestic, the stolid embodiment of her peasant forebears. Gabrielle tended to shun the world, especially its newness, and looked to the past for guidance. She dominated her son, and much of his need for privacy and his suspicion of institutions can be traced to her influence. The tie between mother and son was furthered after the war by Leo Kerouac's physical decline. While the father was slowly succumbing to cancer, the son was writing novels in the kitchen, and the family was supported by

Gabrielle who worked in shoe factories. Kerouac, who had internalized an obligation to replace his father as provider, felt an immense guilt about his inadequacy to do so. He solicitously cared for Leo during the final period of suffering, morbidly fascinated by the process of disintegration and death. Before he died, Leo Kerouac asked his son to swear to care for his mother for the rest of her life, a burden that the son accepted faithfully.

Death had unusual implications for Kerouac. When he was four, his older brother Gerard died from a rheumatic heart condition. The infirmity had been prolonged and painful, and Kerouac retained the memory of many hours spent with Gerard. The effect of the death was traumatic. For months, Kerouac refused to sleep apart from his mother or in the dark. An unusual stress on mortality in Kerouac's fiction may stem to some extent from the impact of Gerard's illness which reinforced both the religious strain in Kerouac's character and the bond between him and his mother. The brooding sense of mutability that Kerouac felt as a child was transformed with passing years into a latent gothicism.

By the time Kerouac had reached school age he was avidly listening to radio programs like "The Shadow," composing and illustrating his own comic books. Another influence during these early years was the movies, especially horror films and the tragicomic burlesques of Chaplin or The Three Stooges. Escorted by his older sister, Kerouac was able to attend the movies frequently for free because Leo Kerouac printed the program for the local theater, and the fantasy world of Hollywood allowed an early adventurous escape.

In high school, Kerouac became a Lowell celebrity because of his track and football feats. In athletics, as with writing, Kerouac was entirely self-motivated, self-taught, and extremely willful. When informed that he was a poor candidate for the football team, he trained on his own, running for hours after school until the pain in his legs became unendurable. In his senior year the collegiate scouts began to make offers. Gabrielle urged her son to attend Notre Dame because of its Roman Catholic affiliation, but Kerouac, with an instinct for excitement like his father's, chose Columbia because it was situated in New York City. Kerouac was required by Columbia to spend an additional preparatory year at Horace Mann, so in 1939 he left Lowell and boarded with an aunt in Brooklyn, taking the long subway ride to upper Manhattan each school day.

While he received good grades at Horace Mann, Kerouac felt disadvantaged because of the privileges of wealth and social class enjoyed by most of his classmates. The cultural shock of New York City, furthermore, was enormous. He had left the intimate nexus of family, school friends, and working-class environment. The overwhelming impersonality of the city, the masses of its inhabitants and their unapproachability, the new rhythms and street sounds, the visible extremes of slum poverty and the Park Avenue residences of some of his classmates, the museums and theaters, both threatened and tantalized him. The result was turmoil.

In his freshman year at Columbia, Kerouac broke his leg early in the football season. The accident became a fulcrum for his loyalties. The drive to excel as an athlete was partly a response to his father's projected ambitions, a way of vicariously gratifying Leo Kerouac, but Gabrielle had been staunchly opposed to football from the start. Kerouac himself had been writing since early childhood and the rigors of training meant there was little time to write or study literature. He later admitted to his friend Joyce Glassman that the accident was extremely fortunate, giving him the leisure to immerse himself in books, read Shakespeare, discover his own capacities. In his second year, while many of Columbia's football stars were enlisting in the armed services, he defiantly walked out on the team when he felt Coach Lou Little was not allowing him sufficient opportunity to demonstrate his running skills. It may not have been so much an act of petulance as it was the confirmation of a direction about which Kerouac had previously been unsure.

The precipitous departure from Columbia, however, created stress and more uncertainty. He went to New Haven, where his parents had temporarily settled, and found work as a gas-station attendant. After a short stay, he went back to Lowell where an old friend helped him get a position as a sportswriter on the *Sun*, but he was to spend more time reading James Joyce and attempting his own stream-of-consciousness passages than attending sports events, and he left the newspaper after two months. It was difficult for him to remain in one place for long. As an index to his impatience and confusion, he enlisted in both the marines and the coast guard on the same day, and then shipped out the next day as a scullion on a merchant-marine vessel taking a bomb run to Greenland. The ship returned in time for him to resume classes at Columbia. When Coach Little failed to let him play in the opening game, Kerouac used it as an excuse to stalk out again. At the end of the semester, responding to the patriotic fever in the nation, and also seeking to escape from Columbia, Kerouac enlisted in the navy. But naval discipline proved intolerable: symbolically, he flung his rifle to the ground one morning during drill and walked to the base library where he was apprehended by men with nets. In June of 1943, just a little past his twenty-first birthday, he was discharged as a paranoid schizophrenic. His six months in the navy had been spent mostly under observation by naval psychiatrists.

Several years later, when Allen Ginsberg wrote to him from Columbia Psychiatric Institute, Kerouac remembered his own fear in the "nuthouse," his feeling of seeing through heads, his habit of sitting with the worst patients to determine the causes of their despair. Kerouac claimed that the "paranoid" part of his diagnosis was caused by his intelligence. His refusal to submit to authority prefigured the way the Beats would employ unconventional behavior as a method of release from confining social expectations. Kerouac hated the brutality of football, and he could not endure the senseless routines of naval regulation; both systems depended on unthinking obedience to mere pattern. His response in both cases was an outburst of anger; instead of permitting himself to be caged by social circumstance, he acted with volatile swiftness. That the rebellion was unpremeditated and spontaneous made it all the more convincing, an expression of powerful individuality that would not be channeled according to familiar societal routes.

This was an especially grim period for Kerouac. His parents were unsympathetic, criticizing him as an idler, dismayed by their son's failure to finish at Columbia. Leo also disapproved of Kerouac's literary intentions. What made his father's disappointment even more painful for Kerouac was Leo's slow physical collapse.

Partly as a relief from the oppressiveness of his home, Kerouac signed on for another bomb run, this time to Liverpool. Returning to his parents' apartment in Ozone Park, Queens, he continued to work on the early versions of *The Town and the City*, a novel intended to explain his past, to justify himself in the eyes of his father, and to clarify the confusions of the war years.

Early in the spring of 1944, Kerouac returned to the Columbia campus and met Edie Parker, a student at Barnard who was studying drawing with George Grosz. Kerouac soon began living with Edie, and by the summer he had met Ginsberg and Burroughs. Before long, they were all sharing an apartment, and Joan Adams had introduced Kerouac to Benzedrine. Kerouac also met Lucien Carr—a friend of Burroughs' who was to become a key link in the Beat circle. Carr was an impulsively arrogant and poised young man of aristocratic lineage. Kerouac frequently spoke of his beauty, his boyish effervescence. Blond, with almond eyes and slight body, Carr provided a striking contrast to Kerouac's stockiness, his broad neck and heavily muscled thighs, his dark look of submerged masculinity. Kerouac admired Carr's Wildean elegance, and the two young men soon became close drinking buddies, meeting at the West End Bar, then a workingmans' pub near Columbia University. Carr was completely taken by Kerouac's enthusiasm for life, by his abundance of intellectual and physical energy. At that time, Kerouac carried the working drafts of *The Town and the City* in little notebooks which he would read eagerly to Carr and others. He would also amaze his friends with his photographic memory, his ability to recite obscure baseball statistics or to remember the Kentucky Derby winner of a particular year.

Carr had met Burroughs through Dave Kammarer, a former

college instructor who had escorted Carr and a group of other young boys on Saturday nature hikes in St. Louis, years earlier. Kammarer and Burroughs had been childhood friends, living within a block from each other and attending the same schools. Kammarer had become infatuated with Carr. Using incorrigible deceptions, he had relentlessly pursued Carr to New York, declaring his love and his desire to possess him exclusively. He would shadow Carr about the streets, haunt the bars that he frequented, ingratiate himself with his friends, and suddenly appear at parties. On August 13, 1944, after an evening of drinking at the West End, Kammarer accosted Carr in Riverside Park, insisting that they make love. Carr retaliated by stabbing his antagonist repeatedly in the chest with his scout knife, then throwing the body into the Hudson River. Dazed by fears of the potential consequences of his action, Carr woke Burroughs who recommended that he immediately surrender himself to the police. Instead, he found Kerouac, who helped dispose of the murder weapon in a sewer grating. The two friends spent the day in curious disregard of the seriousness of Carr's position, drinking in several Harlem bars, and then visiting the Museum of Modern Art. On the following day Carr was arrested, and Kerouac was apprehended in Edie Parker's apartment as a material witness to a homicide and jailed in the Tombs.

Leo Kerouac, with strong regard for his family name, had warned his son of possible disgrace through entanglements with his new city friends. Appalled by his son's arrest, he refused to raise funds for a bail bond. Feeling unjustifiably deserted by his family, Kerouac decided to marry Edie Parker on the day after his arrest. It was Edie, in fact, who bailed him out. The marriage ceremony was performed in City Hall with two detectives acting as witnesses. Then the newlyweds traveled to Grosse Pointe, Michigan.

Unhappy with the idea of living on the bounty of his wife's relatives, Kerouac found a job in a factory counting ball bearings. The decision to take this kind of job typified his uneasiness when confronted by signs of wealth and power. Instead of seeking pa-tronage, his natural inclinations always led him to working-class occupations where he could find comfort in manual activity as well as freedom from pretension. While the choice was as natural for Kerouac as the kind of voice he would discover for his fiction, it also betrayed a lack of confidence in the marriage. Edie, too, was insecure about the relationship from both an emotional and an intellectual perspective. She wrote to Allen Ginsberg, pleading that he become her secret tutor, asking him to suggest books for her to read and to pose questions on them, so that she might try to understand what Kerouac knew.

The marriage only lasted two months and Kerouac returned to New York City. Spending several weeks in Ginsberg's dormitory room, he read voraciously and projected a novel on Carr's act in collaboration with Burroughs. The members of the Beat circle had known each other for a short time, but intense loyalties had been forged in an atmosphere of reading, intellectual discussion, aesthetic exploration, and riotous drinking. In the wake of the murder, more subtle ties were formed. An unresolved tension that was primarily sexual worried various members of the group—especially Ginsberg who was unsure of how to interpret his own desires. In a primal and irrational response to Kammarer's overture, Carr had brought the unmentionable into the open. His act was both pathological and unifying, scarring the front pages of the newspapers and giving the group its first taste of public identity. The act seemed to have a gratuitous grace; it was an exemption from the ordinary, a romantic gauntlet in the bland face of the world. For Kerouac the involvement with the murder was particularly significant—it precipitated a weaning away from his family. From an artistic perspective, it revealed how his life and the lives of his intimates could be as suitable as subject matter for his art as any imagined fiction by Dostoevsky or Gide. His sense of himself and his friends as Nietzchean outlaws was confirmed.

Kerouac's involvement with Burroughs and Ginsberg was intense but full of conflict. Perhaps his uneasiness was the reflection of the suspicions of his parents, who warned him of the evil influence of his friends. Regarding himself as a "madman child," Kerouac recognized in both Burroughs and Ginsberg a commonality of spirit. He admitted to Ginsberg that he felt a demented love for Burroughs whom he considered the most brilliant man he had ever met. But he was repelled by Burroughs' inquisitive sardonicism, and by both Burroughs' and Ginsberg's wallowing in intellectual and emotional egocentricity, their perpetual analysis of motives. In his letters, Kerouac periodically raged with hostility, castigating his friends for what he saw as a decadent absorption with disintegration which he compared unfavorably with his own quest for centers of health, the desire to find godly attributes in himself and others. Kerouac's attitude was partly a protective pose, a way to ensure his independence even from those to whom he was closest as he continued to search for a new artistic method to release his inner life.

In 1946, the initial conjunction of the Beat writers ended. Ginsberg embarked on a long freighter voyage. Burroughs and Joan Adams had left New York to begin farming in Texas. Kerouac returned to his parents' home to watch his father die. The impact of the last wasting months was draining, impeding progress on *The Town and the City*. Kerouac's solace was in omniverous reading. In a letter to Ginsberg, written in French, he listed the books he had finished in one week: *Moby Dick* (a present from Burroughs), *Sons and Lovers*, *The Counterfeiters*, sections of the Bible, of Aquinas' *Ethics*, of Rouchefoucauld's *Maxims* and Pascal's *Pensées*. In order to write, Kerouac began to rely on Benzedrine. He told Ginsberg that the drug shaped new perceptions, but it also made his body flabby and his hair recede. The drug may have contributed to Kerouac's thrombophlebitis which left him with the disquieting foreboding that his own life could be ended at any time by a blood clot in his leg.

Kerouac was still feverishly applying himself to *The Town and the City* when Neal Cassady—who was to become the subject of his next two novels—wrote to him from a reformatory in New Mexico on the recommendation of Hal Chase, one of Kerouac's Columbia classmates. Shortly afterward, Cassady arrived in New York with his sixteen-year-old bride, and invited Kerouac to his tenement flat in Harlem. When Kerouac knocked on the door, Cassady opened it, standing naked in the doorway. Kerouac must have experienced a shock of recognition because of the mirror-image he saw before him—the physical resemblance of the two men was remarkable.

Kerouac once declared that the only way to dissolve neurosis was through the white fire of action—and now Cassady was to provide the necessary heat. He quickly replaced Lucien Carr as a model. Cassady's overwhelming self-confidence, his vast reserves of vigor were entirely unsupported by the rigors of his background. Raised on the Denver skid row by a wino father, riding freight trains and sleeping in hobo jungles as a child, stealing automobiles for joy rides with girls, in and out of reform schools and prisons, Cassady became the prototype of the Rimbaudian adventurer, consumed "by the disease of overlife," as Kerouac would write in his poem on the French poet. Even his speech patterns embodied his frenzied excitement; he would talk in a series of staccato bursts as if his enormous energies were about to erupt volcanically through his mouth. He immediately pursued Kerouac with pleas that he teach him how to write.

Kerouac identified Cassady with his lost older brother Gerard. In later years, he would write a brief novel about himself and Cassady as children, meeting in San Francisco's Chinatown for lunch with their respective fathers who were escorted by sexy blonds. The fantasy, which was composed in French, suggested the peculiar intimacy of their relationship. Cassady was to become a phallic totem for Kerouac very early in their friendship, a projection of an obsessive sexual drive that Kerouac admired but did not share. One of Cassady's first letters to Kerouac, the "great sex letter," described how Cassady almost successfully seduced a woman on the bus to St. Louis only to be foiled by her sister's appearance at the terminal. The next night, traveling to Kansas City, Cassady met a virgin schoolteacher whom he "screwed as never before" in the park early the next morning. Such exploits became the basis of a vicarious identification which Kerouac formulated in his fiction.

Cassady's visit to New York was brief, but his impression on Kerouac was indelible. In Cassady, Kerouac was to recognize a restlessly consuming part of himself that could not be satisfied by his writing alone, and which was frustrated by his responsibility to his mother. Cassady sent Kerouac tirading letters from Denver encouraging him to discover the American landscape through the fortunes of the open road. The effect was contagiously inspiring and in the summer of 1947, Kerouac abruptly discontinued work on *The Town and the City*. Hitchhiking most of the way west, Kerouac began to appreciate the potential of a novel that could capture the vitality of America. His imagination was inflamed by the conception of a hero like Cassady who was capable of the kind of ecstatic outburst Ginsberg was to depict in "Howl":

> who barreled down the highways of the past journeying to each other's
> hotrod-Golgotha jail-solitude watch or Birmingham jazz incarnation
> who drove crosscountry seventytwo hours to find out if I had a vision or
> you had a vision or he had a vision to find out Eternity.

Kerouac may have had more than just a glimpse of how his experiences with Cassady could provide the basis for a picaresque narrative in which he could focus on the points of excitation he felt in the culture: the speeding view of Cassady's hipster outlook balanced by the more old-fashioned decency and self-doubt of a narrator like Sal Paradise. But he was disappointed by his anticipations of Denver. Cassady was preoccupied by interminable discussions with Ginsberg, who had fallen in love with him and also followed him there, and by multiple relationships with women. He had little time to spare. Kerouac decided to cross the rest of the continent, hoping to find a freighter berth in San Francisco. He had no luck, but did meet an old friend from Horace Mann who allowed him to share a shack in Mill Valley.

The trip cross-country was a potent catalyst, and Kerouac returned to New York to complete *The Town and the City*. At the same time, he began preliminary sketches for *On The Road*, feeling that the form of the book he had been writing was too contained for the natural flow he wanted to release. It was then that John Clellon Holmes met Kerouac, and his recollections provide a valuable portrait of Kerouac at this crucial juncture. His first impression of Kerouac was of shyness, a boyish exuberance tempered by deep undertones of moodiness and an unforgettable concentration of consciousness. Holmes had never met another writer as open-hearted and unwary, as willing to share his ideas. In his own journals, Holmes registered his amazement at Kerouac's systematic pursuit of his writing. Kerouac brought Holmes some of his diaries and manuscripts, evidence of the tremendous drive behind his work. He set impossible goals for himself as he had when running track as a schoolboy in Lowell. He would record the number of words he wrote daily, yet feel plagued by terrible doubts about the act of writing while his mother worked in a shoe factory. Despite his guilt, Kerouac persevered, his writing the reflection of an incredibly self-absorbed intensity.

For Kerouac, Holmes became a bedrock of value, a man whose judgment was dependable because he retained a sure sense of rightness despite the confusions of New York. Kerouac confided in Holmes because both were ready to abandon old answers that no longer satisfied or worked, but even more because Holmes was a serious spirit, a man genuinely struggling to find valid responses in an anxious time without resorting to a flagellant nihilism or escaping in acts of absurdist comedy. He was a marker, a buoy, a man on the border between past and present with the sensitivity and intelligence to make discriminations, and with an openness to what might have seemed bizarre to others. While Kerouac respected Holmes as a writer, he often felt his prose and person to be too analytical. In a letter to Ginsberg, Kerouac remarked that Holmes stood properly outside of the Beat movement, observing it more than living it. The fruit of such detachment was Holmes' novel *Go* which sought to embody Beat precepts in characters based on Kerouac and Ginsberg. Kerouac also disagreed with Holmes' leftist political sympathies, just as he denounced and detested Ginsberg's socialist ideals.

He once proclaimed to Holmes what he saw as the perennial artistic creed: revolution is revelation! Like Burroughs, he felt liberalism was merely a comfortable sham for the middle classes, that grief for the suffering in the world was often just a rationalization of guilt, a solace of conscience. Becoming more conservative as he grew older, Kerouac felt nostalgic for the pugnacious freedoms of the virile frontier, and profound regret for the loss of simplicity and spiritual inspiration.

As he was completing *The Town and the City*, Kerouac enjoyed a period of relative peace, continuing his friendship with Holmes as they both took classes at the New School in the Village. During the Christmas holidays of 1948–49, he and his mother visited his sister in Rocky Mount, North Carolina. Kerouac had mentioned his intentions to Cassady in a letter, but was amazed when Cassady suddenly drove up to his sister's home in a new Hudson. Cassady immediately overwhelmed Kerouac, even persuading Mrs. Kerouac that he could move some of her furniture from North Carolina to New York. Cassady and Kerouac made the long trip and returned in a day and a half. Cassady drove virtually nonstop, on amphetamines and talking the entire way—leader of the lost battalion of platonic conversationalists Ginsberg describes in "Howl." This unheralded appearance jarred Kerouac, rupturing the fragile sense of stability he was just beginning to develop which he would seek unsuccessfully afterward. Cassady, the comet from the West, triggered a cyclonic crisscrossing series of travel adventures for Kerouac during the next few years which he would describe in *On The Road* and *Visions of Cody*. This time he agreed to accompany Cassady back to San Francisco, but they detoured to see Burroughs and Joan Adams in New Orleans.

In San Francisco, in the spring of 1949, while working as a construction laborer, Kerouac learned that Robert Giroux had accepted *The Town and the City* for Harcourt Brace, so he returned to New York. When the manuscript was ready, cut almost by a third, Kerouac took the bus back to Denver to work on *On The Road*, feeling he needed a more intimate knowledge of Cassady's early surroundings. When he joined Cassady in San Francisco, both suddenly decided to return to New York, Cassady driving a 1947 Cadillac for an automobile-transport agency, burning the engine out by the time they reached Chicago. In New York, Cassady found work parking cars, and Kerouac rejoined his mother. After *The Town and the City* appeared to favorable reviews but few sales, Kerouac went back to Denver in the summer of 1950 and worked there as a messenger for the Denver Dime Delivery Service in order to familiarize himself with the city. Again, Cassady showed up unexpected, this time convincing Kerouac to drive to Mexico City to see Burroughs. Kerouac felt pursued by Cassady, but found his presence compelling; he could not withstand his manipulative abilities. Kerouac could be withered by a smile, and Cassady knew exactly how to charm him. He also felt that since he was writing about Cassady, each new experience could mean further discovery. But once in Mexico City, Cassady simply deposited Kerouac and sped off to New York. Kerouac lived with Burroughs and Joan Adams, developed a severe case of dysentery, smoked vast quantities of marijuana and used some morphine, all the time working on the growing manuscript of *On The Road*.

Kerouac returned to Ozone Park that fall worn out with illness, his body devastated by the drugs he had been using. After a partial recovery, he resumed his visits to Ginsberg, Holmes, and other friends in the city. One man to whom Kerouac had been particularly attracted was Bill Cannastra, a graduate of Harvard Law School who worked for Random House Encyclopedia, and who had become a rambunctious alcoholic. Cannastra was fond of pranks like running around the block naked. He frequently had huge parties at his loft on 21st Street which Ginsberg, Kerouac, and Holmes attended. Cannastra had the qualities of mercurial energy that Kerouac admired in Cassady; even though that energy was often pathologically destructive, it resulted in self-definition through acts which however randomly motivated, anarchic, or meaningless in design still constituted being in what seemed a vacuous age. Cannastra would dance on broken glass, balance precariously from a window sill and climb to another window, antagonize and belligerently insult his guests, drink himself into a stupor and pass out in his own vomit. He died horribly during the summer of 1950 while Kerouac was in Denver—the manner of his death a striking symbol of the blind intensity motivating the reckless rage of the Beats in their early phase. Cannastra was in a subway near his home when, just as the train was leaving the station, he tried to exit through an open window and was smashed into a platform column and crushed to death. He had been living with a woman named Joan Haverty, a department-store waitress, and she remained in the loft after his death. Kerouac visited Joan on one of his trips to the city, and within two weeks they were married. John Clellon Holmes thought Joan would be good for Kerouac because of her youthful innocence and her inarticulate need to love. But for the second time Kerouac had married a woman he knew insufficiently, confused by an episode of violence involving male friends. Furthermore, this marriage represented a psychic desertion, a betrayal of Leo Kerouac's injunction that Kerouac care for his mother. The marriage only lasted six months with unfortunate repercussions as later Joan plagued Kerouac with her paternity suit. While living with Joan, Kerouac wrote script synopses for Twentieth-Century-Fox, all the time continuing his struggle to find a new form for *On The Road*.

At this point, Cassady influenced Kerouac again, not with a personal appearance this time, but with a sprawling forty-page single-spaced letter—known as the Joan Anderson letter—virtually one long unpunctuated sentence which gave Kerouac the penultimate insight into the form he needed for his novel. He had been "hunched over a typewriter" since he was eleven, he once told Holmes: after years of revising sentences, imitating and mastering various literary styles, his arduous apprenticeship in letters was almost over.

Early that spring, Kerouac was hospitalized for a second time with phlebitis. The enforced bed rest seems to have been a period of final germination for the novel. Released in late March, he began typing on sixteen-foot rolls of thin Japanese drawing paper that he found in the loft, taping them together to form one huge roll. He worked tirelessly for three weeks. When John Holmes visited him on April 9, he had already written thirty-five thousand words.

Kerouac began his marathon linguistic flow in early April, drinking cup after cup of coffee to stay awake, typing his 250-foot single paragraph as it unreeled from his memory of the various versions he had attempted during the past two years, but writing now with a more natural freedom, somehow organically responding to the Zen notion of "artless art." Finally he had found a voice that was much less literary and imitative than that of *The Town and the City* and a way of departing successfully from the earlier novel's conventional restraints, which he now saw as a kind of literary lying.

Holmes has an entry in his journals for April 2, 1951, describing a hilarious conversation with Kerouac on Third Avenue, and a frantic drive with Kerouac with Cassady at the wheel during which Cassady deliberately accelerated his car at a pedestrian who was crossing the street, stopping short just in time. The act typifies Cassady's lifestyle—always like Cannastra's in his last years, bordering the precarious edge between sheer sensation for its own sake and danger courted to develop courage with no regard for consequences. Such daredevil exploits shocked the more rational and disciplined aspects of Kerouac's personality, but he tapped the raw power of these acts for his writing.

Kerouac completed *On The Road* by the end of April, and left Joan Haverty two days later. Restless and highly overexcited, he agreed to accompany his mother to Rocky Mount where she intended to spend the summer with her daughter. Kerouac bought a tape recorder for new literary experiments, and once in his sister's home embarked on a voyage of books to calm himself. In a letter to Holmes he wrote that he was reading Dostoevsky, Proust, and had just completed Lawrence's *The Rainbow*, Faulkner's *Pylon* and *Spotted Horses, Madame Bovary, The Marriage of Heaven and Hell*, and *The Ambassadors* which he disliked. He was also reading Gorky, Whitman, Emily Dickinson, Yeats, and smaller bits of Hawthorne, Sandburg, and Hart Crane. In the same letter, Kerouac predicted that his fate would be not to have an extra dollar until the day he died, and, indeed, for the next six years he would receive essentially no income from writing.

Unconsciously, Kerouac must have known that *On The Road* would not find ready acceptance from publishers. As soon as he had completed the typing of his manuscript, he called Robert Giroux, his editor, in an overflow of exuberance. When he brought the huge scroll over for Giroux to see, he stood in the doorway of his office and rolled it out on the carpet, virtually throwing it at him. Startled, Giroux began to talk about revision, remembering how much he had cut out of *The Town and the City*, and Kerouac rolled up his book and walked out.

Kerouac spent the rest of the year unsuccessfully seeking a freighter berth in New York, and then on the West Coast. In January of 1952 he moved into the Cassadys' attic. Neal was working on the railroad and was able to enroll Kerouac in a training program with the Southern Pacific. Kerouac realized that he would have to do more work on *On The Road*, and he had already begun *Visions of Cody*, an even more ambitious book. Parts of *Cody* grew out of *On The Road*—Kerouac's idea of revision was really expansion. He would remove a section from *On The Road* and elaborate it so that before long he had enough material for another book.

Cassady still wanted to learn about writing, but now he insisted that Kerouac teach him the will to write! Ironically, Cassady seemed more burdened than free. He was working sixteen hours a day to relieve his anxieties and escape entanglements. He encouraged his wife Carolyn to become intimate with Kerouac in an attempt to further the sexual bond he and Kerouac shared, although the strain of this arrangement soon became impossible to endure. Cassady's attitude to Kerouac was also changing: he seemed sullen, resentful, insultingly abrupt—whenever Kerouac tried to discuss literature or writing, Cassady would assume the false toughness and virility of the workingman and shift the subject to bills and money.

Kerouac had been happy working on *Visions of Cody* in the attic, reading the eleventh edition of the *Encyclopædia Britannica* for relaxation, but the new tensions in the Cassady household made him think of returning to Mexico. He had also been introduced to peyote by the poet Philip Lamantia, and the drug experience created a craving for the encircling timelessness of Mexico. For Kerouac, as for Burroughs and Ginsberg, Mexico was an opportunity to free the imagination from conditioning, a way to contradict "invisible exactitudes," as D. H. Lawrence called them, the abstractions of schedules and responsibilities. Cassady drove him to the Arizona border, hardly saying one word during the entire trip, and at dawn Kerouac crossed the wire fence into Sonora.

The return to Mexico coincided with a great change in Kerouac's outlook, the start of a downward emotional spiral caused by the devastating recognition that his own best writing—books like *On The Road* and *Visions of Cody*—might be commercially unacceptable. Yet writing was as essential for Kerouac as eating or breathing. He decided to write exclusively for himself—he would become his own ideal audience. This major shift in perspective from the conception of literature as entertainment to writing as a necessary mode of expressing a personal vision in hostile circumstances was independently perceived by Burroughs, Kerouac, and Ginsberg in the fifties.

The trip from the border to Mexico City was the first subtle indication of Kerouac's new priorities. Even though he had already visited Mexico, he wrote Ginsberg that he felt farther away from home than ever previously—in an oriental land beyond Darwin's chain. It is clear that Kerouac needed to further the distance between his newly emerging self and past ties. The second-class bus jostled over dirt roads, forded rivers, passed through dense jungles. In the small village of Culiacán, Kerouac spent the night in a rude stick hut, drinking pulque and smoking opium while singing bop songs for his Indian hosts.

When Kerouac arrived at 212 Orizaba Street, he found Burroughs writing like a "mad genius in littered rooms." Kerouac wrote Ginsberg that he felt like some beat fool in a land of centipedes, worms, and rats, trapped in a room with the "St. Louis of American aristocracy." Burroughs was injecting heroin, and Kerouac, too, began to use it several times a week. While the drug intensified his depression, the despair he still felt over the public failure of his writing, he began work on *Doctor Sax*, an experimental novel about his Lowell childhood. Most of the book had to be written in a hall bathroom because Burroughs' quarters were so cramped. Kerouac had no money at the time, and Burroughs described him in a letter to Ginsberg as being surly and uncooperative.

Kerouac wrote Holmes that he was destitute and starving, his weight dropped from 170 pounds to 158, but that he was beginning with *Doctor Sax* to discover a "wild form" beyond the arbitrary confines of the novel. He admitted an irrational lust to notate every association and reverberation in his consciousness, a desire to amplify every image and recollection. The circumstances of his life were affecting his sensibility. Burroughs' bathroom was as isolated as a prison cell; the delirium of heroin, of constant marijuana and little food had allowed him to experience, like Rimbaud, the derangement of the senses. In another letter to Holmes he exclaimed under the influence of marijuana: "How's the folks? Who's the hex? What's the hoax? Where's the axe? How's the hix? I got hicks." He was writing with a renewed sense of verbal play, a punning distortion of language that encouraged access to the unconscious.

At the same time that he was remembering his childhood in *Doctor Sax*, he was groping with the problems of identity and anonymity. Burroughs was preparing to leave Mexico for South America and tried to interest Kerouac in the journey, but his spirits were at an absolute nadir. He wrote Holmes that he felt surrounded by doom and death; he was penniless, and hounded by a former wife who wanted him jailed—Joan Haverty had filed her paternity suit. He was the loneliest of writers, having completed three long books in the past year, yet forced to live like a despised bum. Finally, he compared himself to Wilhelm Reich, predicting that like Reich he would die in disgrace, poverty, and isolation.

Exhausted and miserable, he returned to Rocky Mount in August of 1952 only to be jarred by another surprise visit from Cassady who convinced Kerouac to move into his new home in San Jose. Kerouac joined the Cassadys on the West Coast, but his disappointment with Neal's egotism and material concerns, as well as complications with Carolyn, forced him to leave. Impoverished again, he found a room on San Francisco's skid row, worked as a yard clerk for the Southern Pacific, and spent most of his time in his room writing "San Francisco Blues," a series of poems, and "October in the Railroad Earth," one of his finest short pieces. He wrote Holmes that he now felt like an exile in his own country, as he brooded over the past, the inexplicable rejections he had received from Columbia University, from publishers, even from his family—most of all he was haunted by the memory of his mother's warnings that he not dishonor his father's name. He began to work as a brakeman, hoarding his earnings in a resentful, self-pitying mood, feeling nostalgia for a girl named Mary Carney whom he had first loved at sixteen in Lowell. Now he felt he had been seduced from the comforts of life with her—having children, working on the Boston-Maine railroad as her father had done—by the careening hucksterism of Neal Cassady.

Kerouac was back in Mexico City when Burroughs was preparing to depart. Unhappy and desolate as he felt, he thought Burroughs' fate was even worse than his. His friend had lost everything—Joan, children, even his patrimony. Kerouac watched Burroughs pack in the moldy room with its old leather cases and worn holsters. Burroughs gave Bill Garver, wasting away from drugs, a derringer and hurried off into the night, at the last minute throwing a picture of Ginsberg into his bag.

Kerouac returned to New York in time for the Christmas holidays. His mother had found a new apartment in Richmond Hill, Queens, and he remained there through spring writing *Maggie Cassidy*, in which he memorialized Mary Carney. In May he boarded a bus for his brakeman job in California. After a freighter trip to Panama, he was back in New York by August where he had a two-month romance with a black woman that became the subject of *The Subterraneans*. Several weeks after the affair had been disrupted by Gregory Corso, he sat down in his mother's kitchen and on

Benzedrine completed the book in three consecutive days and nights.

These years were among the most fruitful but restless of Kerouac's career. His peripatetic journeys continued until the publication of *On The Road* in 1957. There were several more flights to California, and another Mexican adventure with Ginsberg and Corso. Kerouac had not lost his capacity for revelry despite his discouragements. In a letter to Holmes he described a June day in 1955 in New York City that began with a visit to Anatole Broyard, continued as he got drunk with Corso, and then sang bop songs in Washington Square Park; at sunrise, he found himself on the Morton Street pier with two tenor saxophonists and a trumpet player. That afternoon he drank with Malcolm Cowley, the critic. But the levity was beginning to be tempered by a gnawing despair over his future. After all that he had written, nothing had been published since *The Town and the City*, and he had not earned a cent as a writer since the initial advance of one thousand dollars. That Kerouac was beginning to wonder about his own identity is suggested by the way he kept changing his name as he signed his letters, from Jack, to Jean, to Jean-Louis, to Jack-off or Jockolio.

Kerouac sustained himself spiritually during his years of denial by prolonged study of Buddhism—as his thousand-page manuscript, *The Book of the Dharma*, may suggest if it is published. His interest began in 1954 when Neal Cassady was proselytizing for Edgar Cayce, the psychic medium who claimed the ability to tell a person his past lives. Kerouac felt Cassady was being duped into a belief in ego and self-nature because of a tremendous need to cling to personality. He had been reading Thoreau, and decided to tap the roots of Cayce's views on reincarnation by going directly to Buddhist scripture in the compilation of great texts—the Lancasatara Sutra, the Surangama Sutra, the Diamond Sutra, and many others—in Goddard's *Buddhist Bible*. He spent months reading in libraries, working with both primary and secondary sources, even translating some of the sutras from the French. He wrote Cassady that life itself was as much a dream as the notion of eternity, that the soul had no essence after death, which simply meant the departure of one's consciousness from participation in dream. The true way was nonconceptual, Kerouac argued, and Cayce's system depended on certain arbitrary concepts necessary to preserve the illusion of self. Cayce was "an angel furying in the murks of error," caught in the surface reality of the discriminating, observing, judging mind. Essential Mind, however, was reached by meditation—All-Things realized through dream without selfhood. While Cassady was unprepared to accept such propositions, Kerouac began to apply them to his own life and art. His studies in Mahayana Buddhism confirmed his own literary aesthetic, as well as supporting his spiritual needs. Knowing, the Buddhists taught, was exclusively spontaneous, never a function of past memory. Whatever occurred in innocent spontaneity could become meditative; one could live from moment to moment, relaxed, playful, weightless, without tension or expectation. As the Diamond Sutra which Kerouac read and reread states:

> Stars, darkness, a lamp, a phantom, dew, a bubble,
> A dream, a flash of lightning, or a cloud:
> Thus should one look upon the world.

Meditation, a state of controlled grace as Kerouac felt it, could never be designed, sought, or pursued, but had to happen of its own accord. The time he spent in meditation helped him to reconcile himself to his own essential aloneness, but it also invigorated him with the ecstatic sense of "samadhi" which he described in *The Dharma Bums* as "the state you reach when you stop everything and stop your mind and you actually with your eyes closed see a kind of eternal multiswarm of electrical Power of some kind ululating in place of just pitiful images and forms of objects."

Kerouac outlined his "Chinese position" to Ginsberg in a letter of May 1954, claiming to have reached the center of things "where nothingness resides and does absolutely nothing." He aspired to abandon all evil outflowing of "life" to permit the recognition that he had no self, no ego, and therefore could no longer act as an "I." As he read in the *Tao Te Ching*:

In the pursuit of learning one knows more every day;
in the pursuit of the way one does less everyday.
One does less and less until one does nothing at all,
and when one does nothing at all there is nothing that is undone.

Buddhism served to change the Beat emphasis from defeat in the world to beatific acceptance, from a rage of self-assertion to a quiet watching, an eventual merger with entities larger than the self. Kerouac decided to terminate all activity for the time in order to assimilate his new ideas—all writing, work, friends, sex. Again, reading the *Tao Te Ching*, he must have been moved by passages such as the following:

Without stirring abroad
One can know the whole world;
Without looking out of the window
One can see the way to heaven.
The further one goes
The less one knows.

Kerouac wrote long letters to Ginsberg summarizing his philosophical discoveries and urging the study of Buddhism. But there were consistent signs of the weight of his own sadness. In the summer of 1955 he wrote to Ginsberg that his favorite writers—Emily Dickinson, Blake, and Thoreau—had all ended their lives as recluses. Sleeping on Bill Garver's floor in Mexico that summer, afflicted by his phlebitis, he informed Ginsberg that he felt aimless, ephemeral, without direction or purpose. While Ginsberg responded eagerly to Kerouac's long letters full of advice on Buddhist scripture, Burroughs had very different views. When he heard that Kerouac had planned a period of celibacy, he wrote telling him that:

Buddhism is psychic junk . . . . A man who uses Buddhism or any other involvement to remove love from his being in order to avoid suffering, has committed, in my mind, sacrilege comparable to castration.

Kerouac was impressed by the forcefulness of Burroughs' remarks, but he persevered in his Buddhist studies. Unconsciously, he needed the passivity and distance that Buddhist tenets offered to gain perspective on his own disappointments, delusions, anger, and temporal failures. At the same time that Buddhism became a way of deconditioning, of changing his own expectations, helping him to transcend his old self and to rise from the sloughs of despondence, it must have created as much conflict as it did resolution. Kerouac's very ambition as a writer was tied to his exceptional sense of his own past. Buddhists see the recourse to future ambitions or past memories as an evasion of the immediate; the future is only a projection of the past, and can neither be expected nor desired. Yet Kerouac's literary ambitions were much stronger than the ideology that provided temporary succor. Ironically, the utter anonymity in the face of the world that he had learned to appreciate through Buddhism made the public role that was demanded after *On The Road* appear all the more difficult for him.

With Buddhism, he had weathered his most depressing period. He had also been reconverted to a religious temperament that had been obscured by the existentially rebellious impulses of the Beats. Kerouac, Ginsberg, and some of the West Coast poets like Gary Snyder and Philip Whalen used Buddhism to shift their early stress from disillusion in Moloch's world to an inner voyage, an attempt to pursue alternate value systems. Buddhism helped Kerouac transcend his own artistic ego, the supreme sense of self he had admired in men like Cassady or Cannastra. Writing *Wake Up*, a life of Buddha, and *Some Of The Dharma* became more than simply the relief of his own burdens or a way of preventing total collapse. The hours of study and meditation became a reaffirmation of his own gentleness, his search for a quiet, solitary, continual, and conscious compassion for all sentient beings.

Still, Kerouac's own desperation in 1954 and 1955, the years of his most intense involvement with Buddhism, cannot be minimized. In May of 1955, he related to Ginsberg a dream that occurred in a synagogue library which revealed the extent of his own personal loss and fear. In the dream, Kerouac is suddenly seized with convulsions in front of two men in a synagogue lined with books. Screaming maniacally, flopping about epileptically, Kerouac grovels as the men calmly observe him, neither surprised nor frightened but detached. As he continues to scream, Kerouac is sorry for the men whose worship or contemplation he has disturbed. The scream suggests the unpublished manuscripts; the convulsions are the result of the artist's need for public recognition, and the men are that indifferent audience. At the end of the letter, he begs Ginsberg to pray for him, saying that he is at the end of his tether and is thinking about suicide. He calls himself a wretched paper pauper and blames the New York publishers.

Kerouac's devotion to his craft was his greatest sustenance, the singular connection to the world of a particularly isolated man who yearned for communion and celebration even as he found his respite in desert walks or living in a shack on a mountaintop. From 1950 to 1957, he wrote twelve books, a creative explosion comparable to Melville's great productive period from 1853 to 1857. During these bleak years he was encouraged by friends and to a significant extent by Malcolm Cowley, who criticized *On The Road* for being too Wolfean, but recognized its raw power as early as 1953. Robert Giroux, Carl Solomon, and another editor working for Alfred A. Knopf had all rejected the book for essentially the same reason— what they saw as a formal and structural looseness. Cowley, who was then an advisory editor at Viking, tried to convince the house editors to buy the book. He corresponded with Kerouac and helped get a section of the novel, "The Mexican Girl," printed in the *Paris Review* and another part in *New World Writing*. Finally, in 1955, Viking editor Keith Jennison became interested, possibly because of an account of Ginsberg's reading of "Howl" in San Francisco that appeared in the book section of the Sunday *New York Times* and created a stir.

One year later no progress had been made despite the fact that Kerouac had already spent two years reworking the manuscript. He wrote to Cowley in the summer of 1956 threatening to withdraw his book unless given a contract and an advance, suggesting that rather than being demeaned he would prefer not to have the book published at all. Fortunately, Viking responded favorably and Kerouac heard his good news in Mexico that August. When Cowley also helped Kerouac get a small grant of three hundred dollars from the National Institute of Arts and Letters, Kerouac wrote that Cowley had assisted the "helpless angels."

On The Road was published in the fall of 1957, almost six years after it had been written. Ironically, the timing was perfect. Had the book appeared earlier, it might have received only the transient attention accorded *The Town and the City.* Kerouac sensed this, and in a note to Cowley he remarked that *On The Road* was a hipster novel that would crest on the wave of rock-and-roll. The book was clearly a sign of a new awareness in America. Gilbert Millstein, writing in *The New York Times,* saw it as a "historic occasion" comparable to the publication of Hemingway's *The Sun Also Rises*—another herald of generational identity. While *On The Road* received considerable attention, many of its reviewers were vicious or misinformed. "The Know-Nothing Bohemians," Norman Podhoretz' attack in *Partisan Review,* is an indication of the general reception. Podhoretz realized that a new generation was in the making, and he characterized it as hostile to civilized values, an anti-intellectual reflection of ignorant, populist primitivism. He claimed that the action of *On The Road* was without dramatic validity, that the experiences it recorded were trivial, but worst of all, he deplored Kerouac's "simple inability to say anything in words." Such reviews had a drastic personal effect. From the solitude of meditation in the wilderness to the brutal exposure of public appearances was too great a distance to be traversed without foundering, and Kerouac chose to annihilate himself by withdrawal in the manner of Melville after the failure of *Moby Dick.*

ALLEN GINSBERG

LONG AGO, ALLEN GINSBERG offered an image of himself as "Poet-prophet-friend on the side of love & the Wild Good. That's the karma I wanted—to be Saint." But the way to sanctity and the purification of worldly desires can be painful and treacherous. As Yeats' Crazy Jane tells the moralizing bishop who taunts her in her fallen state, nothing can be whole that has not first been sundered, rent by the disorders of risk in action.

Ginsberg's childhood in Paterson, New Jersey, and early years as a Columbia student were cauterized by intense suffering, anxiety, and the most introspective self-confrontation. He needed years to understand his own identity, and to define himself as a poet. While he employed his shaping powers of articulation and his probing curiosity as means of discovery, these same qualities sometimes became only an aggressive shield, disguises for his insecurities. His sanity was at times in question, precariously balanced on the edge of what he might learn about himself. Even close friends like Burroughs worried about his future ability to function in the world.

Allen Ginsberg's childhood was tormented by the psychological instability of his mother, Naomi. Frequently, he missed school to remain with her, trying to soothe her hysteria. Naomi Ginsberg was an extreme case of the exacerbations suffered by sensitive individuals as a result of political struggle and dissident ideology. She obsessively feared assassination, believing that her mother-in-law was trying to poison her and imagining spies when she looked out of her window. The "mad idealism" (as her son phrased it) of her leftist affiliations reached a peak during the Spanish civil war, when she became convinced that President Roosevelt himself was responsible for placing wires in the ceilings and even in her head to eavesdrop on her most private thoughts. Institutionalized for three years during her son's adolescence, she returned home with amnesia after electric- and insulin-shock therapy, hardly recognizable because of the weight she had gained while under Metrasol. She soon left her family to live with a sister in the Bronx, but was again to be institutionalized in Pilgrim State Hospital on Long Island.

Ginsberg's visits to his mother burdened him with a sense of hopeless frustration. There was little that could alleviate Naomi's misery and isolation. Her letters to him were yet another reminder of the world's pain, strangely mixing poignant despair, berating accusation, and desperate pleas for assistance in obtaining her release. Characteristically, she would combine expressions of terrible loneliness with unexpected twists of affirmation:

> I wish I could feel loving arms around me. I wish I could fall in love and get love in return. When will my sons love me! . . . Make a joy out of everything you do. Don't let anything bother you too much. Only remember the good.

Her mind swung like a pendulum from indictment to benevolence. One particularly distressing factor for her son was Naomi's thoughtless nudity, a certain weird flirtatiousness with her own memory of her former beauty which he found difficult to endure. While Ginsberg identified with his mother as an outcast, he was disturbed and unsettled by her unpredictable changes of mood and her utter inability to comprehend his own intentions in life. Naomi Ginsberg had become the ambivalent mother, more dependent patient than protector, more an object of pity than a source of solace.

Allen's father, Louis Ginsberg, a poet and teacher, was the

stabilizing presence in the household. If Naomi's political aspirations motivated her son's outrage against injustice, his father's
acceptance of the system provided a model to be rejected. For forty
years, Louis Ginsberg taught English at Central High School in
Paterson, and at night at Rutgers University. A conservative liberal,
he valued culture as a vehicle to inculcate traditional values which
would support existing institutions. Where Naomi had been atheis-
tic, Louis stressed the importance of his Jewish heritage; when his
wife belonged to communist fringe groups, Louis feared retribution
just as his Russian grandparents had feared the pogrom.

Jack Kerouac once perceptively observed that to Ginsberg, Louis
represented hateful sanity, and that by playing the madman, the son
could somehow justify his mother. But as with any dangerous game,
the feigning of madness tends to overwhelm the imagination. An
"antic disposition," assumed initially like Hamlet's as a persona, can
ultimately transform consciousness. In Ginsberg's case, the madness
was more courted than inflicted; though it necessarily meant
suffering, it served to relieve him of the obligations of a middle-class
existence.

When Ginsberg began his studies at Columbia University in 1943
at the age of seventeen, he was still able to balance his father's
expectations of respectability with his mother's idealism. Originally
intending to help the masses by working within the labor movement, he studied economics and spoke vehemently for the debating
society. But his interests were already shifting. The course which
most pleased him during his freshman year was a great-books
seminar taught by Lionel Trilling, a novelist and literary critic.
Lucien Carr, one of his classmates, encouraged him to write poems.
Ginsberg began showing his poems to Trilling, even though he
realized that is was unlikely that Trilling would respond to his
subjectively elegiac voice. Another teacher, poet Mark Van Doren,
was generally more receptive although he felt the poems were often
bathetic. Ginsberg admitted to Van Doren that he was unsure about
the poems, that he felt handicapped by ambiguity and an excess of
unfocused feeling.

His father's criticism undoubtedly contributed to his uncertainty. Louis Ginsberg had written and loved poetry all of his life, modestly fashioning a decorous, conventional verse style. Under his influence, his son was imitating Renaissance forms with an ornate, overstylized language that was often woodenly lifeless. When Louis Ginsberg criticized the inadequacies of these early attempts, he also discouraged any tendencies toward experimentation, advising that "unless the shell hold, the kernal is not sweet." The paternal advice on prosody was also intended to protect the son from other possible excesses.

Louis, in his letters, often appeared as a sententious Polonius figure warning his son that revolt could only lead to social disorientation. He stressed caution, reserve, moderation, and pragmatic realism in poetic form as in life. Allen's brother Eugene, who also wrote poetry, accepted such advice. But Allen felt increasing scorn for much of the accepted poetry of his day. During a lengthy correspondence on the aesthetics of poetry, Louis recommended that his son attend to poet Karl Shapiro's ideas on the necessity for absolute moral values in poetry, on order and the danger of disequilibrium. When Louis praised Shapiro's attack on Hart Crane, Allen responded that he had begun his study of Rimbaud.

Ginsberg fully appreciated the weakness of his early attempts to find a suitable poetic voice, even though he edited the *Columbia Review*, and won several university prizes for his poems. The poems were incorporeal, weighted by such abstract concerns as eternity, light, and death. The slow iteratively reflective tonalities, the controlling sense of organization, all reflected his study of Petrarch, Dante, Sidney, and Spenser. Ginsberg acknowledged to Kerouac that he was only a "ventriloquist of other voices," an imitator of *literary* suffering who realized that the false rhetoric of his symbolism only created artificial passions. He told Kerouac that he was so absorbed with "a series of words that I went around abstractly composing odes, until even now I can't tell them apart." Apprenticeship to traditional models is a basic step in an artist's evolution. *Gates Of Wrath*, a collection of Ginsberg's undergraduate poems, shows sincerity in emulation—but the poems are often awkward and amorphous. Lacking the concrete imagistic base of his later work, the early poems are like the academic verse that dominated the poetry journals after the war. Ginsberg was struggling to discover a significant new form, and he connected his inability to grow as a poet to his own turbulently unsettled emotional life. His recognition of his personal inadequacies finally paralyzed his imagination, as he confessed to Van Doren:

> I want to be a saint, a real saint when I am still young, for there is much work to do. However, my poetry is incompetent so far and I will have to work and understand before I can find a way of writing that is right. I do not feel now that I can by myself, and I need help—psychoanalytic help—before I will be able to find myself, and I do not think that I am doing any good by continuing to write poetry, so I have stopped writing in the last month and may continue to do so unless I can break through and work in peace and effectively. I may have to change my mind if nothing ever happens or if I discover that I must still work however empty it seems, but I still do not see any perfection of technique or imagination while I stay as I am.

Ginsberg was to devote considerable energy during the following years to finding appropriate psychoanalytic treatment. His most pressing anxiety was due to a sexual confusion that was compounded by his mother's malady, something which made him mistrust women as vessels of failure. His early inclinations were homosexual—originally, he wanted to attend Columbia because of an unrequited infatuation for a former schoolmate who had enrolled there. The authoritarian culture of the years after the war had categorized homosexuality as a diseased perversion bordering on criminality. Ginsberg was tormented by a repressed yearning for physical contact which could be relieved only through masturbatory fantasy. During his Columbia years, his friendship with Kerouac—whom Ginsberg appreciated as a mellow, trusting figure of infinite sensitivity—afforded him a reliable form of dependence that he desperately needed. Kerouac's tolerance and his genuine capacity for understanding diffused Ginsberg's guilt. The relationship with Burroughs—whom Ginsberg saw as a substitute father—helped open him to an awareness of his own inhibitions and fears. Burroughs' attempt to psychoanalyze Ginsberg illuminated feelings of self-loathing and inferiority. Burroughs emphasized the importance of accepting oneself for what one was, and advised Ginsberg to act according to his own innermost needs, to ignore social dictates. While exposing a series of ingenious defenses and rationalizations, Burroughs demonstrated to Ginsberg the roots of his sexual hesitancy. The recognition that his own "queerness" would not prevent close relations with those he most admired allowed Ginsberg a necessary self-respect, and made him less the victimized voyeur of his own fantasies. When Burroughs later suggested that a Reichian analysis would be helpful, Ginsberg wrote directly to Wilhelm Reich. The letter seems all the more revealing because it was never actually sent:

> My main psychic difficulty, as far as I know, is the usual oedipal entanglement. I have been homosexual for as long as I can remember, and have had a limited number of homosexual affairs, both temporary and protracted. They have been unsatisfactory to me, and I have always approached love affairs with a sort of self contradictory, conscious masochism. I have had a few experiences with women which were unsatisfactory from the start since my motivation was more curiosity than interest, and I have been pretty consistently impotent when with a woman. I have had long periods of depressing guilt feelings—disguised mostly as a sort of Kafkian sordidness of sense of self—melancholy, and the whole gamut I suppose. I have been trying valiantly to get some psychoanalysis for years almost always unsuccessfully, mostly for financial reasons—I live on $15 a week provided by my father, study in school, and could not provide the necessary $40–$50 a week by part-time work.

The Kafkian sordidness to which Ginsberg referred was not eliminated by Burroughs' amateur analysis. Ginsberg realized that although he was now able to see his situation with greater clarity, he remained centrally unchanged, "washed up on the shores of my neurosis," but even more vulnerable than before since his defenses had been destroyed with "nothing to replace the lost armor." The protection Ginsberg desired was less related to ideology or psychological recognition than to sheer experience, more bruising contact with the world of ordinary activity than his student pursuits permitted. On one occasion his abrasive friend Lucien Carr took him to a workingmans' cafeteria, and argued that a Columbia intellectual could not pose as one of Whitman's roughs, and would never be able to communicate with such men. Carr, who habitually mocked Ginsberg's idealistic aspirations, told him that his virginal naïveté and gaucheness resulted from inexperience with life.

Ironically, it was Carr's stabbing of Dave Kammarer that indirectly led to Ginsberg's suspension from Columbia and precipitated him into the world. In the spring of 1945 Carr, who had been expelled after the murder, and then Kerouac, who had been asked to avoid the campus, were discovered to be living in Ginsberg's dormitory room. When a chambermaid reported that "Fuck the Jews" and "Nicholas Murray Butler has no balls" had been inscribed on the dirty film of Ginsberg's window, Dean of Students McKnight was outraged and wanted Ginsberg expelled. Lionel Trilling interceded on Ginsberg's behalf, but the good Dean was so shocked by what Ginsberg had written that he could not even bear to pronounce the words—instead passing them to Trilling on a slip of paper while looking away. Trilling and Van Doren advised McKnight to soften his position, and he agreed to a suspension with readmission through a psychiatrist's letter stating that Ginsberg was fit to resume studies. Ginsberg wrote that he was allowed to "fade into the landscape of the common world," working at a variety of jobs, spot-welder, night porter, dishwasher in Bickford's cafeteria, learning the argot of jazz and Times Square, how to communicate with nonintellectuals, ordinary people, hustlers, and the down and out.

Enrolling in a four-month training course in the Merchant Marine Academy at Sheepshead Bay, Brooklyn, he found his fellow students adolescent. The school fostered anxiety while offering a training in routine, detail work like buffing floors with foot-rags, washing clothes, storing gear neatly. Ginsberg tried to assume the mask of a "regular guy" he told Kerouac, but his disguise ended when his classmates caught him reading Hart Crane's poems. He graduated at the end of 1945 with a case of pneumonia. As soon as he recovered, early in 1946, he embarked on a seven-month voyage on a ship that stopped at various ports on the Atlantic and Gulf coasts. The trip served a dual purpose. In one sense, it became the psychological equivalent of a monastic retreat, severing Ginsberg from the ties of family, friends, school, all vestiges of familiar culture. Ginsberg felt sharp differences from his shipmates—they would play poker while he read—but the close contact with ordinary seamen helped to violate the protective sheath of academic life that had separated him from the world.

In the spring of 1947 Ginsberg began receiving a series of enticingly ambivalent letters from Neal Cassady. Kerouac had introduced them several months earlier when Cassady was in New York. Cassady had been excited intellectually by his relationship with Ginsberg, and he admitted that he had consciously forced himself to accept Ginsberg's amorous advances as compensation for what he had learned. He claimed that upon returning to Denver he felt a neurotically compulsive need for Ginsberg, comparing himself to a "woman about to lose her man." Subsequently, Cassady acknowledged that although he could be bisexual, he preferred women, and his emotional needs were not very strong in the first place. He felt the same brotherly love for Ginsberg that he had shared with Kerouac. However, in the same letter he proposed that they might "assume a responsibility toward each other and entertain a certain erotic attraction (lover idea)." Ginsberg, who saw his relations to friends like Kerouac, Burroughs, and Carr in a sacramental and ritual light, felt the time was appropriate to seal his friendship with Cassady sexually. Expecting a more binding relationship, he left for Denver. But Cassady was unprepared for any total involvement. At best, he could only squeeze Ginsberg into a regular schedule divided up among his wife, other lovers, friends, work, poolroom visits and horse races, and whatever else occurred in his frenetic life. Dejected, feeling that he had been duped and manipulated, Ginsberg vented his rage in a letter written to Cassady that summer:

> The point is that I am the only one capable of mastering you right now and moving you by will and intelligence and insight and presumption out of the sterile round of self-destructive love and work and activities and emotions, the whole impasse of your existence. I do not know but that you need me and may realize it more than I need you though at the moment my practical and partly my emotional need for you gives you some advantage, but not very much. I will break your mind and soul open and I warn you that now, even if it means chaining you to a bed and beating you with that prison belt.

Under the pressure of Ginsberg's appeal, Cassady explained that the urgent tone of his own letters was caused by a habitual need to persuade people to act. Reconciled to the fact that Cassady was unavailable except on his own terms, Ginsberg agreed to hitchhike south with him to visit Burroughs and Huncke at New Waverly. They remained only one week. While Cassady drove Burroughs and Huncke back to New York City, Ginsberg shipped out on the *John Blair*, a freighter carrying wheat to Africa via Marseilles. The voyage lasted almost two months, with forty days at sea, so Ginsberg was unable to register for fall classes at Columbia. He assured his father that he had every intention of completing his degree, but that he needed money for psychoanalysis. He stressed the importance of such assistance, writing that the Denver experience had so perturbed him, filled him with such irritation, ennui, and self-lacerating introspectiveness that he needed the isolation of a long sea trip as a prelude to the certain pain awaiting him when he began analysis.

Returning to classes in the spring session, he started a novel about his years at Columbia University. He sent several chapters to his father who deplored the eccentricities expressed by the characters, finding their actions generally barbarous. Ginsberg responded that his point was that the entire society was decadent, that bourgeois "normalcy" was diseased. To disapprove of a novel because its characters are irresponsible or eccentric, he argued, was to avoid an aesthetic judgment. His intention was not to "prettify" the community of free spirits he was trying to depict. Like Kerouac and Burroughs, he would employ no euphemism, nor would he censor any crucial language or detail to make his work more palatable. At least his characters were aware of their imperfections while the rest of society was "unconscious that it exhibited its repression in social sadism." Ginsberg's attempt to write honestly about his life at Columbia marks a turning point in his own development away from the romantic longings of his earlier poetry, but he still needed more time to absorb Kerouac's and Burroughs' lessons before he could find his own poetic voice.

When Ginsberg reached the end of his years at Columbia, he felt a sense of dead-end hopelessness. As he faced his future, he was very much alone. His friends had scattered. Burroughs had departed for Mexico. Kerouac was sequestered with his mother in virtual isolation, completing *The Town and the City*. Cassady had just declared that there was no hope that their former intimacy could be renewed on any terms. Looking for work like an "eccentric dope in a world of mechanical supermen," Ginsberg was miserable and lost in the vastness of New York City. He defined his *accidie* in a letter to Kerouac:

> I long for death more than ever, but am afraid to take my life. My soul does not want to take any action, exist or die. I can't find the way out by thought, even action is useless it seems. My action is always balked and untrustworthy. I haven't even the guts or the clarity and resolution to pray for forgiveness because I am tonguetied and will not name my true sins.

Ginsberg spent a long, dreary summer working two hours a day as a file clerk at the American Academy of Political Science, returning to his East Harlem tenement to idle, read, and sleep away the time. He compared himself to Joseph K who is suddenly awakened, accused of unknown crimes, and put on trial for having led a meaningless existence. Increasingly, he felt the inadequacy of his poetry. Reading the manuscript of *The Town and the City*, where he was portrayed as the Rimbaudian poet Levinsky, intensified his sense of artistic failure, and even more, of his own inability to rebuild his personality.

Ginsberg had previously endured what he called his "Denver Doldrums" because of the emotional fiasco with Neal Cassady, but his present depression was even worse; now he felt utterly isolated and worthless. One day he was relaxing in bed, reading Blake while masturbating, and as he came he experienced a sweepingly blissful revelation. He saw "Ah! Sun-Flower," the poem over which he had been musing, as a manifestation of the universe freed from body, that is, as a psychospiritual transportation, a departure from corporeal awareness that allowed ineffably ecstatic energies to pervade his consciousness—something between what Buddhists might call Nirvana and the "terrible beauty" of Yeats' "Easter 1916." Simultaneously, he heard a deep, grave voice sounding like "tender rock" reciting "Ah! Sun-Flower," and a few moments later, "The Sick Rose." Hearing these lyrics of mutability rendered through no apparent physical agency that Ginsberg could perceive shocked him out of his torpor, the lethargy caused by refusing to end a phase of his life. Catalyzed to the vitality of the universe, he would now see his own poetic attempts as part of a tradition of magic prophecy. Later, he would understand the experience in more psychological terms, as an inner mental projection of his own desired but then only latent physiological voice. In the following weeks, Ginsberg deliberately tried to reevoke the Blake spirit in order to confirm his initial sense of cosmic depth and of a shaping intelligence in the universe, but he soon learned that the act of invocation itself was not his proper path, that it could easily lead to the monstrous horrors of a bad psychedelic trip. Years later he recalled his "vastation" in a book of prose jottings called *Indian Journals*:

> The four different visions . . . ending with a crawling sensation, horror in my skull & the sky black closing down on me—uncanny & horrible apparition of —what—of nothing describable in specific: A feeling, which was sudden, relating to the black crawling appearance of the sky—the sky the farther universe itself—yet there was nothing apparent physical crawling in the sky. But the sensation of a living presence—Uncanny—a non-human, implacably alien presence—to eat me up—then & there— Similar this 1948 vision to Ayahuasca horrors in Peru the night of the falling star & the God-blob. Since this the last sign from Blake or whatever might be named of that 1948 time—Perhaps schematized to indicate the limits of human perception—beyond that—bordering off into the non-human—If you want to see *that*—It's serious—maybe death— naturally—being beyond the nature of mental flesh perception—thus perhaps telling me—"sign"—to shut up & live in the present temporary form.

John Clellon Holmes first met Ginsberg that summer, shortly after the Blake visions. In *Nothing More To Declare*, he offers a vivid picture of Ginsberg who on one particular visit spoke about God, Blake, and Cezanne, emanations and transfiguration, visions, madness, and prophecy with maniacally feverish energy, seemingly undulating a single winding sentence. Holmes was haunted by Ginsberg's penetrating eyes, his ingratiating laugh, his chattering combination of the erudite and the fantastic. Ginsberg's powerful impression was reflected in a journal entry of May 1949 which became the germ of *Go*, Holmes' novel. Holmes saw Ginsberg as a combination of oracle and jester, a man of disturbing intensities and hysteria suffering from the inverted egoism of the spiritually wounded. According to Holmes, Ginsberg's relationship with his mother was the source of his wound, the axis around which his madness, homosexuality, and poet-nature all revolved. Holmes may have been a little envious and bewildered by what Ginsberg had learned since his suspension from Columbia: a style that blended a hipster's awareness of the street with more intellectual proclivities. Ginsberg had consciously decided to demolish his old self of defensive arrogance and superiority, attempting to obviate his ego through drugs, sex, and friends like Cassady who would encourage the irrational and impetuous in him to violate the inhibitions of reason and control.

One man in particular, Herbert Huncke, who initially introduced Ginsberg and Burroughs to morphine and the underworld of New York, was to wrench Ginsberg from the middle-class insulations of his early conditioning, to rupture the final dikes of restraint and discipline. The relationship was to end with Huncke's arraignment on felony charges, and Ginsberg's arrest and detention in the Columbia Psychiatric Institute. In 1949, Ginsberg moved from East Harlem to a small apartment at 1401 York Avenue where he lived frugally on thirty dollars a week earned as a copyboy at Associated Press. Partly because of the Blake experience, he felt a need for assimilation, a fear of flux, surprise, and even joy. He needed to withdraw from the distractions of the city, and he was satisfied with his solitude. One bitter day in early February, Huncke appeared at his door in a delirious and suicidal state. Recently released from jail, he had walked the streets of the city for nights and days without rest or food. His feet were bruised, bloody, and sore; his skin was blistered and festering. Despite his own desire for seclusion, Ginsberg charitably bathed Huncke's feet, and gave him his bed where he slept for several days. Ginsberg was intrigued by an ominous aura of danger that enveloped Huncke. Here was a man who seemed self-damned, who believed death was imminent and regarded that eventuality with morbid complacence, a man who suffered greatly, and who possessed what seemed almost supersensory perceptions. Huncke was egoless, completely rootless, with no sense of permanence, possession, or property. Ginsberg saw in his state a metaphor for what he was trying to express in his poetry, and he was impelled, as was Kerouac with Cassady, to mythologize such a character. He also realized a special kinship with Huncke because they both shared the same problem—an inability to accomplish direct, natural love. Despite warnings from his father and his friends, he allowed Huncke to dominate his life and his apartment, rearranging the furniture and wearing his clothes. Burroughs wrote him that Huncke was parasitical, that the more he was given, the greater his unconscious resentment of his benefactor.

When Huncke recuperated, Ginsberg delivered an ultimatum to either find work or leave. Huncke's answer was a huge psychosomatic boil, incapacitating his leg and requiring several more weeks to heal. During this time two of Huncke's friends, a paroled ex-convict named Little Jack Melody and a tall, auburn-haired beauty named Priscilla Arminger began to visit. Melody, who favored pink slacks and a zoot-suit hat, had a reputation as a Lower East Side gangster but Ginsberg felt a doelike gentility in him. Priscilla was a former heroin addict who had been cured by Melody's patient attendance. The visitors brought marijuana and a Victrola, and the group spent several nights talking and listening to jazz. Later that month Ginsberg developed a severe bronchial illness, and was solicitously cared for by Huncke and his friends. Depressed after his recovery, Ginsberg thought of leaving his job at Associated Press to visit Burroughs and Joan in order to galvanize Burroughs out of his heroin addiction. Melody proposed to assume responsibility for the apartment with Huncke, and in April he installed himself and Priscilla. The key had always been in the hall bathroom so that anyone—especially Kerouac when he was in the city—would be free to enter.

Melody, Priscilla, and Huncke had been breaking into cars and apartments, and they began to bring carved chairs, expensive cabinets, even a cigarette machine for the kitchen, into the already crowded area. On one occasion, they persuaded Ginsberg, his hands clammy with fear, to join them in a stolen car as they cruised midtown and took a woman's coat from a car parked on Third Avenue. Just then, Burroughs was arrested in New Orleans for possession of narcotics, and Ginsberg's plans to visit had to be canceled. Lucien Carr, still on parole himself, became concerned about Ginsberg's company, and worried about letters that he had written to Ginsberg which were being kept in a house of criminals. During an all-night walk around the city, Carr persuaded Ginsberg that the situation was dangerous. Finally, the three burglars agreed to clear Ginsberg's apartment of all compromising goods. Ginsberg wanted to deposit his own personal papers at his brother's house on Long Island, and Melody and Priscilla drove him there in another stolen car which was filled with stolen suits and other incriminating articles. In Queens, Melody took a wrong turn off Northern Boulevard, driving in the opposite direction on a one-way street. A policeman appeared, motioning him to stop. Melody panicked, backed up, and swerved the car around the policeman and back to Northern Boulevard. Irrationally believing that a police car was in pursuit, he drove wildly and lost control, crashing the car into a telephone pole. Little Jack and Priscilla, with instinctive criminal reactions, fled from the scene instantly. But Ginsberg was dazed, his glasses broken, his personal papers scattered all over the wreckage. He wandered about the area despairing and desolate with seven cents in his pocket, recalling the warnings he had received from those whom he most trusted, and realizing that what had occurred was inexorably connected to his earlier choices.

Gradually, he had permitted Huncke to involve him with a band of petty thieves. Instead of the "landscape of the common world," he had stumbled into an inferno of senseless illegality. Still, Huncke had imparted his particular lesson in the transient significance of material objects. With his skin disease, his face "spectralized the color of blue cheese" as Cassady put it, Huncke was an object of pity, as much an untouchable as Naomi. He had impressed Ginsberg with a marvelous knack at telling tales, with his curiosity, compassion, and demonic dreaminess. Huncke wrote short stories and would read them to Ginsberg; later, Ginsberg would dedicate to Huncke his book of early poems, *Empty Mirror*, both for the opportunity of hearing the stories and because Huncke epitomized the quality of vacant despondence that Ginsberg captured in the poems. Ginsberg had learned from Huncke's directness of language, a narrative written in "naked city man speech, clear and magnanimous as personal conversation," and this had been the direction Kerouac encouraged. Huncke was also a model of an unanalytical approach to daily life, but although the ultimate implications of deemphasizing the intellect were to be fruitful for Ginsberg's poetry, they did immediately precipitate a descent from the ivory tower of Columbia University to the threat of jail on a felony charge.

On the morning after the crash, the police arrived and arrested Ginsberg—his address, of course, had been found in the car. Trilling took Ginsberg to see Herbert Wechsler, a Columbia professor specializing in criminal law who counseled Ginsberg to plead guilty and serve his sentence. This scandal and the earlier involvement with Carr's murder of Kammarer had created a satanic reputation for Ginsberg at Columbia. Van Doren sternly advised that this "ring of iron" was a warning against further investigations of evil. But Ginsberg's faculty friends felt what Trilling has described as an aristocratic bond with him, and they were reluctant to see one of their best students imprisoned. Harry Carman, Dean of Columbia College, called District Attorney Frank Hogan, a loyal graduate of Columbia, and Hogan suggested grounds for a plea of psychological disability provided that Ginsberg received psychoanalytic therapy. Dean Carman arranged to have Ginsberg treated at Columbia Psychiatric Institute free of charge.

Almost as soon as he arrived at the Institute, Ginsberg met Carl Solomon, another man who was to influence him. Ginsberg was nervous, anxious to be assigned to his room, wondering what it would be like to live with a group of men who were supposed to be crazy. The tension of facing criminal indictment had made him unsure of his own grip on reality. When he entered his ward he saw a large man being wheeled in on a stretcher. Emerging from an insulin-shock coma, Solomon asked Ginsberg who he was in a literate tone. Testing Solomon's sensibility, Ginsberg answered that he was Prince Myshkin, the saintly character in Dostoevsky's *The Idiot.* Solomon retorted that he was Kirilov, the suicidal nihilist in *The Possessed* who is unable to tolerate any signs of ecstasy. The characterization was respectively exact, defining a continuing tension in their friendship. They met freely on the ward for several months, writing imaginary letters to figures like T. S. Eliot and reading aloud to each other. Ginsberg read Yeats and Melville, and told Solomon about Kerouac and Burroughs; Solomon introduced Ginsberg to his favorite French Surrealist writers, Michaux, Isou, Artaud, and also Genêt. Ginsberg took notes on Solomon's curious adventures and his aphoristic exclamations. Later, he would dedicate "Howl" to him. Solomon had been admitted to City College when he was fifteen in 1943, the same year that Ginsberg entered Columbia. Going through a Marxist phase, he joined the American Youth for Democracy, a communist-front organization known as the Tom Paine Club. His inquisitive nature caused him to begin shipping out on merchant-marine vessels after the war. In Paris, he searched for Existentialists and Surrealists, learning about them before they became esoteric. In 1947 he had jumped ship in France and witnessed an Artaud reading in Saint-Germain-des-Prés. He became interested in Artaud's book on Van Gogh, *The Man Suicided By Society*, where Artaud condemned all psychiatry, arguing that most mental patients were gifted with superior insight and lucidity that allowed them to see through social shams. When he returned to New York, Solomon was in a very negative, nihilistic state, thinking about suicide and lobotomy. Reading Gide's *Lafcadio's Adventures*, he became fascinated by the idea of gratuitous crime, stole a sandwich from the school cafeteria, showed it to a policeman, was sent to a psychologist and then to Psychiatric Institute.

When Carl Solomon first met Ginsberg he characterized him as a "dopey daffodil" because Ginsberg seemed to represent a Words-worthian projection of sensitivity rather than Artaud's Surrealist conception of the poet as brute. In Psychiatric Institute, Ginsberg seemed entirely conventional with a neat haircut and horn-rimmed glasses. The two friends fought continually over every intellectual and aesthetic point: Ginsberg, for example, saw Whitman as a sexual revolutionary, and Solomon would argue that his political ideas were more significant. They also disputed the relative merits of their analysts: Solomon was being analyzed by a woman, a disciple of

Harry Stack Sullivan, and Ginsberg by a Freudian. Ginsberg described the doctors in a letter to Kerouac as "ghouls of mediocrity," claiming that the staff interpreted absurd or eccentric action as madness. According to John Clellon Holmes, Ginsberg's analyst was soon left confused and completely at a loss, feeling that his patient was saner and surely more honest than he was. Ginsberg was released after eight months.

Out of Psychiatric Institute, Ginsberg introduced Solomon to some of his other friends. He persuaded Carl to rent a cold-water flat on 17th Street where they held a New Year's Eve party. Ginsberg introduced Solomon to Jay Landesman, a patron of the arts from St. Louis who edited a magazine called *Neurotica*, one of the earliest postwar publications to anticipate the sexual revolution. Landesman was to print both Ginsberg's and Solomon's work. Solomon later had two books published by City Lights Press, *Mishaps Perhaps* and *More Mishaps*. The books are comprised of staccato routines, strange anecdotes, and pithy essays, all reflecting Solomon's self-imposed and quixotic role of the world's intellectual antagonist. Called the "lunatic saint" by his friends, Solomon would fulfill their expectations by performing all kinds of weird acts: the perfect Dadaist gesture of throwing potato salad at novelist Wallace Markfield who was lecturing on Mallarmé, an act commemorated in "Howl"; pretending to be W. H. Auden at an exhibition and gleefully signing autographs in Auden's name; selling ice cream in front of the United Nations after leaving his position as an editor for Ace Books. "Every man lives by a set of rules to which he is the only exception," Solomon once wrote. To Ginsberg, Solomon was an instance of the artist as outrage, a man capable of an intuitively quick surrealistic buffoonery that exposed the pretentious stuffiness of the world. Like Huncke, he was an outcast artist, an exile within the culture.

Ginsberg returned to Paterson to live with his father after his release from Psychiatric Institute, and it was at this time that he met William Carlos Williams. He visited the older poet, ostensibly to interview him for a local labor newspaper. Williams did not then share the reputations of his friend Pound, or of Eliot, and pursued a contrary aesthetic. Ginsberg wanted to meet him both because he lived in Paterson and because he had been confused by lines in his poetry that sounded almost like prose. Earlier, he had written to Williams to describe his own youthful attempts "to perfect, renew, transfigure and make contemporarily real an old style of lyric machinery." Williams found the poems full of potential, but flawed by a language that was fashioned in literary terms. This was his point of difference with Pound and Eliot. Ginsberg wondered, when he interviewed him, why so many of Williams' lines approached a prose base, and the older poet responded with the recent memory of overhearing a Polish laborer in the streets of Paterson exclaiming "I'll kick yuh eye!" Williams asked how one could render such a line in iambic pentameter, and Ginsberg realized that Williams was listening for pure sounds and rhythm as derived from actual speech, not as dictated by a metronome or any preconceived literary pattern:

> I suddenly realized that his poetry was absolutely identical with speech, the highest speech, but absolutely identical, rhythmically and syntactically. And then I suddenly realized that if you began right where you are, with your own speech, then obviously you would have to create a whole new world of speech, that had never been written down before, which was what he was doing and what anybody could do. But it also meant that you had to listen, as he advised, very carefully, to your own sound, and to other people's talk-sound and talk-rhythms—and if you listened to "I'll kick yuh eye" or "plunging on a pissmire, uhhh . . . "! you would arrive at all sorts of new unknown rhythms.

After the interview, Ginsberg perused his own writing and sent Williams several fragments that corresponded to Williams' notions of "speak-talk-thinking." The older poet admired the lines, and Ginsberg understood what at the same time had inspired the projective-verse movement of the Black Mountain poets, the pragmatic American tradition of Emerson and John Dewey that urged artists to employ the materials of their own environment rather than looking abroad as James, Eliot, and Pound did. Williams enjoyed Ginsberg's spirit and they met on several occasions. Once, they visited a bar on River Street in Paterson that Williams wanted to use as a locale in his long poem *Paterson*, into which he was to weave his friendship with Ginsberg by quoting from his letters. Another time, they got slightly drunk in downtown Paterson, talking about Pound, Genêt, and Marianne Moore. When they went to look for an old swimming hole lost in the midst of factories, they paused at a riverbank to make a poem about a piece of old concrete, a sliver of tin, a pin from a loom, and some ancient dogshit. This accidental combination perfectly illustrated Williams' theory that objects actually surrounding the poet could be assembled into the stuff of poetry as effectively as myth or history. Williams, then in his late sixties, was depressed about aging and fearful of death. Kerouac encouraged Ginsberg to learn all he could from the older master, agreeing with Williams' idea that the best poetry resulted from the original impulse of the mind, the "prose seed" or first wild draft of the poem. Ginsberg acknowledged to his friend that Williams did know much that could help free him from traditional poetic affectation, but he didn't have the "whole naked junkyard in the moonlight of his intelligence like you."

Ginsberg's resilience during this period was strong enough to compensate for his lack of recognition as a poet. His friends were being published, they were even using him as a character in their books, but his own work was consistently rejected. Before the Huncke fiasco, prodded by Mark Van Doren, he had assembled a collection of his poetry called *The Book Of Doldrums*. In 1950, it was rejected by Robert Giroux, Kerouac's editor at Harcourt Brace. In 1952, Random House turned down *Empty Mirror* despite a generous preface by Williams. Ginsberg had been sending poems to *The Kenyon Review*, but John Crowe Ransom wrote him that he wanted a more compacted poetry. Around this time, in a letter of introduction for Ginsberg to Marianne Moore, William Carlos Williams wrote that he was "instinctively drawn" to Ginsberg without exactly knowing why, but he was confident that Ginsberg had a "clean, rigorously unrelenting mind that would do outstanding work" if he could survive. Williams emphasized that the exceptional sensitivity that he discerned could be lost if unnoticed. Moore responded that *Empty Mirror*, a collection especially influenced by Williams' short line, depressed her terribly because it only projected an unredeemable disgust and despair. She insisted that more affirmation was necessary. Another letter of introduction was sent by Williams to Ezra Pound—whom Ginsberg was to meet years later on Pound's eighty-second birthday.

New Directions had accepted several of Ginsberg's prose poems for their annual issue in the summer of 1952, but he was still dissatisfied by his lack of progress as a poet. He now knew the direction he wanted to take: Kerouac's "uncharted verbal rhetorical seas" of lush imagery and weaving rhythms. But his voice had not yet manifested itself in his work. In a letter to Cassady, Ginsberg admitted that he was still living in an egotistic grayness and squalor which now displeased him: "I must stop *playing* with my life in a disappointed gray world." He felt resigned to a condition where lack of love, tenderness, or meaningful relationship had forced a "blank withdrawal into myself." He told Cassady that he would have to leave New York City to escape the rut of his existence. It was at this time that Kerouac had begun writing to Ginsberg, interesting him in Buddhist ideas. Ginsberg, who often apprehends ideas visually, could make little sense of Kerouac's new concerns until he began studying Japanese and Chinese art in various libraries. He was particularly attracted to Zen, comparing its impact to Carl Solomon, seeing that its essence was to exhaust words so as to see the world new.

In December of 1953 Ginsberg hitchhiked south to Key West. His subsequent travel, his intellectual, emotional, and aesthetic growth were outlined in a long letter which he wrote to Mark Van Doren on May 19, 1956:

> . . . plane to rotting Havana, plane to Yucatan, then four months in the jungle near Palenque, old Mayan ruin, exploring, writing, swinging in hammocks and playing log drums, cutting bananas off trees and working on a plantation of a woman who used to play Jane in the Tarzan pictures

around 1933 (Karena Shields), a religious minded grandmother now who preferred to hide her face with wrinkles multiplied. Then wrote a long poem still Williams style ["Siesta In Xbalba"], blocks of observations separated by ellipses, though rather romantic in feeling. Then up to San Francisco where I worked for a year in market research and earned a flannel suit and had two secretaries and strode down Wall St. (Montgomery here) whistling in the morning. Then half a year supported by Govt. unemployment $$ putting together another book of sketches and prosy poems, tho this time a lot more developed than before and more spontaneous too. Then met a bunch of Buddhists (Zen) who are very nice, and entered Berkeley to take a masters and threw up my hands inside of a month and was back on wine and poetry with the zen lunatics. Never again. I swear I begin to realize the mistake I made in your office with the lawyer, I was scared and had nothing to be scared about really. Life is marvellous to me. Anyway I have gone mad again in a happy sort way and besides Whitman is a vast mountain so big I never saw him before. Be that as it may read my poems. They seem to me to be a kind of original blow struck for freedom, my own certainly. I don't know what to think. Are they not better than what you'd been led to expect? I have an immense pile of unpublished mss sitting around now and just begun to explore the possibilities of the long line—several experiments in which this mss is. But as far as I can see everybody else around is dead. Out here there are a few hidden and excellent poets—a kind of buddhist influenced post Pound post Williams classicism full of independence and humor AND gift of gab, native wordslinging. Well anyway I am off to the Arctic right now with a govt. cargo ship (I'm a civilian) going to resupply the DEW line (defense radar hemisphere paranoia on which all things hang like a drop of) at salary of $5040 per annum, back in Oct. and return to NYC visit family and take off leisurely & rich (plenty money) tour of Europe, will go to Moscow and write rhapsodies under the Kremlin wall. The arctic trip is in north Alaska, great icebergs, white auroras and sheets of light ices from heaven I expect. Actual pole.

. . . I have been reading Smart, Apollinaire, Lorca, Crane, Whitman, Catullus. Some Dylan Thomas—all this last year, since writing these poems. Building on a dry base of imagism, then the surreal but sensible superstructure of imagination. Pound and Eliot are in a way classicists, Popes and Drydens. What is coming ahead I imagine is an assertion of individual feeling again. Nothing could be healthier. But why Whitman has been so misunderstood and ignored, I'll never know. Nobody in Columbia seems to have actually read him, Chase hardly, tho I remember you were always partisan. I wonder if you see what I'm seeing here, I guess you must. But if so why is Tropic Of Cancer (by gosh henry miller) not read in Columbia? There is a continuation in a direct line, with inspired personal pages. I just read that for the first time short while back and realized he was never even so much as sniffed at in school. By hindsight and thru experience I feel an enormous gulf between what I really believe in and the kind of literary inanity developed on campus. And look what's happened to Hollander—a bright buoyant spirit— everything's crabbed and crosseyed and silly and formal to a point of absurdity—and so on down the line. No wonder someone like R. Weitzner could not breathe. As for me it has taken years to dig the sunflower which was there all along as you know. I'm not talking mysterious just generalizing rapidly in case I sound vague. But a lot of it is in the technique, the line, the conception of what a poem is. Nobody takes it as the direct expression of a simple truth, nobody believes in truth or something. And I was supposed to be the degenerate? Well I'm still wobbling around happily digging freedom. More to say all the way along the line: anyway I am well and have been living it up since I left New York and deepening my awareness of who I am and my understanding of who god might be. Dont all those madmen hem you in. I mean I see Kerouac now happily writing like an archangel lying around in the woods, gloomy and laughing, but at least DEVOTED to life and not camping around rearranging social moral ideas etc. Burroughs—you may remember—suffering in Tangier and London but writing an enormous great original book. And poor Huncke, he's I hear in Sing Sing. He was really alright, there was no need to scare me. Accidents and mistakes are accidents and mistakes but lambs are lambs. What's left is compassion, mercy—might as well accept it, unremitting, even when embarrassing. Love to you, write me what you think of the poems. Note the long line and variations thereof—it's all bop . . . . Unworried wild poetry, full of perception, that's the lillipop. Who of my age are daring even?

Ginsberg's long letter accompanied an odd-sized paperback called *Howl* that had been published by a small press in California. The book might not have been written without certain personal developments which led to a resolution of his sexual anxieties. Through a painter in San Francisco named Robert LaVigne, Ginsberg met Peter Orlovsky. LaVigne had taken Ginsberg to his apartment to show him his work after an all-night conversation in Foster's Cafeteria. The first painting Ginsberg saw was a large, seven-by-seven portrait of a naked boy, legs spread, with some onions at his feet. The lyrical power of the painting was epiphanous, triggering the homoeroticism that would soon be expressed in "Howl":

> who let themselves be fucked in the ass by saintly motorcyclists,
>   and screamed with joy,
> who blew and were blown by those human seraphim, the sailors,
>   caresses of Atlantic and Caribbean love,

The emphasis of these lines is ecstatic—screaming with joy rather than pain. Such lines declared the end of Ginsberg's sexual ambivalence—the shy hesitancy that prevented him from fulfilling desires that seemed natural. Approaching thirty when he saw LaVigne's painting, Ginsberg had been defeated by repeated failures to establish lasting relationships with lovers like Neal Cassady, his search for male tenderness frustrated by guilt. Almost as a symbolic token of liberation and as a rejoinder to repressed yearnings, the subject of LaVigne's painting walked into the room while Ginsberg was admiring it. Peter Orlovsky was seven years younger than Ginsberg, and with him Ginsberg felt a frankness and open responsiveness he had never previously shared with another man. A year later, they accepted a total commitment to each other:

> We made a vow to each other that he could own me, my mind and everything I knew, and my body, and I could own him and all he knew and all his body; and that we would give each other ourselves, so that we possessed each other as property, to do everything we wanted to, sexually or intellectually, and in a sense explore each other until we reached the mystical "X" together, emerging two merged souls. We had the understanding that when our (my particularly) erotic desire was ultimately

satisfied by being satiated (rather than denied), there would be a lessening of desire, grasp, holding on, craving and attachment; and that ultimately we would be delivered free in heaven together. And so the vow was that neither of us would go into heaven unless we could get the other one in—like a mutual bodhisattva's vow.

Orlovsky replaced the dream of Neal Cassady, answering a tremendous need. Ginsberg had written to Kerouac a decade earlier that "if I overreach myself for love, it is because I crave it so much, and have known so little of it." Orlovsky was young and receptive; Cassady had already changed greatly. Ginsberg wrote Kerouac on September 7, 1954, that Cassady seemed as if he were suffering from a blankness, that he claimed to be without feelings, and that his speech was especially disassociated. Cassady was no longer sweetly carefree, no longer the fount of mental gaiety, but pathetically rushing around feeling trapped by his ties to family and the railroad. Ginsberg influenced Orlovsky as he initially had stimulated Cassady—acting as a tutor, engaging him in long, intense discussions, offering suggestions for reading and study that substituted for more formal training.

As the relationship with Peter took time to become permanent, Ginsberg decided to continue his own education at Berkeley. Kerouac, then living on the West Coast, told Ginsberg that the university might provide a proper atmosphere for him, and that he should not fear becoming a college professor, teaching literature, Buddhism, oriental art, and poetry. Kerouac soon changed his advice, but Ginsberg had already realized, despite encouragement from professors Mark Schorer and Thomas Parkinson, that graduate study meant years of plodding that would not help him as a poet.

At Berkeley, however, Ginsberg was to discover a community of writers whose work he admired. Ginsberg met Gary Snyder who was doing graduate work in oriental languages, and Kenneth Rexroth, an older poet whom Ginsberg characterized as a "crazy W. C. Fields literary hullaballoos." Rexroth conducted a sort of western salon, a weekly literary gathering where Ginsberg met

Robert Duncan, Philip Lamantia, Michael McClure who was then Duncan's student at San Francisco State, and Lawrence Ferlinghetti, a poet who had opened the first paperbound-book store in the country and had established City Lights Press. Ginsberg was most impressed by Duncan, but felt his poems were too involved with sensibility. Duncan visited Ginsberg and reacted enthusiastically to Kerouac's "Essentials of Spontaneous Prose," which he read on Ginsberg's wall. Through Duncan, Ginsberg got interested in the readings at the San Francisco Poetry Center.

In the fall of 1955, Ginsberg organized a group reading at the Six Gallery in San Francisco. Rexroth was to read and to introduce the other poets: Ginsberg, Lamantia, McClure, Snyder, and his friend Philip Whalen. Ginsberg wrote "Howl" two weeks before the occasion and astounded the audience—which was passing around jugs of wine brought by Kerouac—with the power and brilliance of his delivery. The reading quickly became legendary and Ginsberg was repeatedly requested to read in the San Francisco area. Although "Howl" recorded the despair and desperation of a generation, Ginsberg's reading was like a detonation in a museum, the surging exhilaration of his voice itself an exhortation of future promise. The poem was a crucible of cultural change. Except for the response to Dylan Thomas' readings in America, never before had a modern audience reacted so passionately, or identified so completely with a poet's message. Ginsberg called "Howl" his "original blow for freedom": it was also the germinating public seed of the Beat movement.

"To be wise is to suffer" Tiresias warns Oedipus, and the biography of the generation portrayed on these pages is often an account of pain. Testing the limits of personality after the Second World War, the Beats felt the loneliness of cultural exile in a world intent on fulfilling its most disastrous potentials and the anguish of artists struggling with form to convey a vision of apocalypse. By the time Howl, On The Road, *and* Naked Lunch *were in print, the Beats had their audience despite the timidity of publishers and the asperity of critics. Learning to see with the perspective of outsiders, they described the incipient fascism of values induced by corporate structures and the military mentality. Though un-unanimous in their politics, they challenged the conformist obedience to a warrior psychology that frightened so many in the fifties. Writing to Jack Kerouac from Paris on January 4, 1957, Allen Ginsberg commented on the puzzled malaise of Americans who had seen the interconnecting fibers of national purpose unraveled by the lies of goblins:*

> *It's as if all our madness will come home to roost—all the bad books, yelling at Einstein and Chaplin, bad movies, mean newspapers—have built up bad karma & will have to be accounted for by awful groans of unbelievable history . . . . We've supported too many monsters too long. We were right all along, I mean my own sweet socialistic angelic dreams were not pipedreams but the only thing the wide world dreaming on things to come demanded. Now the bitter American reality encounters the Oriental century to come.*

Jack Kerouac was one of the most baffled and betrayed. Ginsberg once tried to console him with the counsel that genius must suffer the burdens of the world. Ironically, the most optimistic of the Beats was to feel that the "bitter American reality" was fused with his own destiny. Fatalism was a mournful chord in Kerouac's letters, where he frequently predicted his own catastrophe. Just before On The Road *appeared, he secluded himself in a room in Mexico for three weeks while staring at the walls, writing Alan Ansen that although he was only thirty-five, he felt seventy. Hypersensitive to hostile reviews, he found it difficult to face the world. Photographs taken during the sixties are the visual clue to Kerouac's self-annihilation through alcohol, the "joyous disease" he called it: face and body puffing with flesh, spirit soured in incommunicabil-*

ity. Taciturn and brooding, he felt he was surrounded by a generation of despisers. The disgust exudes through his last published piece, "I'm a Bippie in the Middle." The scene is a gluttonous banquet of American affluence where every handshake is a soiled pact in hypocrisy, concupiscence, waste, and dollar lust reminiscent of the disillusioned tone of Melville's The Confidence Man. *Ginsberg has tried to explain Kerouac's final estrangement from the country he loved. Like Whitman, Kerouac proposed "the noble ideal American open-mind sensibility, open road, open energy" but his country took the reverse track of militant heartlessness, and Kerouac's artistic soul was rejected:*

> *I think that crushed him in the sense of making him pessimistic, making him realize how really unrelievably awful American destiny was, and I think he just took the hint and retired from the scene seeing that the condition of America was hopeless.*

That Ginsberg shares Kerouac's despair is evident in The Fall Of America, *the collection for which he received the National Book Award for poetry in 1974. But the paradoxical touchstone of Ginsberg's sensibility has been that its jeremiad has been fired in affirmation. Kerouac once commented to Peter Orlovsky that Ginsberg belonged to the "springtime soul" of eastern Russia whose image was the limitless flat plain of* Alexander Nevsky, *dotted with endless brothers. Unlike Kerouac who decided to withdraw entirely, Ginsberg's evangelical populism made him a conscience of the sixties, a promulgator of such transcendental ideals as Whitman's "adhesiveness." One confrontation in particular seems emblematic of the potency of Ginsberg's style. Early in the sixties, he invited the Russian Delegation to the United Nations to attend a poetry reading by himself and Peter Orlovsky at the Judson Church on Washington Square. The twenty men in gray suits and close-cropped hair looked like anxious policemen as Orlovsky stripped to his shorts to accent the sense of personal revelation in the diary he was reading. A little later, as Ginsberg was passionately reading the Moloch section of "Howl," the stolid descendents of Mayakovsky stiffly rose and filed out of the room. It was a symbolic lesson in the politics of the word.*

Ginsberg continued to project his "sweet socialistic angelic dreams" during the internecine rancors of the midsixties. He became an energy center for the antiwar movement, helping to organize marches, appealing to rallies, finally participating in the historic protest at the Democratic Convention in Chicago in 1968. The enemy was the war on nature, what Ginsberg called "International Biocide," and he tempered the movement with a spiritual asceticism, urging a reduction in consumption and an end to the growth mania of industrial capitalism. As a luminary of liberation, he appealed for tolerance, for an opening of the narrowness that so afflicted the fifties, and he continued to search for ways to recover meaningful communal rituals.

William Burroughs, the Beat fugitive of the fifties, became more overtly political in the sixties as indicated by his presence with Ginsberg and Jean Genêt at the Democratic Convention in Chicago. When Kerouac visited Burroughs in Tangier in 1957, he characterized him as the "Forgotten American" who would telepathically seek to combat dictatorship. Writing to Ginsberg in Chile in 1960, Burroughs stated that politics was a trap for the writer; by 1970, he admitted that American writers could no longer pretend indifference to political questions which were now essential to survival. Rejecting Ginsberg's communal, back-to-nature approach as retrogressive, Burroughs now argues that technology has evolved to the point that precludes escape in the pastoral. The planet is threatened by what he calls the "control madness" of power used for destructive purposes. The problem is not inherent in scientific advance, but in the principles of secrecy and control. Burroughs' antidote is a resistance based on openness, on the release of all secrets—the writer's function is to decipher the incredible, to clarify the inevitable. In Naked Lunch, Burroughs viewed the artist as a passive recording instrument, but he now believes that the purpose of writing is to move an audience, and that its future lies in seeing how close the writer can come to affecting events. Depending on the magical powers of language to suggest a picture of impending cataclysm, his method has always been the arabesque of apocalypse, and his main linguistic concern has been to end Western verbal conditioning and the faith in progress it inspires.

The choices and actions of the members of the Beat Generation, unusual as they may be, are the record of trials to overcome oppressive circumstance. But the fleshly lives pale before the conviction of the works themselves, and it is to the novels and poems that we must turn for the genuine source of imaginative excitement.

Hal Chase, Jack Kerouac, Allen Ginsberg, William Burroughs, Riverside Drive, New York, 1944. (*Courtesy Marshall Clements*)

Neal Cassady and Jack Kerouac, San Francisco, 1949. (*Courtesy Allen Ginsberg*)

Herbert Huncke on Burroughs' farm in New Waverly, Texas, 1947. (*Courtesy Allen Ginsberg*)

Allen Ginsberg and Jack Kerouac, East 7th Street, New York, 1953. (*Courtesy Allen Ginsberg*)

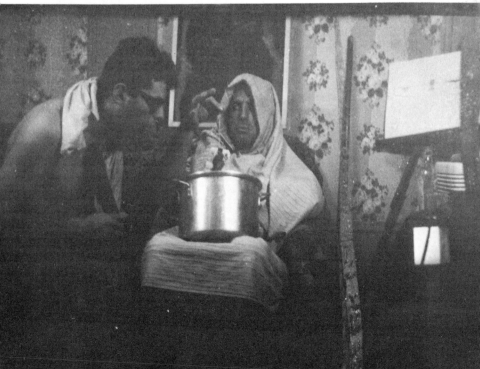

William Burroughs on East 7th Street, New York, 1953. (*Courtesy Allen Ginsberg*)

Jack Kerouac on fire escape, New York, 1953. (*Courtesy Allen Ginsberg*)

Jack Kerouac at
Villa Muniria in
Tangier, 1957.
(*Courtesy Allen
Ginsberg*)

Jack Kerouac, Allen
Ginsberg, Peter
Orlovsky, Gregory
Corso, and Lafcadio
Orlovsky, Mexico City
Zocalo, 1956. (*Courtesy
Allen Ginsberg*)

Peter Orlovsky, Allen Ginsberg, Allen Ansen, Paul Bowles (*seated*), Gregory Corso, and Ian Summerville, garden of Villa Muniria, 1957. (*Courtesy Allen Ginsberg*)

Jack Kerouac in last years. (*Courtesy Allen Ginsberg*)

OPPOSITE: Allen Ginsberg on upstate New York farm, Labor Day, 1973. (*Courtesy MELLON*)

FOLLOWING PAGE: William Burroughs at The West End Bar, New York, 1974. (*Courtesy MELLON*)

PART III

THE BLACK BEAUTY
OF WILLIAM BURROUGHS

They have no conversation, properly speaking. They make use
of the spoken word the same way that the guard of the train makes
use of his flags or his lantern.

—Samuel Beckett
Malone Dies

"TWILIGHT'S LAST GLEAMINGS," written by Burroughs at Harvard
in 1938, but not published until 1964 in *Nova Express*, offers a clear
illustration of his intentions as a writer. The story is a painful but
hilarious parody of the sinking of the *Titanic*, except that Burroughs'
vessel is allegorically named the S.S. *America*. An explosion occurs
in the boiler room, but an "air-conditioned" voice advises that there
is no cause for alarm. Ship's Doctor Benway, drunkenly lurching
through an emergency operation, dropping cigarette ashes on his
patient, sweeps his instruments and drugs into his bag and boards
the first lifeboat. A politician from Clayton, Missouri (the suburb of
St. Louis where Burroughs was raised), rushes into the first-class
lounge and orders the musicians to play "The Star-Spangled
Banner." The captain, confronted by Lady Bradshinkel, owner of
the ship, seizes her wig as the deck tilts and shoots her to obtain her

kimono. On his way to the lifeboats, he finds the purser ransacking money and jewels from the safe, draws a gun hidden in his brassiere, shoots him, seizes the valuables, then forces his way onto the lifeboat. The scene is hysterical pandemonium as wealthy American passengers attempt to flee. Burroughs' eye moves along the decks, burlesquing the tragedy, punctuating the mayhem with fragments of the national anthem. The parable is a premonition of the fall of America—everyone desperate for escape, but stealing, pillaging, abusing their authority at the end as they have been doing all along. Just as in Burroughs' mature works, there is no organizing narrative presence, no explaining omniscient intelligence, no judgment. The author's eye moves swiftly, cinematically, uninterested in formal transitions or artificial connections, concerned primarily with capturing the sense of chaotic flux, the terror of disaster; the exposure of false disguises is brutally candid, scathingly comedic.

Burroughs' vision is the most impersonal of all the Beat writers. As early as 1948, Burroughs announced in a letter to Allen Ginsberg a philosophy he termed "factualism:"

> All arguments, all nonsensical condemnations as to what people 'should do' are irrelevant. Ultimately there is only fact on all levels, and the more one argues, verbalizes, moralizes, the less he will see and feel of fact. Needless to say I will not write any formal statement on the subject. Talk is incompatible with factualism.

Although Burroughs has never deserted the factualist ideal, his aesthetic has evolved from the bare documentary realism of his first book, *Junkie,* to the structural intricacies of *Naked Lunch* and the complex textures of the cut-up technique. His inventive art has been infused with what Allen Ginsberg has aptly called a Yankee practicality, but its features have been difficult to decipher. Burroughs is the most experimental of the Beats, a writer who, like Henry James, is first read by other writers greedy to learn the secrets of the craft, and then later by a larger audience. "An advance in art" Harold Rosenberg has argued, "is considered to take place to the degree that art divests itself of the characteristics of art." In this sense Burroughs may be a novelist of the future, but one with a compelling message for us now.

For many readers, William Burroughs' complexity is a formidable, sometimes intimidating obstacle. His novels are composed of scenes which are often without the narrative focus provided by recognizable characters, or the scenic unity provided by a particular locale. Characters metamorphose into other characters, appear without introduction only to disappear without explanation; scenes shift sharply from New York City to South American jungles without transition. Such difficulties are compounded by the presence of alien forms that seem derived from the world of science fiction—annihilating insects, viral parasites, succubi and other demons, all merging with humans, invading their bodies and manipulating their minds, acting through their beings bizarrely, disruptively creating what Burroughs calls *nova*: the aggravation of insoluble conflicts and incompatible political situations resulting in a planetary explosion.

Burroughs continues the experimental tradition in fiction, the modernist movement of Gertrude Stein, Joyce, Gide, and others who sought to free fiction from the confining boundaries of the conventional novel. His novels court to the ultimate limits an idea expressed by William James in *A Pluralistic Universe* that can stand as a keynote for modernist fiction: "In the end nothing less than the whole of everything can be the truth of anything at all." It was the simultaneous truth of this "whole" that Burroughs, like Kerouac and Ginsberg, was dedicated to capture. As he told Ginsberg when he sent him examples of what was to become *Naked Lunch*, he was not trying to compose a historical novel where the events had already transpired, but writing narrative that "is happening."

Burroughs' experiments with narrative forms have profoundly developed the dimensions of fiction. Just as the cut-up extends Joyce's stream of consciousness, Burroughs' exceptional fluidity is a magnification of Henry James' principle of shifting point of view.

The Jamesian tradition as developed by Conrad, Ford Madox Ford, Virginia Woolf, successfully ruptured the umbilical passivity of a reader dependent on an omniscient narrator, and placed that reader in the active center of a situation that could not be resolved by absolute judgments. The events of the story, the facts of the milieu, would swirl about the reader with all the contradictions and misunderstandings felt in any real situation. The demands on the reader's intelligence amounted to a combination of the detective's perspicacity and the psychoanalyst's intuition. Clues, vitally meaningful signs, would form the basis of interpretation. But the masters of modern fiction, from James to Faulkner, despite their intensive development of technique, were all still predominantly interested in telling a story.

Burroughs, like Poe or the French Symbolists, creates an ambiance, an atmosphere of conflicting particles whose points of contact reveal a dark and hidden interior. His medium may best be approached through analogies to the new physics. Whereas Newton's mechanical view of the cosmos, like Victorian omniscience in the novel, resulted in a morality of predictable absolutes, Burroughs' world, like Einstein's, projects a relativity of endless exfoliation. What first intrigued Einstein and led to his theory of relativity was the very unpredictability of the rate at which atoms absorb or emit electrical energy. Before the assumptions of quantum mechanics, the ultimate constituents of matter were thought to be the negatively charged electron, the positively charged proton, and the chargeless neutron. Today, instead of a determinable universe, scientists are faced with an immeasurable uncertainty. Quantum mechanics successfully destroyed the possibility of absolutes for our time, but also revealed a baffling array of highly relative bodies acting without evident controls. Take the case of the neutrino, which offers a perfect analogy for the way in which Burroughs treats many of his characters: it has no physical properties, neither mass nor electric charge nor magnetic field; it is neither attracted by gravity, nor captured or repelled by the electromagnetic fields of other particles, even as it may fly past or through those particles. The neutrino, unlimited by any apparent boundaries, deepens our understanding of dimension in space just as the positron—an electron temporarily engaged in moving backward in time—challenges our linear and chronological concepts of history. And space and time in Burroughs' work correspond to such cosmological laws.

In *Improvised Poetics*, Ginsberg suggested that Burroughs does not conceive of words as he writes, but instead sees flashing pictures. In a lecture at Tufts University, Ginsberg spoke of observing Burroughs while writing with his eyes gazing into a "middle distance." Ginsberg asked Burroughs what he was thinking about, and he answered "Hands pulling in nets from the ocean." Ginsberg explained that this was a "pictograph" of what they had seen on the shore that night.

Burroughs' speed of observation moves too quickly for sequential prose or the unit of the paragraph. The three books that complete the *Naked Lunch* tetralogy, *Nova Express*, *The Soft Machine*, *The Ticket That Exploded*, have a labryinthine density deriving from Burroughs' use of the cut-up—a technique that juxtaposes fragments collected from random reading, snatches of conversation, newspaper items, quotations from writers like Rimbaud and T. S. Eliot, recurring motifs from Burroughs' own work, all rearranged into a mosaic with no overtly centralizing idea. Burroughs learned the cut-up from his friend Brion Gysin, a painter who tape-recorded a message that became a touchstone for Burroughs:

> I come to free the words
> The words are free to come
> I come freely to the words
> The free come to the words

Burroughs wrote Ginsberg in September of 1960 that the cut-up was a tool, a transitional bridge for passages that could not be logically connected. Often, from a page of cut-ups, he might select a line to be merged into his text. The technique was extended by a process he called the fold-in, where he would take a page of his text and someone else's, fold each down the middle, and place them side by side on the same page. The result, he felt, was analogous to the flashback in film.

Both the cut-up and the fold-in can be seen as a response to Kerouac's ideal of spontaneity. While Burroughs believes the spontaneous cannot be willed, the unpredictable can result from a dextrous use of scissors. The cut-up was to become a means through which he would objectively detach himself from romantic images, from tenderness, from personal associations and ties to his own words. It eliminated habitual reactions and conditioned reflexes, separated words from traditional referents, violated the normal syntax that influences rational behavior. It was also, curiously, a step in the direction of Eastern thought with its basis in chance and coincidence.

Burroughs' intention as a writer, beginning with *Naked Lunch*, has been to show how certain word combinations produce specific effects on the nervous system. By "cutting the word-lines," he believes he can find clues to the nature and function of words, as well as anticipate, suggest, or predict future events. As such, the cut-up threatens what Burroughs calls the Control Machine: any political system that through repression and social stratification ensures the power of the few and the subjection of the many, reinforcing the situation with such institutional means as police, religion, education, patriotic indoctrination through mass media.

Burroughs argues that media is now able to control events by emphasizing certain news stories, by editorializing, advertising, and selecting entertainment. "Cutting the word-lines" means severing the hypnotizing authority of newspapers, magazines, radio, and television, whose sources of power are obscured. It becomes a way of resisting the constant bombardment of images to which modern city man is subject that blunts his receptivity, dazes his senses with a permanent image haze. As a means of exploring subliminal awareness, the cut-up can establish fresh connections between images.

Burroughs has pointed to antecedents of the cut-up in the work of the Surrealist poet Tristan Tzara (who caused a riot in a theater when he pulled the lines of a poem from a hat) and T. S. Eliot. Another possible influence was a tape Burroughs heard by Jerry Newman, a friend of Kerouac's who was a record producer. The tape was called "The Drunken Newscaster," and on it a tipsy announcer confused the news with the interpolation of unrelated fragments of anecdotes. According to Ginsberg, Burroughs laughed so hard when he heard Newman in 1953 that he nearly fell out of his chair.

The form of the cut-up perfectly captures the disorder and confusion of madness, and Burroughs (like Borges, or Nabokov in *Pale Fire*) metaphysically refutes any distinctions between reality and fantasy. He writes from the viewpoint of the deranged drug addict whom he has compared to the schizophrenic. Madness becomes the expected behavior of the authorities, the political and institutional powers of the Control Machine. Their activities are a barrier, an obstacle to be overcome, and this premise motivates the swift metamorphoses of Burroughs' absurdist characters.

The result is less a world of sensibility than one of hallucinatory fear, a kind of para-awareness, for Burroughs articulates what Conrad's Kurtz would barely utter as "the horror, the horror!" The comparison is not fortuitous: Burroughs' voyage is into the miasma of Conradian darkness, though without the empathy that Marlowe's naïve journeyman's perspective affords in *Heart of Darkness*. Burroughs' landscape is a grotesque version of Conrad's exotic terrain, a spectacle of horrid insects and parasites, crabs emerging from chemical gardens, piles of rotting garbage, molds and fungi, diseased flesh and decaying carrion, weeds and rancid swamps.

T. S. Eliot, of course, first realized the value of the Conradian inferno and used it as a correlative for his own time. And Burroughs quotes from "The Love Song of J. Alfred Prufrock," from "Preludes," from "Rhapsody On A Windy Night," from "The Waste Land" itself, as he fashions a neon version of Eliot's vision of sterility with irridescence gleaming out of offal, mysterious energy sources congealing in places of death. By *The Ticket That Exploded*, Burroughs seems to have assimilated Eliot's dessicating, ascerbically ironic view of nature in an entropic state of decomposition and rottenness. Burroughs' vision, like Eliot's, feeds on precise, clinically observed and unemotionally rendered details; these objects are presented cinematically, with all the speed of the motion-picture lens, and all transitions, even the formalities of infinitives, prepositions, and definite articles are omitted for the sake of increased tempo. It is speed that most characterizes Burroughs' prose, an accelerating quality demanding brevity of focus, appropriate surely to the surprising dislocations of the surrealistic eye as well as to Burroughs' proposition (like the Buddhist notion of *maya*) that all apparent sensory feelings, thoughts, and impressions are illusory. The rapidity of shifts of points of view and transformations of character creates an exceptional momentum that leaves the reader in the center of a maelstrom, caught in an exhilarating dance of desperation that invariably leads to death and obliteration—through the addict's needle, through the orgiastic excesses implied by Burroughs' favorite hanging metaphor, through a number of violent avenues that Burroughs has imagined with the ferocity of his contemporary, Jean Genêt.

The response to so excremental a vision may be one of simple revulsion, and it is true that many readers cannot bear much of Burroughs' incessant flagellation, sexual torture and mutilation, terrible deprivations of body and spirit all set in so fetid an environment. The initial depiction of the addict Lee (Burroughs' pseudonym in his first book, and a figure who recurs throughout his work) in *Naked Lunch* is typical:

> Lee lived in a permanent third-day kick, with, of course, certain uh essential intermissions to refuel the fires that burned through his yellow-pink-brown gelatinous substance and kept off the hovering flesh. In the beginning his flesh was simply soft, so soft that he was cut to the bone by dust particles, air currents and brushing overcoats while direct

contact with doors and chairs seemed to occasion no discomfort. No wound healed in his soft, tentative flesh. . . . Long white tendrils of fungus curled round the naked bones. Mold odors of atrophied testicles quilted his body in a fuzzy grey fog. . . .

Lionel Abel, when reviewing *Naked Lunch* in *Partisan Review*, grudgingly accorded the book "only a tiny bit of literary merit," and quarreled with Norman Mailer's view (offered in *Advertisements For Myself*) of its beauty. Burroughs is so excessive in the above description of Lee's decomposition as to approach a kind of lushness, a richness and profusion that one finds in Poe's stories of hysteria, or in Baudelaire's *Les Fleurs du Mal*. Abel judged *Naked Lunch* from a rather heavy-handed moral perspective, and for him the novel had no aesthetic. In the way that "black comedy" describes the ironically sinister laughter of writers like Beckett, the term "black beauty" evokes the tone of joyous terror in Burroughs' work. "Beauty," Rilke has written, "is nothing but the beginning of terror that we are still just able to bear," and behind the psychology of such a remark lies an aesthetic that has eluded many of Burroughs' critics.

Consider another illustration of Burroughs' kind of beauty, this time from the "black fruit" chapter of *The Ticket That Exploded*:

From an enormous distance he heard the golden hunting horns of the Aeons and he was free of a body traveling in the echoing shell of sound as herds of mystic animals galloped through dripping primeval forests, pursued by the silver hunters in chariots of bone and vine—Lonely lemur calls whispered in the walls of silent obsidian temples in a land of black lagoons, the ancient rotting kingdom of Jupiter—smelling the black berry smoke drifting through huge spiderwebs in ruined courtyards under eternal moonlight—ghost hands at the paneless windows weaving memories of blood and war in stone shapes—A host of dead warriors stand as petrified statues in vast charred black plains—Silent ebony eyes turned toward a horizon of always, waiting with a patience born of a million years, for the dawn that never rises—Thousands of voices muttered the beating of his heart—gurgling sounds from soaring lungs trailing the neon ghost writing—Lykin lay gasping. . . .

Two notes are necessary for clarification: Lemurs, in Burroughs' world, are beings so spontaneous as to die when confined; black berry smoke signifies drug intoxication. The passage depends on a variety of sensuous experiences and several striking images. The bone and vine chariots, the golden hunting horns, the obsidian temples are set in the frozen splendor of a Keatsian eternal moment that recalls the picture on the Grecian urn. The dominant color of the passage, as it is throughout Burroughs' work, is black: the temples of obsidian, the lagoons, berries, charred plains, and ebony eyes function as signs of the death-in-life which forms Burroughs' typical moment. Yet, near the end of the passage, a strange sense of disembodied force, a transfer of secret energies, creates a haunting if peculiar animation. It is this sense of vitality in the very throes of death that informs Burroughs' world with its eerie, morbid beauty. Burroughs enacts a fragile balance between the most extreme instances of suffering and the kind of transported radiance that excess of pain provides in Mantegna's *Saint Sebastian*, in the Renaissance paintings of martyrdom and crucifixion, even in the more spasmodic visions of Breugel and Bosch whose entangled horrors are presented with the same calm certainty as Burroughs'.

To Poe's belief that the death of a beautiful woman was the ideal subject for poetry, Wallace Stevens has offered the modern symbolist corollary, "death is the mother of beauty." Stevens' formula is surely useful when considering how much of twentieth-century fiction and poetry emanates despair and points to death, and Burroughs, more than any other writer of his time, has sought death as an end, for and of itself. This search is characterized by a brutal self-immolation in explosions of pain. As André Breton prophesied during World War II, "Beauty will be convulsive, or not be." And Burroughs' distortions of the body and spirit create a spectacle of suffering in the Dadaist and Surrealist tradition. The apocalyptic intensity of Burroughs' blackness reminds us of the uncontainable fury of Antonin Artaud, another doomed addict, who warned that for theater to have meaning it would have to signal through the flames like some desperate victim being burned at the stake.

Artaud's demand for a "theater of cruelty" offers a proper analogue for Burroughs' parabola of violence and mounting degradation, and just as Artaud's visions in the thirties presaged the inquisitorial terrors of the concentration camps, Burroughs' antennae may be tuned into strange circuits revealing the future. His compressed, obscure, and extremely visual sequences are like flashes of a barely glimpsed and terrifying extraterritorial existence. It is intriguing to remember, in this connection, that at the end of *Junkie* Burroughs declared that his "final fix" would be yage, a drug used by Indians at the headwaters of the Amazon that supposedly increases telepathic sensitivity.

The relationship of savage torture and sensuous pleasure is integral to Burroughs' fiction. A characteristically repeated scene describes a man being hung during an orgy; as he is homosexually ravished, his neck snaps in conjunction with orgasm. There are occasions when passion and violence have been interfused with a transcendentally regenerative power—as when Nietzsche accounts for the origins of classical tragedy in pre-Doric Dionysian rites—but such higher possibilities are not as easily derived from Burroughs' bloody dismemberments. Yet the demonic drive of scenes like the hanging sequences is rendered with a compulsion that is total and convincing as fantasy.

A typical illustration of what Burroughs sarcastically calls the "Garden of Delights" occurs as a screenplay, the section of *Naked Lunch* called "A.J.'s Annual Party." The film begins with Mary, a thin brunette, performing fellatio on Johnny, front and rear. She then straps on a rubber penis and assaults him. Mark enters and forces Johnny to commit similar homosexual acts, culminating on a vibrating chair as Johnny screams. Johnny is then escorted to a gallows platform covered with moldy jockstraps and hung as Mary impales herself on his erect member. In contrast, we may recall Beckett's more passive tramps who, in *Waiting For Godot*, only speculate on the possibilities of hanging. Since they barely exist, they can hardly muster the courage to be, to perform so decisive an act, and the ensuing tone is ironic. But Burroughs' figures enact a frenzy of perpetual becoming. Mary, after Johnny has been hung, cannibalistically sucks out his eyes, and bites away his nose, lips, and sexual parts. Mark then leaps on her and "they roll from one end of the room to the other, pinwheel end-over-end and leap high in the air like great hooked fish." Mark then hangs Mary during intercourse, and is transformed into Johnny. Up to this point the scene borders on pornography; it is ecstatically kinetic in its depiction of violence, giving us no explanation of its significance—only the speed of flashing sensation. The resurrected Johnny then leaps madly about the room and out into space, fulfilling the impulse of the symbolist hero to narcissistically embrace his image while plunging into an abyss:

> Masturbating end-over-end, three thousand feet down, his sperm floating beside him, he screams all the way against the shattering blue of sky, the rising sun burning over his body like gasoline, down past great oaks and persimmons, swamp cypress and mahogany, to shatter in liquid relief in a ruined square paved with limestone. Weeds and vines grow between the stones, and rusty iron bolts three feet thick penetrate the white stone, stain it shit-brown of rust.

Burroughs then rewrites his ending. First Johnny and Mary embrace sexually after being anointed with gasoline and they both burst into flames; then Johnny douches her with jungle bone-softener and transfixes her with neon nails. It is an ever-accelerating pattern of violence and horror, the intensity increasing with each new barbaric act. The scene is finally resolved with a note of gothic lyricism sounding like a perverse parody of D. H. Lawrence:

> Damp hairs on the back of his balls dry to grass in the warm spring wind. High jungle valley, vines creep in the window. . . . A long tuber root creeps from Mary's cunt, feels for the earth. The bodies disintegrate in green explosions. The hut falls in ruins of broken stone. The boy is a limestone statue, a plant sprouting from his cock, lips parted in the half-smile of a junky on the nod.

Scenes like this one may be appalling to some sensibilities, overtly pornographic and shocking, but the lines are imbued with a phosphorescent luminosity and rendered in a spurting rhythm. In exaggerating sexual fantasy, Burroughs has gone further than predecessors like Joyce and Henry Miller. The Beats believed that absolutely anything was suitable as subject matter. The idea of taste was something they distrusted entirely, seeing it as a polite rationalization for elements of life that could not be faced artistically, the result of a legacy of Victorian prudishness that persisted far into the twentieth century. If Burroughs challenges the socially acceptable in his hanging scenes, pursuing them with reckless obsessiveness as if their horror—what he has called "terminal sewage"—was too great for a single exposure and required the cumulative impact of successive visits, his effort should be appreciated within the context of the tradition created by de Sade, Joyce, Lawrence, and Henry Miller, all writers who have tried to redeem our repressed fears and desires.

Burroughs has always treated taboo subjects with clinical candor. His use of physical abuse, of obscene detail and language is partly his correlative for a failed civilization. He introduced homosexuality and drug addiction as subjects in the fifties, but refused to exploit this material naturalistically. He writes with a devastating nightmarish flatness as if out of some hopeless vacuum—like the oracle in a bottle providing Eliot's epigraph to "The Waste Land"—of "human aggregates disintegrating in cosmic insanity, random events in a dying universe," as he observed in *Junkie*, his first book.

Junkie is a realistic account of Burroughs' initiation into the drug experience. The book's preface suggests how his perpetual childhood fear of nightmare, his tendency to hallucinate, and an awareness of some omnipresent impinging supernatural horror were premonitions of the underworld of drug addiction. But what is most revealing about *Junkie*, written when Burroughs was thirty-five and after several years on drugs, is the manner in which a realistic mode is extended almost to the surrealistic intensity of *Naked Lunch* and the following works. Early in the book Burroughs compares his first morphine experience to floating without outlines, and recalls a series of pictures passing, as on the cinema screen; these qualities become essential characteristics of his later fiction. As he describes the horrors of withdrawal, Burroughs imagines New York City in ruins, with huge centipedes and scorpions (later favorite images) crawling in and out of empty bars, cafeterias, and drugstores on 42nd Street. Burroughs' critics have not observed the extent to which the key motifs of the later fiction are anticipated in *Junkie*. Some of these are offered with a realistic reserve and a precise attention to details—as when Burroughs explains how difficult it is for the addict to locate a vein—that makes sadism seem casual. Burroughs relates how he once supported his drug habit by stealing from helpless drunks, men susceptible to a hierarchy of scavengers who eventually will strip away all possessions as if robbing a corpse. These marauders anticipate the Liquifactionists of *Naked Lunch* who absorb one's protoplasmic being, and the hostile intruders of *Nova Express* and *The Ticket That Exploded* who take over human bodies.

Two typical images occur during the withdrawal process, a condition explaining many of the surreal dislocations of Burroughs' later imagery. The first image, of orgasm experienced after hanging, first appears after Burroughs has been arrested in New Orleans for possession of an unregistered pistol:

> I lay on the narrow wood bench, twisting from one side to the other. My body was raw, twitching, tumescent, the junk-frozen flesh in agonizing thaw. I turned over on my stomach and one leg slipped off the bench. I pitched forward and the rounded edge of the bench, polished smooth by the friction of cloth, slid along my crotch. There was a sudden rush of blood to the genitals at the slippery contact. Sparks exploded behind my eyes; my legs twitched—the orgasm of a hanged man when the neck snaps.

The second image, basic to Burroughs' imagination, presents a dissolving amoeboid mass. Burroughs, now in Mexico, has with-drawn from morphine, but has regressed to an alcoholic stupor:

> When I closed my eyes I saw an Oriental face, the lips and nose eaten away by disease. The disease spread, melting the face into an amoeboid mass in which the eyes floated, dull crustacean eyes. Slowly, a new face formed around the eyes. A series of faces, hieroglyphs, distorted and leading to the final place where the human road ends, where the human form can no longer contain the crustacean horror that has grown inside it.

Junkie may be considered a blueprint for all of Burroughs' work: it offers an introduction to the macabre and bizarre characters who reappear in his later fiction. There is Subway Mike who looked like "some specialized kind of underground animal that preys on animals of the surface." Or Mary, whose system could not absorb calcium so that "there was something boneless about her, like a deep sea creature. Her eyes were cold fish-eyes that looked at you through a viscous medium she carried about her. I could see those eyes in a shapeless, protoplasmic mass undulating over the dark sea floor." Or Doolie, who became for Burroughs "the focal point for a hostile intrusive force. You could feel him walk right into your psyche and look around to see if anything was there he could make use of." In his later fiction Burroughs calls this point of entry a coordinate, a place where an alien controling agent would enter. And Doolie becomes the prototype of the carriers in the later fiction: "The envelope of personality was gone, dissolved by his junk-hungry cells. Viscera and cells, galvanized into loathsome insect-like activity." The insect image, a fusion of Gothic fantasy and science fiction, dominates all of Burroughs' work, and it is presented with remarkable force in his picture of the typical drug pusher:

> This man walks around in the places where he once exercised his obsolete and unthinkable trade. But he is unperturbed. His eyes are black with an insect's unseeing calm. He looks as if he nourished himself on honey and Levantine syrups that he sucks up through a proboscis.

What is his lost trade? Definitely of a servant class and something to do with the dead, though he is not an embalmer. Perhaps he stores something in his body—a substance to prolong life—of which he is periodically milked by his masters. He is as specialized as an insect, for the performance of some inconceivably vile function.

Junkie, unlike the rest of Burroughs' work, is an ordered narrative, and the full grotesquerie of death as the ultimate reality is not felt with the force of the later fiction. Burroughs traces his involvement with addictive chemicals along a linear route from New York City to New Orleans to Mexico. While the experiences are quite painful, especially during the instances of drug deprivation, the horrors are cushioned by the narrator's journalistic presence, his retrospection, his guiding perspective through the infernal regions of drug abuse. When the same experiences are presented in the later books through the vehicle of the terminal addict, the difficulties for the reader are comparable to those confronted in Joyce's attempt to articulate the language of dreams in *Finnegans Wake* or Faulkner's use of the idiot Benjy in *The Sound and the Fury*. Drugs, Burroughs explains in his *Paris Review* interview, create a "random craving for images," and his cinematic sequences which seem to float across the page and almost evanesce respond to such a need. The reader searching for patterns, contrasts, or the thematic connections of conventional fiction must waive such expectations.

Burroughs cannot be fully appreciated by reading only *Naked Lunch*, for he develops crucial situations in *The Soft Machine*, *Nova Express*, and *The Ticket That Exploded*. The cumulative message of these novels is a warning of throttling controls on freedom and a world ruled by robot forces. Burroughs never really specifies the origins of this evil. In *Nova Express* and *The Ticket That Exploded*, the evil consists of agents planted by other galaxies to foment clashes on earth; later, the source is a virus from Venus. It is tempting to classify Burroughs as a writer of science fiction. However, because the content of science fiction is usually so difficult to believe, the writers of the genre have tended to employ conventional narrative techniques. None are as fragmentary as Burroughs, who will present a series of disconnected, unintegrated episodes without the narrative framework of plot or story.

Modern experimental novelists have struggled to reject classical notions of harmony, though some, like Joyce in *Ulysses*, have substituted cohering unities that greatly facilitate the reading of their works. In *Ulysses*, for example, the Homeric myth parallels Stephen Dedalus' flights and Bloom's more dogged pursuits, giving substance and meaning to the whole, just as the concentration on a day in Dublin provides additional focus and direction. Burroughs deliberately excludes such unifying conceptions from his books although, like Joyce, he uses stream of consciousness to enter deeply internalized states of being. In his *Paris Review* interview he claimed that he thought in "association blocks" rather than words, rejecting ordinary logic; and he asserted that the "Aristotelian construct is one of the great shackles of Western Civilization."

In what he calls an "atrophied preface" near the end of *Naked Lunch*, Burroughs offers several insights into his idea of the novel and the writer's role in composition. The writer can only record what exists in front of his senses; he cannot presume the imposition of plot or continuity. Burroughs implies that he has been possessed in the process of composition by alien agents. His characters are "subject to say the same thing in the same words" at different points in the narrative because their multiple disguises form the fused identity necessary to reveal the drug experience. As a result, readers can "cut into *Naked Lunch* at any intersection point." The book becomes a "kaleidoscope of vistas"; the world cannot be expressed directly, but requires a "mosaic of juxtaposition like articles abandoned in a hotel drawer, defined by negatives and absence. . . . " In *The Ticket That Exploded*, a character observes that "This is a novel presented in a series of oblique references," and the comment stands for all of Burroughs' work after *Junkie*.

Burroughs has commented that his experiences with drugs did not induce a visionary quality as much as a sense of "moving at a high speed through space." This results in the floating metaphor first distinguished in *Junkie*, but becoming more pronounced as Burroughs progresses as a writer. Except for Pound's *Cantos*, no modern writer presents so rapid a series of transformations as Burroughs, and this is a feature that in Burroughs' case may be derived from film. Much as film exclusively captures the immediate presence of what is being photographed, Burroughs uses no past or future. Instead he relies on juxtaposition to create dimension and body. Since he has no real central characters, since his figures fade out of his narratives so quickly, since events change so rapidly, he violates all the ordinary features of novelistic perspective, what most readers take for "reality" in fiction—that is, a mirror of the familiar world. The result is as difficult to comprehend as Cubist painting was when it first exploded the logic of representational construction in art.

A good illustration of Burroughs' presentation occurs in *Nova Express*. Called "Shift Coordinate Points," it is an account of the struggle between different galactic forces for control of earth and the universe. K 9 is William Lee, the agent who detects and tracks down other hostile and threatening figures like The Subliminal Kid, Sammy The Butcher, and Izzy The Push, all of whom occupy drug addicts and work through their bodies:

K 9 was in combat with the alien mind screen—Magnetic claws feeling for virus punch cards—pulling him into vertiginous spins—

"Back—Stay out of those claws—Shift coordinate points"—By Town Hall Square long stop for the red light—A boy stood in front of the hot dog stand and blew water from his face—Pieces of grey vapor drifted back across wine gas and brown hair as hotel faded photo showed a brass bed—Unknown mornings blew rain in cobwebs—Summer evenings feel to a room with rose wallpaper—Sick dawn whisper of clock hands and brown hair—Morning blew rain on copper roofs in a slow haze of apples—Summer light on rose wallpaper—Iron mesas lit by a pink volcano—Snow slopes under the Northern shirt—Unknown street stirring sick dawn whispers of junk—Flutes of Ramadan in the distance—St. Louis lights wet cobblestones of future life—Fell through urinal and the bicycle races—On the bar wall the clock hands—My death across his face faded through the soccer scores—Smell of dust on the surplus army blankets—Stiff jeans against one wall—And Kiki went away like a cat—Some clean shirt and walked out—He is gone through unknown morning blew—"No good—No bueno—Hustling myself—" Such wisdom in gusts—

K 9 moved back into the combat area—Standing now in the Chinese youth sent the resistance message jolting clicking tilting through the pinball machine—Enemy plans exploded in a burst of rapid calculations—Clicking in punch cards of redirected orders—Crackling shortwave static—Bleeeeeeeeeeeeeep—Sound of thinking metal—

"Calling partisans of all nations—Word falling—Photo falling—Break through in Grey Room—Pinball led streets—Free Doorways—Shift coordinate points—"

This example of what Burroughs calls an "association block" with its sense of eerie dislocation, and its events that seem so unordered by ordinary logic, realized shapes, or recognizable places, depends upon an unusually free notion of juxtaposition. When such evidently lyrical images as that of the rose wallpaper or the rain in cobwebs are yoked to an environment of electronic combat, some gap in expectation is widened, intending to diffuse and broaden the reader's focus rather than attempting to concentrate it as most fiction conventionally does. The result may be an unfamiliar music, rather like John Cage's dissonant compositions that almost impale ordinary sounds onto a musical structure.

Perhaps the most cogent analysis of Burroughs' method may be achieved by applying Charles Olson's descriptions of projective verse. Olson was fascinated by the kinetics of poetic movement since he saw the poem as an energy transfer, highly potent, very special, and, if successful, as meaningful as the most profound spiritual insights or messages. He claimed that the problem for the poet was an awareness of the process through which the energy that prompted the writing becomes the energy in which the reader participates. He believed that this interchange best occurred in as open a literary structure as possible, and Olson's key was transformation:

ONE PERCEPTION MUST IMMEDIATELY AND DIRECTLY
LEAD TO A FURTHER PERCEPTION. It means exactly what it
says, is a matter of, at *all* points (even, I should say, of our management of
daily reality as of the daily work) get on with it, keep moving, keep in,
speed, the nerves, their speed, the perceptions, theirs, the acts, the split
second acts, the whole business, keep it moving as fast as you can citizen.
And if you also set up as a poet, USE USE USE the process at all points,
in any given poem always, always one perception must must must
MOVE, INSTANTER, ON ANOTHER!

Reacting like Pound against the nineteenth-century poets' tendency
to flat statement, Olson, concerned with the artistic process of
becoming, carries the tenets of Pound's Imagism to its logical
extreme.

Burroughs, however, has another purpose that exists in particular
accord with the Beats' desire to transform language so that it cannot
be used as a conditioning agent. Since the eighteenth century,
writers have appreciated the ability of the word to determine
morality. In our own time, writers with such divergent political
outlooks as George Orwell and Ezra Pound have agreed on how
media corrupts language, reducing its efficacy by confusing the
meaning of words. Orwell's fear, like McLuhan's anticipations of the
end of fiction, is that language will be replaced by pictures as the
chief conditioning agent, and the world of modern advertising seems
to support this view. In *Tristes Tropiques*, Claude Levi Strauss
asserted that writing itself has historically favored the exploitation
rather than the enlightenment of mankind. From its original connections with early architectural enterprises, as a form of artificial
memory and a method for organizing the present and future, writing
became a source of power, ultimately a tool whose primary function
was "to facilitate the enslavement of other human beings" through
colonization or the internal regulations which all had to obey. In
The Ticket That Exploded, Burroughs compares the present state of
language to a viral infection caused by a parasitic organism. He
agrees that "what we see is determined to a large extent by what we
hear," and advocates a linguistic purge. In his final chapter (called

"the invisible generation" and written in collaboration with Brion Gysin) he proposes a number of ways in which the conditioning influences of language can be reduced, such as playing a tape recorder backward slowly so that one can "learn to unsay what you just said. . .such exercises bring you a liberation from old association locks." Burroughs and Gysin recommend a variety of such methods: running tapes at different speeds to hear new words being formed, and splicing in body or animal sounds. Burroughs' point is that "the use of irrelevant response will be found effective in breaking obsessional association tracks," and sometimes his own anarchy of references in the cut-ups seems directed to this end.

Of course, the paradox of writing to end dependence on the word can be extended to Burroughs' centripetal rather than centrifugal conception of narrative structure. If his field is as vast as it is, if readers cannot find plot or story on which to focus, can he teach them to destroy the "control machine?" Actually, reading Burroughs, experiencing the circularity of his broadened field of reference, does serve to reshape perceptions so that the conditioning influences of the ordinary linguistic system become more apparent, and therefore less effective. But to successfully read the novels in the first place one has to want to be freed from those prejudices, and thus to have been partly liberated already.

In a sense, the unusual degree of violence in Burroughs' world—corresponding, of course, to the excesses of a spectacularly violent nation—frees the reader from normal expectations. The violence may itself be regarded as an assault on conditioning. In *Nova Express*, Burroughs reflects that "some ugly noxious disgusting act sharply recorded becomes now part of 'Photo falling—Word falling,' " that is, Burroughs' refrain for the breakdown of the supportive structures for our present technological civilization.

Burroughs himself provides the barest amount of thematic statement to bolster his views: indeed, if this is possible, he is a writer almost without a point of view, purely existing as a kind of supercharged literary centralizing and focusing neutrino in a world of ordinary movement. Occasionally he will comment directly, the very sparsity of such remarks giving them added weight and importance. In his *Paris Review* interview, for example, he equates the nova police he imagines in *Nova Express* with the forces of technology. Burroughs (like Conrad in *The Secret Agent*, Chesterton in *The Man Who Was Thursday*, or Mailer in *An American Dream*) believes that police and criminal elements share a similar mentality. The point of his equation of nova with technology is that both separate man from his naturally supportive conditions, replacing them with the antagonisms of competition and specialization.

The fear of control and pattern is endemic to Burroughs' vision. In *Naked Lunch*, he speculates on the future of biocontrol, a system of bioelectric signals injected into the nervous system which will telepathically regulate physical movement, mental processes, emotional reactions, and sensory impressions. The result would be robotized existence, for as he warns, "*You see control can never be a means to any practical end. . . . It can never be a means to anything but more control. . . .*" Burroughs feels that the United States is particularly the place for such an unhappy transformation, despite its myths of freedom and independence, because it has almost invented the thinking machine and as he advises near the end of *Naked Lunch*, "Americans have a special horror of giving up control, of letting things happen in their own way without interference. They would like to jump down into their stomachs and digest the food and shovel the shit out."

Burroughs' more overt declarations usually occur near the beginnings or ends of his novels. For instance, *The Ticket That Exploded* begins with the revelation of a biological weapon that reduces men to slobbering, inhuman things, and ends with an illustration of the effects of word conditioning:

> what are newspapers doing but selecting the ugliest sounds for playback by and large if its ugly its news and if that isn't enough i quote from the editorial page of the new york daily news we can take care of china and if russia intervenes we can take care of that nation too the only good communist is a dead communist lets take care of slave driver castro next

what are we waiting for let's bomb china now and let's stay armed to the
teeth for centuries this ugly vulgar bray put out for mass playback you
want to spread hysteria record and playback the most stupid hysterical
reactions. marijuana marijuana why that's deadlier than cocaine.

Such direct imitations are infrequent in Burroughs' fiction. His
indirectness is characteristically conveyed by allegory. The descriptions of the various political groups in *Naked Lunch*'s Interzone, a
complex of rooms forming one huge building like a vast beehive,
exemplifies Burroughs' allegorical tendencies. The Liquifactionists
believe in the "merging of everyone into One Man by a process of
protoplasmic absorption." The Divisionists are similar products of
conformist homogeneity: they cut off tiny bits of their flesh and
nurture exact replicas of themselves in embryo jelly. Opposed to
these groups are the Factualists who struggle against the use of
control to "exploit or annihilate the individuality of another living
creature." Motivating such fantasies is a paranoid vision of Western
competitiveness, like Kerouac's more direct prediction in *Big Sur*:
"like raving baboons we'll all be piled on top of each other. . . .
Hundreds of millions of hungry mouths raving for more more
more."

Burroughs' mode is parody. His ambition to expose the controls
created by institutions, his exaggerated allegories of hospital operating rooms, of police and customs bureaucracies, result, as John
Clellon Holmes has observed in *Nothing More To Declare*, in a
rewriting of *1984* by W. C. Fields. The carnival mood of Burroughs'
burlesque does balance the sense of violent terror in his work. The
best illustration of Burroughs' grotesque humor is the figure of Dr.
Benway in *Naked Lunch*, a man who deplores brutality only because
of its inefficiency. Benway, who directs a Reconditioning Center in
the Freeland Republic, is an expert on interrogation, brainwashing,
and control. His macabre medicinal machinations are an ironic
reflection of Burroughs' belief that there is no technological cure for
spiritual disease. Burroughs' description of a typical operation
stands as a primal influence on more recent absurdist fiction:

I had a Yage hangover, me, and in no condition to take any of Browbeck's shit. First thing he comes on with I should start the incision from the back instead of the front, muttering some garbled nonsense about being sure to cut out the gall bladder it would fuck up the meat. Thought he was on the farm cleaning a chicken. I told him to go put his head back in the oven, whereupon he had the effrontery to push my hand severing the patient's femoral artery. Blood spurted up and blinded the anesthetist, who ran out through the halls screaming. Browbeck tried to knee me in the groin, and I managed to hamstring him with my scalpel. He crawled about the floor stabbing at my feet and legs. Violet, that's my baboon assistant—only woman I ever cared a damn about—really wigged. I climbed up on the table and poise myself to jump on Browbeck with both feet and stomp him when the cops rushed in.

Burroughs' comedy of hilarious excess is frequently tinged by nausea and sickness, like the menu for transcendental cuisine in *Naked Lunch*: "The After-Birth Suprême de Boeuf, cooked in drained crank case oil, served with a piquant sauce of rotten egg yolks and crushed bed bugs." It is a comedy that always verges on death, disease, and excrement. Surely no writer since Swift has expressed contempt and disgust in such brazenly uncomplimentary terms, and the Yahoos of *Gulliver's Travels* become the perfect model for Burroughs' view of man. Of course this sort of comic indulgence in ugliness and bestiality, in misfortune and maladjustment, is complementary to what I termed "black beauty" near the beginning of this essay. In this sense Burroughs does manage a unity of tone as he insists on a cruel pessimism, and the absolute lack of hope. Burroughs' characters will leap ferociously like Violet, Dr. Benway's baboon assistant, or will grovel like the president of Interzone who, in an annual Swiftian parody of the political process, crawls across the municipal garbage heap and in full view of the entire populace delivers the renewed lease to the British governor. The point is that human features in Burroughs' world are blurred, distorted, and eventually disappear.

The criticism that in *Nova Express*, *The Soft Machine*, and *The*

Ticket That Exploded, Burroughs does not develop beyond the techniques of *Naked Lunch* is invalid: the three subsequent books form part of a larger whole, compiled partly from the same original manuscript, continuing the same vision, but always extending it. Developed after *Naked Lunch*, the cut-up adds a major difference in texture and atmosphere, creating its own strange profusions and impassable blocks. Sacrificing clarity and the element of narrative, it increases the chaos Burroughs wants his reader to feel. In the more recent works, *Exterminator!* and *The Wild Boys*, Burroughs uses the cut-up much more sparingly, mostly in isolated instances to create poetic bridges, integrating refrains, repeated passages that emphasize material in new perspectives. The result is generally an increase in coherence and continuity.

The two recent books represent a definite departure from the aesthetic of the objective recording instrument announced near the end of *Naked Lunch*. Burroughs' own political views have become more pronounced and visible, and accordingly his own sense of self is felt with greater presence in his writing now. While the *Naked Lunch* tetralogy has practically no identifiable persona, no single voice speaking for the author—due to the rapid metamorphoses and the obscuring miasma of junk—certain characters like Audrey in *Exterminator!* and *Wild Boys* directly reflect aspects of Burroughs' own past—his study of medicine in Vienna, for example, or his early sketch "The Autobiography of a Wolf." The strength of these later books is due less to experimentation than to power of vision. Both books are composed of brief sketches relating to a common anticipation of apocalypse.

In *Exterminator!*, the wind stops blowing in a Caribbean town called "Puerto de los Santos"; monstrous scorpion women appear in a pastoral English town; ladies are ravished on Fifth Avenue in New York City by American soldiers. Such omens of final disaster are counterpointed by quotations from songs like "The Battle Hymn of the Republic" or Burroughs' favorite, "The Star-Spangled Banner." The first sketch is a straightforward account, in the manner of *Junkie*, of Burroughs working as an exterminator of rats and roaches in Chicago. The following pieces reinforce this subject, except that the extinction becomes human.

In "The Perfect Servant," a Pentagon official's butler is a Chinese agent who employs mind control to send a group of CIA agents into paroxysms, and releases a secret virus that will cause unborn children to speak Chinese at birth. In another sketch, a guerrilla group tries to explode a train carrying nerve gas. Another character stores electricity during shock treatment and releases it as a death ray. In "Seeing Red," a brilliantly effective short parable on obscenity and politics, Lee imports a red picture through customs, the very sight of which enrages the police to the point of asphyxiation. In "The Coming of the Purple Assed Better One," Burroughs mixes his observations of the 1968 Chicago Democratic convention with a fantasy on the political process, as Homer Mandrill, a demagogic baboon, runs for president on an ultraconservative platform. The book's tone is incongrously grotesque and bizarre: a Yiddish grandmother passionately protests the visit of the bedbug exterminator, moaning "like the Gestapo is murdering her nubile daughter engaged to a dentist"; the Queen of England supports herself by running a small grocery and lives in a semidetached cottage in a suburb.

The humor in *The Wild Boys* is more laconic and sadistic: the Green Nun assumes her Christ costume every night and visits one of the young nuns in her convent with a dildo while imagining herself in a poem by Sara Teasdale. The book begins and ends with a procession of stunted, maimed figures, and throughout there is the narrative tension of victims rising to murder their exploiters. The first piece is about Mexicans who love to humiliate Americans, and near the end of the book an old servile gardener stabs his master, a general who has just screamed that "Man is made to submit and obey." Ironically, the cult of the wild boys succeeds because they agree with their enemy, the general. Hints of their presence—a tribal affiliation of young homosexual guerrillas—appear through the early parts of the book, juxtaposed to the many signs of imminent disaster for those still in power. The time is the last decades of the twentieth century. Famine and plague have widened the gaps between rich and poor. In North Africa, where the wild boys originate, all institutional procedures have collapsed: the wealthy are protected by private mercenaries; travel is by stagecoach or mule since there is no longer much oil available. An American expeditionary force of twenty thousand soldiers is annihilated by the extraordinarily savage tactics of the wild boys who fight like animals and spread over the world. Their battle skills are in the tradition of the *lútíyeh*, the eighteenth-century bands of marauding sodomites in India who attacked rich travelers and merchant caravans, or the Pariah women of the same time and place, followers of the goddess Kali, who hunted men in packs and raped them. Like the satyrs and sirens of sodomite and Amazonian myth, the wild boys are impervious to ordinary needs. They descend from the Moslem *gházíyeh*, the berserkers, founded by Hassan-ben-Sabah-Momairi who appears in *Naked Lunch* as an obvious source of admiration for Burroughs. Hassan's followers believed in him as a messiah; they were pledged to complete obedience, and would eat hashish before battle to become indifferent to pain or death. The wild boys are a highly ritualized group whose sacraments are sex and hashish. Using eighteen-inch bowie knives, crossbows, karate, claws treated with cyanide, they develop a mixture of primitive battle tactics and sophisticated technology. Some of them use no language at all, others have developed "cries, songs, words as weapons":

Words that cut like buzz saws. Words that vibrate the entrails to jelly. Cold strange words that fall like icy nets on the mind. Virus words that eat the brain to muttering shreds. Idiot tunes that stick in the throat round and round night and day.

Attacking with fanatical devotion, the wild boys take no prisoners, instead making hash pouches from human testicles. They renounce women and are exclusively homosexual. The tension in the book is between scenes of incredible violence and homoeroticism without love, existing almost for the sake of sensation itself. The world of

The Wild Boys is as frightening as the drug-deranged environment of *Naked Lunch*, and it is Burroughs' best book since then.

Like the image of vultures swooping down a black funnel near the beginning of *Naked Lunch*, Burroughs' vision is intensely surreal. He transmits a feeling of desperate urgency, of apocalyptic disaster and warning. Tony Tanner, in *City of Words*, has interpreted this message in terms of entropy, the idea of matter returning to lower forms of organization. According to this point of view, the night-mares Burroughs concocts are recidivistic, a return to some primitive feared state. As Burroughs writes in *Naked Lunch* on the ritual role of untouchables in India, who "perform a priestly function in taking on themselves all human vileness," so, too, this aspect of his art is shamanistic, a warding off of evil through the public exorcism of his fiction.

But another view of Burroughs' art is possible. According to the new physics that seems to have informed Burroughs' world, as well as the possibility of telepathy induced by the drug experience, Burroughs may be introducing us to a futuristic vision of the cybernetic reality slowly replacing human perspectives in the West. Living organisms form open systems (unlike the Deist view of the world as clock, running down in time because of friction), and feed on energies and materials found in the environment. Instead of dissipating energy—which as Einstein argued cannot be destroyed—the organism builds up more complex chemicals from the chemicals nourishing it, more complex forms of energy from the energy it absorbs, and more complex forms of information—perceptions, memories, ideas—from the input of its receptors. In Burroughs' fiction, the human form is "building up" to a perceptual level that suggests a new stage of experience. Yeats, who used automatic writing and a kind of telepathy in experiments with his wife, felt that man would pass into a new unrecognizable stage in the year 2000, the time that ecologists currently claim is the approximate limit of nature's sustenance of human growth. Burroughs' books point to some new time when communication will occur through combinations of intense sensory but nonverbal experience, where we may wander through existence like neutrinos, unhampered in our flight and connecting only in silence. Rimbaud called for the hallucination of the word. As Gertrude Stein was for the Lost Generation, Burroughs is our theoretician of language, our cabalist of the word. He has deconditioned himself with drugs, and purifying his vision, has used the cut-up as a way of objectively reproducing the process of his own consciousness. His reputation has depended on one book, *Naked Lunch*. Since then the critics have failed to understand his accomplishments. Marshall McLuhan was amused by reviews of Burroughs' work which regarded it as failed science fiction: "It is a little like trying to criticize the sartorial and verbal manifestations of a man who is knocking on the door to explain that flames are leaping from the roof of our house." Burroughs is the Beat archangel of apocalypse: though his content will always be obscene to those still trapped in the legacy of puritanism, his method is cleansing and purgative, however terrifying in implication.

JACK KEROUAC: EULOGIST OF SPONTANEITY

And just for a moment I had reached the point of ecstasy I had always wanted to reach, which was the complete step across chronological time into timeless shadows, and wonderment in the bleakness of the mortal realm, and the sensation of death kicking at my heels, and myself hurrying to a plank where all the angels dove off and flew into the holy void of uncreated emptiness, the potent and inconceivable radiances shining in bright Mind essence, innumerable lotuslands falling in the magic mothswarm of heaven.

Dean and I swayed to the rhythm of the It of our final excited joy in talking and living to the tranced end of all innumerable riotous angelic particulars that had been lurking in our souls all our lives.

—Jack Kerouac
On The Road

JACK KEROUAC—even now our most misunderstood and underestimated writer—is still seen in the narrow category of chronicler of the Beat Generation. His true subject was America itself. He expressed extraordinary sensitivity to the nascent tensions, emerging mores, and the beginnings of a new consciousness in American life, recording the darker aspects of conformity and materialism even as he anticipated and charted the changes in lifestyle that were only to be realized during his declining years, and which were to bewilder him as much as anyone else.

In so many ways there is something quintessentially American about the restless energy of Kerouac's prose. Never settling for a final form, he demonstrated in each of his novels an eagerness to try the new, to vary from conventional expectations of fictional form. Like Henry Miller, Kerouac was uninterested in the ideal of "literary" perfection, or in a fictitious "order" that had little relation to the flux of reality. He stubbornly believed in his writing, expecting that even seemingly immutable literary tastes would change. His reactions to what he saw were often raw and impulsive, yet he was able to tap certain hidden vitalities of the future, verities far beyond the ken of the middle class. His great discovery was the bared power of the actual and the ordinary, the natural and the commonplace—like the road that became his primal metaphor.

In jazz, drugs, and a ruinous thirst for alcohol, he discovered a source of ecstatic release. Like the Buddhists, he believed that "all life is suffering" and indeed a mysterious sadness balances the sheer joy in being that animates so much of his prose. Intuitive, unpredictable, often desperately insecure in his relations with others, he retained a tender affection for all living things. Almost in willful compensation for his shy sweetness, he became an inveterate voyager. Invariably, after each trip and its travail, there was the return to his mother, partly because of the security she represented, but even more because of the writer's need to assimilate his experiences in a place of quiet retreat. Perhaps paradoxically, he lived primarily for words and the rhythms of his work, and not for the bohemian adventures associated with his books.

It was not merely what he saw, but *how* he perceived it and wrote it down that distinguished Kerouac from others who were able to register some of the ambiance of the new hip freedom. In his aesthetic of spontaneity, Kerouac extended the romantic tradition to its logical ends, far beyond the Wordsworthian idea that the writer's function was to *re*capture an action, a strongly felt emotion, in tranquility. Kerouac's model was closer to the opium transport that inspired Coleridge's "Kubla Khan," an ecstatic abandonment of conscious control of language, an intuitive response to the inner voice. Such a heightened state usurps normal consciousness with its filtering processes, soars beyond the intellectual capabilities of reason and choice and selectivity to achieve what Kerouac called "an undisturbed flow from the mind" or what Ginsberg termed in his own work an "undifferentiated consciousness." Kerouac told Malcolm Cowley that spontaneity meant the very sound of the mind, and insisted that craft, revision, resulted in obscuring what a man most needed to write, in leaving unsaid precisely what most needed to be written down. He quoted the Surangama Sutra as an example of his intentions:

> If you are now desirous of more perfectly understanding Supreme Enlightenment and the enlightening nature of pure mind-Essence, you must learn to answer questions spontaneously with no recourse to discriminating thinking. For the Tathagatas in the ten quarters of the universes have been delivered from the ever-returning cycle of deaths and rebirths by this same single way, namely by reliance upon their own intuitive minds.

In "The Essentials of Spontaneous Prose," Kerouac compared the particular mental attitude that nurtured his creation to orgasm—a moment of utterness, of simultaneous mingling sensations when the thought process is obliterated, the body's music is resonant and loud, and the individual is "submissive to everything, open, listening":

> If possible write "without consciousness" in semitrance (as Yeats' later trance writing) allowing subconscious to admit in its own uninhibited interesting necessary and so "modern" language what conscious art would censor, and write excitedly, swiftly, with writing-or-typing-cramps, in accordance (as from center to periphery) with laws of orgasm, Reich's

"beclouding of consciousness." *Come* from within, out—to relaxed and said.

He maintained that the writer's purpose should be to "sketch the flow that already exists intact in mind." The method would be ecstatic: "wild, undisciplined, pure, coming in from under, crazier the better." Swimming in a furious sea of language, the writer would plummet to a place near the "bottom of the mind" to release "unspeakable visions of the individual," the usually unarticulated insights reserved for one's most private moments.

Kerouac termed this procedure "sketching" and it originated in 1951 when the writing of *On The Road* turned from a conventional narrative of road trips to a thickly layered multidimensional conscious and unconscious invocation of Neal Cassady's character in his whirlwind changes. Kerouac's friend, Ed White, had once suggested to Kerouac, "Why don't you just sketch in the streets like a painter but with words?" Kerouac tried this, discovering that the myriad profusion of everything he saw was activated as long as he purified his mind and let the words pour forth with complete honesty, transcribing without shame so rapidly that the writer could forget that he was writing, like Yeats' dancer merging with the dance. The technique was especially suited to Kerouac's own talents—an amazing sense of recall that is matched only by Thomas Wolfe in American letters and an exceptional impressionability. The best writing, Kerouac advised, would be the "most painful personal wrung-out tossed from cradle warm protective mind—tap from yourself the song of yourself—blow!" With the removal of all literary, grammatical, and syntactical inhibitions (as he had learned by reading Joyce) as well as the arbitrary barriers of conventional punctuation, sentences could correspond to rhetorical breath notations, and to the actual inner flow of experience as recorded by the mind. In the early forties Kerouac had been listening to the bebop of Charlie Parker, Lester Young, Dizzy Gillespie, and Thelonius Monk, and their music formed the basis of a new sense of rhythm which he adapted to his own prose line. Charlie Parker taught that music was the result of the artist's own experience, thought, and wisdom. "If you don't live it," he is reputed to have said, "it won't come out of your horn. They teach you there's a boundary line to music. But man, there's no boundary line to art." Kerouac was to explode many of the remaining boundaries for fiction in his time.

Kerouac knew that the integrity of pure experience and the feelings that actually attended the moment of occurrence could best be achieved when the writer removed all procedural lags, when his momentum was such as to obviate the Flaubertian obsession with the precise word; instead, the writer should release an "infantile pileup of scatalogical buildup words," relying on the freest of associations rather than selectivity of expression. Thus he struck at the sacred cow, the very cornerstone of aesthetic theory. The writer was not to revise his original impulses, for revision was a function of conditioning, a concession to standards of taste and propriety that belonged to the temporal community and not to the universal strains that Kerouac sought to capture. Revision was inhibition, the censoring of the purity of the writer's vision, the betrayal of immediacy, the lie in the face of actual experience.

With his rejection of revision and the traditional idea of the writer's selectivity, Kerouac was deemphasizing the element of process in writing, and attempting prose that would communicate unequivocally through the sheer ignition of felt energy. By refusing to revise, he asserted in his *Paris Review* interview, the writer could give his reader "the actual workings of the mind during the writing itself: you confess your thoughts about events in your own unchangeable way." In his interview, Kerouac acknowledged that he had spent his "entire youth writing slowly with revisions and endless re-hashing speculation and deleting and got so I was writing one sentence a day and the sentence had no FEELINGS."

Having written his first million words even before Burroughs met him in 1944, Kerouac had mastered his medium so that expression could be released without the restraints of revision. So he could invent spontaneously—creating instant haiku, as he demonstrated to poets Ted Berrigan and Aram Saroyan when they interviewed him for *Paris Review*, or when he composed the entire sound track for the film *Pull My Daisy* in one sitting after seeing the film for the first time.

Writing whatever "comes into your head as it comes," Kerouac was inspired by the directness and emotional honesty he found in letters he received from Neal Cassady, letters whose racy colloquialism and syntactical ellipses affected his own style. Kerouac saw such exposure of feeling as a crucially significant opposition to the escape from emotion, the impersonality defined by T. S. Eliot in "Tradition and the Individual Talent." In a brief but characteristically pungent piece called "The Origins of Joy in Poetry," Kerouac—while admiring Eliot's poetry—castigated such negative theories as the objective correlative as "a lot of constipation and ultimately emasculation of the pure masculine urge to freely sing." In *The Subterraneans*, he saliently stressed the descriptive bias of his own eye, advising that "the details are the life of it, I insist, say everything, don't hold it back, don't analyze or anything as you go along." This avoidance of judgment or commentary was central to Kerouac's writing, representing an important difference between him and naturalistic writers to whom he might ordinarily be compared.

The animation of spontaneity required a new sense of sentence structure, and Kerouac defined his intentions in a piece called "The Last Word" that was reprinted in the *Saturday Review*:

> My position in the current literary scene is simply that I got sick and tired of the conventional English sentence which seemed to me so ironbound, so inadmissible with reference to the actual format of my mind as I had learned to probe it in the spirit of Freud and Jung, that I couldn't express myself through it anymore.
>
> How many sentences do you see in earnest novels that say, "The snow was on the ground, and it was difficult for the car to climb the hill."? By the childish device of taking what was originally two short sentences and sticking in a comma with an "and" these contemporary prose "craftsmen" think they have labored out a sentence. As far as I can see, it is two short

sets of imagery belonging to a much longer sentence, the total imagery of which would finally say something we never heard before if the writer dared to utter it out.
Shame seems to be the key to repression in writing as well as in psychological malady. If you don't stick to what you first thought, and the words the thought brought what's the sense of bothering with it anyway, what's the sense of foisting your little lies on others? What I find to be really "stupefying in its unreadability" is this laborious and dreary lying called craft and revision by writers and certainly recognized by the sharpest psychologists as sheer blockage of the mental spontaneous process known 2500 years ago as "The seven Streams of Swiftness."

In *Desolation Angels*, Kerouac dramatized his concern with spontaneity by refusing to attend a poetry reading, preferring the power of "uncontrollable involuntary thoughts" to the craft of careful arrangement which implied craftiness, evasiveness, and dishonesty. In the same novel he described his own method:

Clinically, at the time of the beginning of this story, on the roof over Gaines [Bill Garver's in Mexico City], I was an Ambitious Paranoid. —Nothing could stop me from writing big books of prose and poetry for nothing, that is with no hope of ever having them published—I was simply writing them because I was an 'Idealist' and I believed in 'Life' and I was going about justifying it with my earnest scribblings—Strangely enough, these scribblings were the first of their kind in the world, I was originating (without knowing it, you say?) a new way of writing about life, no fiction, no craft, no revising afterthoughts, the heartbreaking discipline of the veritable fire ordeal where you can't go back but have made the vow of "speak now or forever hold your tongue" and all of it innocent go-ahead confession, the discipline of making the mind the slave of the tongue with no chance to lie or reelaborate. . . .

Returning to the unfulfilled linguistic intentions of the British Lake poets, Kerouac sought a diction that would be compatible with the natural flow he wanted to release. Instead of the complexity of Pound or Eliot, and the elitist sense of audience their work implied, instead of the endless ramification and tortuously analytical sensibility of the Jamesian tradition which found its perfect expression in the voice of Eliot, Kerouac believed in the romantic imperative of a language fashioned from ordinary speech. His own voice was representative of an endemic colloquialism in the American character: to listen to the recordings of Kerouac reading his own poems and prose is to attend to a purely natural inflection, one completely without literary affectation. In his voice there was a laughter and closeness to dialect unheard in American letters since Mark Twain. As Kerouac himself put it in a poem he wrote called "Daydreams for Ginsberg":

> . . . . i will write
> it, all the talk of the world
> everywhere in this morning, leav-
> ing open parentheses sections
> for my own accompanying inner
> thoughts—with roars of me
> all brain—vibrating—I put
> it down, swiftly, 1,000 words
> (of pages) compressed into one second
> of time. . . .

Kerouac's ability to record actual sounds sometimes resulted in a native word music, a verve and gusto that departed from the stultifying preciousness of much of the verse of his time:

> Old Navajoa shit dog, you,
> your goodies are the goodiest
> goodies I ever did see, how
> dog you shore look mad
> when yer bayin
>
> Hoo Hound-dog!
> don't eat that dead rabbit
> in front of my face raw
> —Cook it a lil bit

The demotic, however, was only one of Kerouac's voices. As John Clellon Holmes has asserted, Kerouac was gifted with an extraordinary vocal range, almost corresponding stylistically to his personal awe at the geographical variety of the American continent. From the vernacular idiom as it was actually spoken, Kerouac fashioned sentences that were like musical constructions. In *Allen Verbatim*, Ginsberg has commented on the quality of this sound:

> It was that he was suddenly aware of the sound of language, and got swimming in the seas of sound, and guided his intellect on sound rather than on dictionary associations with the meaning of sounds. In other words, another kind of intelligence—still consciousness, still reasonable, but another kind of reason, a reason founded on sounds rather than a reason founded on conceptual associations.

Kerouac's own exuberant bravado and gloomy sloughs were expressed in his great playfulness with words (like the sexual innuendo in his poem, "Pull My Daisy"), in the baroque intricacies of a book like *Doctor Sax*, or his getting high with language as in "Old Angel Midnight" where cascading rhythms were resolved into Joycean word games. At one extreme, there was the surreal solipsism of sound existing for its own sweet sake, as in the poem on the sounds of the sea at the end of *Big Sur*, or the description of the railroad chugging in "October in the Railroad Earth," or the 230th chorus in *Mexico City Blues*, "Love's multitudinous boneyard of decay," written on morphine and parading its "conceptions of delicate kneecaps" like blocks of sculptural sound too burdensome and huge for any single poem. At the other extreme, the tactility of haiku with its fusion of compressed strength and quiet fragility:

> In my medicine cabinet
> the winter fly
> has died of old age

The sudden surprise of haiku was a source of inspiration for all of Kerouac's prose. Poets like Shiki or Basho, as Ray Smith explains in

The Dharma Bums, perceived "as fresh as children writing down what they saw without literary devices or fanciness of expression." While Kerouac's poetry itself has received virtually no recognition (except from Ginsberg), the important point about Kerouac as poet is that there should be little distinction made between what he called his poetry and his prose, where the techniques that inspired the poems were even more effectively utilized.

Jack Kerouac's first published novel was an example of all the conventional possibilities in fiction which Kerouac was to reject. Thematically, it anticipated the rootless bohemian freedom Kerouac was to explore in later novels while explaining why cherished older ways founded in a nineteenth-century sense of family harmony, continuity, and loyalty to place were confounded by the "broken circuit" of World War II. Kerouac began writing the novel in 1942, working at it for six years, writing mostly at night.

When *The Town and the City* finally appeared in 1950, it received generally favorable reviews, several critics noticing a power similar to Thomas Wolfe's. Although only the early parts of the book were written with the cool, judicious detachment that critics expected in the early fifties, they were pleased by its recognizable structure, its finely balanced and crafted scenes, its exceptionally rich sense of place and character. In five parts of approximately a dozen chapters each, Kerouac traced the declining fortunes of his own family, neutrally named the Martins, from their home in the old New England town of Galloway (Lowell) to a tenement railroad flat in Brooklyn, New York.

The novel begins with an omniscient overview of the town and the main characters in the old-fashioned manner of Fielding or Thackeray. The second section ends with a Christmas family reunion and New Year's celebration that provides an ironic reverberation for the confusion of values reflected in the two following parts; the final part centers on the death of George Martin, head of the family, who is based on Leo Kerouac. The *Town and the City* is a domestic tragedy sympathetic to the view that accepts a character like Willy Loman, in Arthur Miller's *Death Of A Salesman*, as tragic victim, absurdly hopeful, pathetically faithful to an unreal ideal, and unremitting, even stoical in pursuit of that ideal.

Kerouac's George Martin is father of five sons and three daughters. A bluff, independent, and generous man who loves horse racing, Martin owns a printing establishment but is unambitious. Forced into bankruptcy, he loses his business and his home, and eventually moves to Brooklyn during the war after his children have left. The change in Martin's sense of himself is clearly a reflection of Leo Kerouac's story: used to walking to work in a small town where he could greet his friends, he now hurtles underground to work in a huge printing plant in Manhattan. Martin's spiritual despair is his discovery of the anonymity of the modern worker. His incipient lung cancer is a naturalistic symbol of his inability to breathe under such conditions. Supported by his sturdy wife, Marge, who works in a shoe factory, Martin sees his formerly thriving family disintegrate just as his own once robust body succumbs to cancer.

For his five sons, especially for Peter Martin, the football hero who most resembles Kerouac himself, the father's failure signals the end of a fixed and static social situation which had served to perpetuate family bonds and community ties. Biographically, the story is a retelling of Kerouac's own childhood, and it presents a revealing parallel to Joyce's. Both received their early education in Jesuit parochial schools. Each writer, while still very young, achieved a painful awareness of the social fabric when declining family fortunes made the father less of a formidable buttress against the world. The result in each case was also an exceptional vulnerability. Joyce abandoned traditional allegiance to the institutional trinity of family, state, and religion, asserting that his devotion to his art was more important to him. Kerouac, in the footsteps of Rimbaud and Jack London, intuitively responded to the spirit of André Breton's *"Lâcher tout"*—and dropped everything, family, football, Columbia, to experience adventure for its own sake. At the same time, however, the loss of his family home in Lowell must have been deeply unsettling: for the rest of his life, whenever he wasn't on the road, he would yearn for a secure haven without finding a satisfactory place, buying several homes on Long Island after selling the film rights to *On The Road*, moving to California with his mother, then to Florida, then returning to Long Island. Like Joyce, Kerouac felt estranged from Lowell as he approached manhood, but was to return to his hometown in several novels.

The tone of *The Town and the City* is one of pervasive brooding sadness. The wholesome verities which sustain the Martin family early in the novel are proven empty by the disorder of the war; an awful sense of meaninglessness incapacitates and paralyzes each of the five sons, frustrating their early promise. The refrain of *On The Road*—"everything is collapsing"—is documented in *The Town and the City* as the very underpinning that once sustained middle-class ambitions of security in family and of upward mobility through education or enterprise becomes illusion.

The evolution of the Martin boys, especially Joe, Peter, and Francis, the three eldest sons, is particularly interesting in that each reflects some aspect of the basic circumstances of Kerouac's life as a gifted young provincial growing up in a decaying industrial town where opportunities for self-expression were limited. Peter Martin, the high-school football hero who makes the team (as Kerouac himself did) through sheer effort, stubborn endurance, and penitent self-discipline, is the most autobiographical character. Peter is the model naturalistic hero, Zola's brute strength overcoming all odds:

> In his deepest soul, deeper than the regret of his heart, he gloated and boasted because he had almost broken Red Magee's neck: for Red Magee had tried to smash Peter Martin to a pulp and everybody had seen the result, everybody knew Peter Martin was the vanquisher.
>
> In the strong autumnal winds he rushed along ignoring the new dark knowledge he now half understood—that to triumph was also to wreak havoc.

When Peter breaks his leg at Columbia (as Kerouac did) he begins to experience the life of the mind and becomes stymied by his own awareness, realizing a level of consciousness that is alien to the brute being of the football field. Peter becomes a projection of the gregariously engaging aspects of Kerouac's personality (the parts that became more difficult to sustain without alcohol as Kerouac grew older), but he is also the only character in the novel whose awareness is focused and self-directed. Sometimes, through Peter, Kerouac seems to be forecasting a program for the rest of his own life, as when Peter glooms over Pearl Harbor: "He was certain his life was over, that he was going to die a young death, and that his last days were going to be spent in striding, silent, scowling enigmatical greatness." Later in the novel, when George Martin is sick and dying, and as Peter tends his father while his mother goes to work, Peter realizes the welding continuity of the old order that the sophistications of university life made him resist. The result is a sense of responsibility that becomes an anxious moral, an ironic measure of guilt to which the Kerouac hero would always bow in later novels.

Francis, contemplative, decadently intellectual, and narcissistically withdrawn, suggests lonelier aspects of Kerouac's character. Francis is first to leave the family. A gawky misfit Sherwood Anderson–type character, he is too locked within himself to share love. Despite his Harvard degree, he is rejected by the navy. When he cannot tolerate military discipline, he feigns madness to get discharged. Moving to New York, living with a woman whom he carelessly rejects, he becomes the caricature of the futile Greenwich Village intellectual. Later on, he begins taking Benzedrine to end his numbness. Kerouac's depiction changes from initial sympathy to scorn as Francis' weaknesses become a function of self-pity rather than circumstance. Francis is Peter's foil, almost an alter-ego, and the two brothers dramatize a conflict that Kerouac himself realized (and repeated with Sal Paradise and Dean Moriarty) between the observing life of the mind and the participating agency of experience. Francis' cynicism becomes an ennui that is translated into a feeling of superiority, but which actually results in an evasion of life. Francis' bad faith and Peter's refusal to acquiesce to hopelessness occur in a strongly etched scene near the end of the second part of the novel. The two brothers are home from college for Christmas, and Francis is reading Gide's *The Counterfeiters* (Kerouac disliked Gide; in *Desolation Angels,* he called him a "postmortem bore"). Peter innocently asks his brother about the book and Francis pendantically discourses on the falsity of appearances. Peter, intuitive but unpoised, retorts that the world is too complex to be reduced to any formula; Francis, persistent, assures Peter that God is dead, and that the principles of the diabolic night will ultimately devour men (a notion to which Kerouac would return in *Doctor Sax*).

The scene is suffused with the kind of intellectuality that Kerouac deplored in his friends Burroughs and Ginsberg. Francis illustrates what Sartre defined as "bad faith," the refusal to struggle because of the conviction that no good can result from life. He exemplifies the conformist academic anemia which precipitated Kerouac's own departure from the university—"colleges being nothing but grooming schools for the middleclass nonidentity" as he was later to write in *The Dharma Bums.* Peter, although he finds few signs of redeeming generosity in the world, other than his mother's staunch family loyalty, is always hoping for something better.

The eldest son, Joe, shares none of Francis' intellectual pretensions, having more of Peter's heart without the capability to direct it. Joe is a truckdriver, and in an outburst that anticipates Dean in *On The Road*, impulsively takes his truck while on a job to South Carolina. He then becomes the first of Kerouac's characters to go on the road, traveling west to work on ranches. Good-natured and easygoing, Joe is reminiscent of Dos Passos' Mac in *U.S.A.* Like Kerouac at the end of his athletic career, Joe knows he can never live out the expectations others have for him. He enlists in the army, spends four brutal years, and returns after the war to urge Peter to succor their dying father. He is now shaken and stunned with an almost pathological potential for arbitrary violence, sullen and resentful of changes he cannot fathom. Peter, Francis, Joe, and George Martin all seem trapped in the same conspiracy of change caused by the war. John Clellon Holmes' image of the "broken circuit" is particularly applicable to *The Town and the City*. The book exposed a new wound in the American soul; Kerouac's later books would be an attempt to mend, to build bridges to past values he thought were worth preserving.

A mixture of ebullient gaiety and depressed brooding about the future ties Kerouac to Thomas Wolfe in the novel. At one point, for instance, Peter sees Joe "standing there all wild and gaunt and racked with loneliness," or George Martin wonders what "it was that was so strange, beautiful, sad, raggedly real, so hurt and unconsolable" about his life. The tumultuousness of emotion, the impulsive irrepressibility of so many of the anguished, tortured conversations between father and son, or brother and brother, the reckless effusions of Kerouac's adjectival streams—"something furiously sad, angry, mute and piteous was in the air. . . . Something strange had happened to Joe in England, something like exasperation, disgust, terrific moody joylessness"—all recall Wolfe's style. In his *Paris Review* interview, Kerouac admitted that Wolfe was "a torrent of American heaven and hell that opened my eyes to America as a subject in itself." In *Vanity of Duluoz*, his last book, he recalled living in Brooklyn (with his aunt while attending Horace Mann) and staring at the same bleak landscape of warehouses that Wolfe saw. Kerouac's tone in *The Town and the City* was the tender lyricism for which Wolfe was known:

> A child, a child, hiding in a corner, peeking, infolded in veils, in swirling shrouds and mystery, all tee-hee, all earnest, all innocent with shiny love, sweeter than a bird, pure with pretty gleaming eyes and rosy lips and the crazy little grin shining out, all writhing and quivering with phantasy and understanding, and the possibility of tears. Unaware of duskish birds with disillusioned eyes flying nearer, but not now—the child, unknowing, yet best knowing, Godly all-knowing, the child crieth—'I see you. . . .'

But Wolfe's influence never dominates *The Town and the City*. The controlled restraint of its early sections is unlike the repetitive delirium of language, the intoxication with obvious poetic effects like alliteration which limit Wolfe's style.

The Town and the City is an evidently imitative novel, and Kerouac uses various voices in it, partly because of his large group of characters, partly because his own true voice had not yet been conceived. As he was to write later in The Subterraneans, The Town and the City as a novel had guts but a dreariness in its prose style. At times, Kerouac consciously emulates the nostalgic sadness of Fitzgerald; other times he imitates Melville (as in a funny encounter between Peter and a Negro cook on a sea voyage), or Stephen Crane's absurd confrontations (especially one very poignant scene where the Martin children collect scrap metal in a dump), but without the insouciant bitterness, always more endearing. When Joe returns from the war, full of disillusioned and confused helplessness, caught by the continuum of his own rage, the mood is appropriately influenced by Hemingway.

The Town and the City is remarkable for its sense of the warmth and rich family cohesiveness of life in a small New England town. But in the second half of the novel some of its most powerful scenes describe the chaotic energies of the city seen through the eyes of old George Martin. His son Peter, returning from a freighter voyage, also discovers a new world that is to become the center of Kerouac's interest in succeeding books. Peter's new city friends are modeled after Kerouac's own friends of this period: Ginsberg (Leon Levinsky), Burroughs (Dennison), Huncke (Junkey), and others. There is a convincing authenticity in Kerouac's descriptions of meeting Levinsky in cafeterias, taking one hilarious subway ride as Levinsky tears a hole through his newspaper and makes faces at the other riders (an episode which Ginsberg has commemorated in a poem called "Memory Gardens," an elegy for Kerouac that appears in The Fall of America). Levinsky assumes an omniscient voice, often categorically judging, berating Peter into consciousness, stimulating, provoking, endlessly arguing.

The anticipations of the later fiction, however, are not restricted to the portraits of Ginsberg and Burroughs, but begin with the brothers. Joe's carefree youthfulness, his proclivity for fast cars, long trips, his uncontrollable whoops of laughter, all suggest that Kerouac's friendship with Cassady, which ripened just as Kerouac was working on the novel, influenced the development of Joe:

> Women loved him because he was boyish, and men slapped him on the back and bought him drinks because he was manly. And all the time he whooped with laughter, told interminable stories, strode about insouciantly, and passed everything off as great fun and good times.
>
> But in all this whirl of long blazing white highways with their roadhouses and diners, the men and women eating and drinking, the laughter, the love-making, the raucous jokes, the beer, the jukebox music, the miles of smooth macadam through pine woods and the roar and rush of the driving, the huge presence of the truck, the weary ecstatic nights—in all this, the swashbuckling Joe was also a kind of grim, workaday, lonely Joe.

Joe had always dreamed of a motorcycle that would take him across the broad expanse of the country so that he could discover a sense of the frontier past, "when you rode on horseback and all you had ahead of you was this big unexplored space." Peter, also, fulfills such ambitions when he hitchhikes to Washington after a freighter trip to North Africa to visit his younger brother Charley in the army: "He thumbed big trucks that started rolling at eleven o'clock across Louisiana. . . . all the way to Richmond blurry-eyed and dazed, boozing his way along until he was one shattered ecstatic nerve." Finally, another anticipation of *On The Road* is the hipster scene of jazz and drugs which Kerouac develops through Liz Martin, Peter's younger sister who elopes with a jazz pianist, and leaves him to become a small-time nightclub singer. The portrait of Liz is comparable to the vignettes Dos Passos sketches in *U.S.A.* to quicken the pulse of excitement:

> She had become one of the many girls in America who flit from city to city in search of something they hope to find and never even name, girls who "know all the ropes," know a thousand people in a hundred cities and

places, girls who work at all kinds of jobs, impulsive, desperately gay, lonely, hardened girls.

Liz speaks in the argot of jazz musicians, using words like "goofing off," "kick," "beat," "loot," "gold," "hung up," and "drag," which add to the effect of New York City that Kerouac was trying to achieve—of some mysterious and vast energy center with its private resources of pleasure that a curious young man from the provinces like Peter Martin would have to work to decipher.

More than fifteen years after its publication, *On The Road* still has a large and growing audience. For many, it was *the* book that most motivated dissatisfaction with the atmosphere of unquestioning acceptance that stifled the fifties; remarkably, despite the passage of time and its relative unpopularity among older university instructors, its audience grows, and young people especially gravitate to a force in it that seems to be propelled by the material itself, almost as if its author did not exist as an outside agency of creation.

Kerouac's trouble in finding a publisher for the book is not surprising. As Henry Miller noted in his preface to *The Subterraneans:* "We say that the poet, or genius, is always ahead of his time. True, but only because he's so thoroughly *of* his time." Completed in 1951, *On The Road* appeared six years later, only after Malcolm Cowley succeeded in persuading the Viking editorial board to publish it and in convincing Kerouac to make or allow numerous changes like eliminating the *actual* names of characters which Viking felt could be libelous, but which Kerouac wanted for authenticity. The original manuscript was a 250-foot roll of paper (which Kerouac compared to a football field). It was one long paragraph, single-spaced with almost no margins, and the punctuation was haphazard. Keith Jennison, the editor who pushed the book through at Viking, said the book impressed him for its flow of language. Allen Ginsberg has commented on the formal breakthrough of the original version of *On The Road:*

An attempt to tell completely, all at once, everything on his mind in relation to the hero Dean Moriarty, spill it all out at once and follow the convolutions of the active mind for direction as to the "structure of the confession." And discover the rhythm of the mind at work at high speed in prose. An attempt to trap the prose of truth mind by means of a highly scientific attack on new prose method. The result was a magnificent single paragraph several blocks long, rolling, like the Road itself, the length of an entire onionskin teletype roll. The sadness that this was never published in its most exciting form—its original discovery—but hacked and punctuated and broken—the rhythms and swing of it broken—by presumptuous literary critics in publishing houses. The original mad version is greater than the published version, the manuscript still exists and someday when everybody's dead be published as it is. Its greatness (like the opening pages of Miller's *Cancer*)—the great spirit of adventure into poetic composition. And greater tender delicacy of language.

According to Jennison, the editorial board at Viking insisted on a more conventionally presentable manuscript, and Kerouac was eager to see the book in print. He had written Ginsberg that Viking believed they had received the product of a five-year revision, but that the book was still much as originally written. Instead of revision, he had purged all material not directly related to Cassady, and had accepted Malcolm Cowley's suggestion to fuse the various trips for the sake of focus. But Kerouac never saw the final galley proofs, Jennison claimed, seeing nothing between the manuscript he submitted and the finished book. Cowley and Helen Taylor, a Viking editor, did the final editorial work on the book after preliminary copyediting. Though Cowley was the major figure in getting the book published, Jennison has admitted to sharing the defeat of not having it printed the way it was written, stating that he thought it would have been much better to publish the original version.

On The Road was unprecedented both formally and thematically, but most of all in depicting an underground subculture that departed entirely from the dominant middle-class mores of the fifties, and instead offered as an ideal the sense of release and joy experienced by the less materially privileged segments of the society. Part of the genius of Kerouac's art was his ability to record the emerging values of his age without obtrusive commentary or overt judgments. Like Burroughs, he rarely expressed his own social views, but instead dramatized alternatives to the accepted through the nascence of the new. As he put it later in *Desolation Angels*:

Hold still, man, regain your love of life and go down from this mountain and simply *be—be*—be the infinite fertilities of the one mind of infinity, make no comments, complaints, criticisms, appraisals, avowals, sayings, shooting stars of thought, just *flow, flow,* be you all, be you what it is, it is only what it always is—

The Town and the City had been a Galsworthian novel of family and place, the Martin brothers projections of Kerouac's own needs, fears, and aspirations. *On The Road* was much more general in scope, a record of a new kind of existence in postwar America, a novel whose atmosphere suggested the new cultural forces destined to further erode the loyalties to place and family that Kerouac had shown disintegrating in his earlier book. The new hedonism with its contagious excitement, its unmannered recklessness, its enthusiasm in activity, in turmoil for the sake of denying complacency and middle-class notions of propriety and status, seemed incomprehensible in 1957. One of the readers for Viking, for example, while appreciating Kerouac's lavish power, was dismayed by the raw sociology of the book, finding it the quintessence of "everything that is bad and horrible about this otherwise wonderful age we live in." The characters were irredeemable psychopaths and hopeless neurotics who lived exclusively for sensation. This judgment, delivered prior to publication, can stand as a sign of how those born before the war would see the book.

But the novel had different appeal for other sensibilities. For those who felt trapped in the bind of societal or parental expectations, bound by the ethos of personal secrecy and self-containment that was prevalent when the novel was written, the puritan notion that one's inner being was really suspect, a source of embarrassment or liability, shame or incrimination, the tumultuous adventurousness of the book had a liberating impact. In *On The Road,* the circumspect caution of an age was entirely shattered. Sometimes, this occurred with all the pain of direct revelation that characterizes Kerouac's fiction; sometimes with an absurd freedom, as when Dean Moriarty answers his door naked. In the way that *Notes From Underground* anticipated the estrangement of modern intellectuals and artists, Dean Moriarty is an early prototype of a new Nietzchean, Dionysian irresponsibility, an example of a transvaluation of values. His first priority is freedom from socially imposed roles or expectations. Since he was raised on the Denver skid row in the company of derelicts and a wino father, he was never subjected to the conditioning of career, family, and country that so impresses most of us in childhood with the need for security and obedience. He had never learned how to achieve status by fabricating a persona to suit a preconceived role. Dean greets Sal Paradise naked at his door to signify animal being. When dressed he wears baggy trousers and torn T-shirts. Instead of making himself an instrument tuned to comply to the goals of a corporation, an institution, or the state, Dean challenges any official authority with his radical subjectivity. Instead of conforming to general expectations, Dean exults in his uniqueness, revels in his eccentricity, his freakiness.

At one point early in the novel, on Sal Paradise's first trip to Denver, Sal encounters Carlo Marx (Allen Ginsberg during the period of the "Denver Doldrums") who reveals that he and Dean have been "trying to communicate with absolute honesty and absolute completeness everything on our minds. We've had to take benzedrine. We sit on the bed crosslegged, facing each other." The intensity suggested by this description is verified by Moriarty's person, although always without focus or sustained purposeful direction, as chaotic as the universe. Dean is a complex figure and some of the especially hostile reactions to him by many of the original reviewers of the novel are understandable. He is as much a projection of Kerouac as he is a reflection of Neal Cassady. In Ann

Charters' *Bibliography of the Works of Jack Kerouac,* she quotes Professor Charles Jarvis' account of a taped radio interview with Kerouac that he conducted in Lowell in 1962. According to Jarvis, talking with Kerouac was like conducting ten conversations simultaneously as his moods vacillated from euphoric peaks to "chasms of ecstatic melancholia." Jarvis concluded that Kerouac himself was the "epitome of Dean Moriarty with all the fits, stops and all the forces which compelled Moriarty to try to corner IT, to burn, burn, burn." The idea the Kerouac shared the swirling contradictory confusions of Moriarty's abrupt digressions, his whirling tangents in a dozen unfulfilled directions, is all the more interesting when the close physical resemblance of the two men is considered.

Dean is an undecipherable puzzle of contradiction; "Do I contradict myself? I contain multitudes," Whitman wrote, a formula that could easily be applied to Dean. He exists as Kerouac's response to the stress of reason, adjustment, order, and conformity that later became so pronounced in the Eisenhower era. Dean violates such qualities with his disarming irresponsibility, his anarchic flow of inexhaustible activity. Although he has been in reform schools and prison, he has a schedule for self-improvement (like Jay Gatsby). Living in a time when sexuality was repressed and associated with evil, for Dean "sex was the one and only holy and important thing in life." No wonder, then, that Dean, "cocksman and Adonis of Denver," is the secret hero of "Howl":

> who copulated ecstatic and insatiate with a bottle of beer a sweetheart a package of cigarettes a candle and fell off the bed, and continued along the floor and down the hall and ended fainting on the wall with a vision of ultimate cunt and come eluding the last gyzym of consciousness

> who sweetened the snatches of a million girls trembling in the sunset, and were red eyed in the morning but prepared to sweeten the snatch of the sunrise, flashing buttocks under barns and naked in the lake.

For Dean, as for Kerouac, sex represented the sweet return to the protective sanctuary and succor of the womb: Dean was "mad with a completely physical realization of the origins of life-bliss; blindly seeking to return the way he came." At the same time, Dean is utterly indifferent to women as women, his Priapic and primal urge making him inconsiderate of any feeling other than the desire in his loins.

For Sal Paradise, the novel's narrator and a projection of the withdrawn Kerouac who lived at home with his mother, Dean had all the unconscious appeal of an alter ego. Dean's particular ability is to become tremendously excited by life in an affirmative "wild yea-saying overburst of American joy." Neither intellectually pretentious nor artistically precious, Dean could earn a living by working on the railroad, parking cars, or recapping tires, but could still become interested in Proust. His infectious enthusiasm contradicted the pessimistic and gloomy Spenglerian view of the future expressed by many of Kerouac's closest friends, and by Carlo Marx and old Bull Lee (Burroughs) in the novel. Kerouac's own partly saturnine disposition welcomed the innocent naïveté of Dean who could accept anything on faith, who answered with an open acceptance the suspiciousness of anything that seemed strange or different that dominated the fifties. Instead of giving way to despair, self-pity, or resignation, Dean acts with passionate abandon.

This energy, however, although admirable as an ideal, is mindless and narcissistically devouring. Representing the momentum of energy for its own sake, Dean seems maddened by the urge to be everywhere at the same time, to love several women, to conduct various searches while fulfilling none. So the negative, some might say the demonic, aspects of Dean play their role in elevating the character from simply a figure based on Neal Cassady to something much larger in scope, a Promethean version of the holy primitive, a shaman's shaman, a combination of the opposite tensions that reveal the crucible of creativity: Yin and Yang, Nirvana and Samsara, Eros and Thanatos.

Practically every character that Sal meets in *On The Road* is either preparing to depart, just returning from somewhere, or planning a journey; cumulatively, they express a vast and restless dissatisfaction with their lives. In all this movement there is no defined center, and Dean's hyperactivity exemplifies the atmosphere itself:

> He leaped out of the car. Furiously he hustled into the railroad station; we followed sheepishly. He bought cigarettes. He had become absolutely mad in his movements; he seemed to be doing everything at the same time. It was a shaking of the head, up and down, sideways; jerky, vigorous hands; quick walking, sitting, crossing the legs, uncrossing, getting up, rubbing the hands, rubbing his fly, hitching his pants, looking up and saying "Am," and sudden slitting of the eyes to see everywhere; and all the time he was grabbing me by the ribs and talking, talking.

On one of their five frenetic jaunts across the country, at the novel's very center, they stop in New Orleans to visit Bull Lee who advises Sal that Dean suffers from a "compulsive psychosis dashed with a jigger of psychopathic irresponsibility and violence." Actually, on January 30, 1949, Burroughs wrote Kerouac that Cassady never disguised his machinations and exploitations of others, warning that he was "the very soul of this voyage into pure abstract, meaningless motion. He is the mover, compulsive, dedicated, ready to sacrifice family, friends, even his very car itself to the necessity of moving from one place to another."

From this juncture in the book, the view of Dean begins to change. Sal senses a pathetic absurdity in Dean's predicaments, especially after he hits one of his girlfriends, bizarrely breaking and infecting his thumb so that part of it must be amputated. After this Sal begins to see Dean as "the Angel of Terror," and then as "a burning, frightful Angel, palpitating toward me across the road, approaching like a cloud, with enormous speed, pursuing me like the Shrouded Traveler on the plain." Near the end of the novel, this life-force that has become the death principle, a "Mad Ahab at the wheel," loses his uncanny volubility, the very power of speech to defend himself, and like some Samson in distress assumes the aura of the scapegoat. Sal never denies his friend, in a sense his spiritual lover, his "Holy Goof" comedic companion who blithely refuses to admit the seriousness of any event, whether it be an automobile collision or a divorce. Dean makes no distinctions, offers no judgments, is removed somehow beyond ordinary standards of measurement. At the same time, his careless impunity is the epitome of American waste; he treats his mistresses like his cars, with an all-consuming speed.

But Dean's childish impetuosity provokes Sal into an awareness of social reality. For example, when the police apprehend Dean, Sal sees what perfect products of social conditioning they are as they judge purely on the basis of external appearances and then act with arbitrary and ruthless power. Neal Cassady hated police, who symbolized repressive authority for him. In a letter to Kerouac written in February of 1951, he pictured them as instruments of potential fascist brutality:

> I recall as I passed the State Police barracks two stern troopers left its well-lit interior and crunched their swank boots on the gravel driveway for brief seconds before they piled me into their radio-dispatched car with automatic motions of tough efficiency. This flashing glimpse of their hard gestures and unslack jaws, clamped so tightly against the grim upper lip, and their faces immobile as steel emphasizing the sheen of their merciless eyes glittering with zeal to perform their duty made me shudder. . . .

Kerouac, like Dean, is more the observer than the commentator, and had an especially acute eye for the changing American scene. As Sal and Dean race back and forth cross-country, they notice alarming manifestations of national suspicion (of course, this is the beginning of the McCarthy period of Cold War international paranoia). At one point they drive into Washington, D.C. during Truman's inauguration to see a display of tanks, planes, and military power, and they wonder what all this defense is for. The answer is implicit at the end of the first part of the novel:

> Suddenly I found myself on Times Square. I had travelled eight thousand miles around the American continent and I was back on Times Square;

and right in the middle of a rush hour, too, seeing with my innocent road-eyes the fantastic hoorair of New York with its millions and millions hustling forever for a buck among themselves, the mad dream—grabbing, taking, giving, sighing, dying, just so they could be buried in those awful cemetery cities beyond Long Island City. The high towers of the land—the other end of the land, the place where Paper America is born.

The materialism that feeds on armament and the need for protection is an obvious symbol of what Dean's candor rebels against. Later, in *The Dharma Bums*, Kerouac was more categorical: "I wished the whole world was dead serious about food instead of silly rockets and machines and explosives using everybody's food money to blow their heads off anyway."

Instead of identifying with wealth and power, Kerouac chooses the American untouchable, the hobo, who exists as a brazen refutation of careerism and competition. The hobo was a descendant of the frontier prospector who once lived in the hills searching for gold, always hoping for an unexpected gift from nature, wandering from mountain lode to washed-out stream in the hope of some momentous discovery. Of course, the stubborn faith of such men did as much to open the West as the efforts of the cattle farmers or the capitalists who built the railroads. Kerouac preferred the risk and adventure inherent in their lives of constant journey and insecurity to the smug complacencies of urban living:

I slept till noon; when I looked out the window I suddenly saw an SP freight going by with hundreds of hobos reclining on the flatcars rolling along merrily along with packs for pillows and funny papers before their noses, and some munching on good California grapes picked up by the siding. "Damn!" I yelled. "Hooee! It *is* the promised land." They were all coming from Frisco; in a week they'd all be going back in the same grand style.

While it is a familiar feature of naturalism in fiction to expose the life of the underprivileged and exploited, it is usually with the intention of seeking redress or reform. The classic illustration is

Upton Sinclair's *The Jungle,* a book that showed the exploitation of an immigrant family while documenting the scandalously unhealthy practices of the meat-packing industry in Chicago. But Kerouac's total identification with the downtrodden does not adhere to naturalistic formulae. He omits the deprivation, humiliation, the hopelessness and victimization that a writer like James Baldwin would magnify, to emphasize a romantic sense of brotherly community and joy in simple pleasures. At the point in the novel where he sees the hobos passing on the freight, Sal has been having an affair with a Mexican girl named Terry, living with her and her son in a tent surrounded by migrant workers. To support them, he picks cotton:

> My back began to ache. But it was beautiful kneeling and hiding in that earth. If I felt like resting I did, with my face on the pillow of moist brown earth. Birds sang an accompaniment. I thought I had found my life's work.

This Lawrencian appreciation of the efforts of manual labor is reflected in Kerouac's generous depiction of the workingman throughout the novel, especially some of the truckdrivers who stop for Sal when he is hitchhiking. As Jaffe Ryder exclaims in *The Dharma Bums,* "You've woke me up to the true language of this country which is the language of the working men, railroad men, loggers." The best illustration of Kerouac's romantic idealization occurs in the beginning of the third part of the novel when he describes the black section of Denver, a passage that Eldridge Cleaver called remarkable in *Soul On Ice:*

> At lilac evening I walked with every muscle aching among the lights of 27th and Whelton in the Denver colored section, wishing I were a Negro, feeling that the best the white world had offered was not enough for me, not enough life, joy, kicks, darkness, music, not enough night. I stopped at a little shack where a man sold hot red chili in paper containers; I bought some and ate it, strolling in the dark mysterious streets. I wished I were a Denver Mexican or even a poor overworked Jap, anything but

what I was so drearily, a 'white man' disillusioned. . . . I was only myself, Sal Paradise, sad, strolling in this violent dark, this unbearably sweet night, wishing I could exchange worlds with the happy, true-hearted Negroes of America.

The black man expressed Dean's existence—without direction because there was nowhere to go and no vision of success, just the ability to enjoy the surroundings no matter what the circumstances. The activity and energy in motion that Sal sees in Dean is found in the black man's music, bop and jazz. Kerouac was to eulogize the "raw wild joy" of jazz more elaborately in *Visions of Cody,* but all through *On The Road* Sal and Dean haunt jazz places and pursue jazz musicians anticipating the absorption of young people in rock-and-roll in the sixties:

And Shearing began to rock; a smile broke over his elastic face; he began to rock in the piano seat, back and forth, slowly at first, then the beat went up, and he began rocking fast, his left foot jumped up with every beat, his neck began to rock crookedly, he brought his face down to the keys, he pushed his hair back, his combed hair dissolved, he began to sweat. The music picked up. The bass-player hunched over and socked it in, faster and faster, it seemed faster and faster, that's all. Shearing began to play his chords; they rolled out of the piano in great rich showers, you'd think the man wouldn't have time to line them up. They rolled and rolled like the sea. Folks yelled for him to "Go!" Dean was sweating; the sweat poured down his collar. "There he is! That's him! Old God! Old God Shearing! Yes! Yes! Yes!" And Shearing was conscious of the madman behind him, he could hear every one of Dean's gasps and imprecations. . . .

There are many unsavory aspects of Dean's jaunts through America, like the frequent thefts that Sal rationalizes by claiming that everyone in America is involved with stealing: these thefts are a dismal anticipation of the youth culture that began in the sixties, an absolute disregard for property, especially when institutionally owned, and the concomitant argument that property rights are invalid because the entire economic system is based on exploitation. In this sense Sal and Dean become the first "dropouts," the renegade vanguard of a new culture. The self-destructiveness and disregard for others reach an apex on their final trip to the "end of the road," to Mexico on the "route of the old American outlaws who used to skip over the border. . . ." Mexico proves to be a welcome contrast to the States. The Mexicans are without suspicion, even police and customs officials seem friendly. But Dean and Sal act without grace, as "self-important moneybag Americans." Despite the sordid environment, Sal senses the significance of the Fellaheen, the Indians whom he sees as the "source of mankind" with the mysterious admiration of D. H. Lawrence in *The Plumed Serpent.* Kerouac, who believed Indian blood was mixed in his French-Canadian past, felt deep sympathy for Indians, a feeling which was to find its fullest articulation in a long Faulknerian eulogy in *The Subterraneans* for Mardou Fox's father, a half-breed Cherokee black man.

The degradations of the Mexican experience are very powerfully realized. As Kerouac revealed in *Visions of Cody,* "Mexico drove me mad. Cody was in ecstasies sweating over it. We were innocent." The section ends with a magnificent debauch in a whorehouse which occurs as the culmination of a crisis of identity that has afflicted Sal throughout the novel, which has been provoked by Dean, but which in a larger sense is a foreboding fatalistic prediction of doom for the old culture. Early in the novel, when Sal first reaches Denver, he loses his keys at a wild party, and even earlier, on his way out West, he wakes up in a cheap hotel room near the railroad depot in Des Moines in a vacuum of unknowing:

> I woke up as the sun was reddening; and that was the one distinct time in my life, the strangest moment of all, when I didn't know who I was—I was far away from home, haunted and tired with travel, in a cheap hotel room I'd never seen, hearing the hiss of steam outside, and the creak of the old wood of the hotel, and footsteps upstairs, and all the sad sounds, and I looked at the cracked high ceiling and really didn't know who I was for about fifteen strange seconds. I wasn't scared; I was just somebody

else, some stranger, and my whole life was a haunted life, the life of a ghost. I was halfway across America, at the dividing line between the East of my youth and the West of my future, and maybe that's why it happened right there and then, that strange red afternoon.

Later in the novel, while Sal and Dean are sleeping in an all-night movie on Detroit's skid row, Sal has a fantasy of being swept up with the garbage, where later Dean would find him embryonically curled in a rubbish womb. The progression is clear. Whenever Sal finds himself in bed with a woman, he asks her "What do you want out of life?" It is not a rhetorical question, but the very point of the cyclonic vortex of Dean's world into which Sal has been sucked. Until Sal can direct that question to himself, he cannot achieve self-knowledge, and must thrash madly with Dean. Sal Paradise, ironic name, never finds the answer in *On The Road*. For Kerouac, the free open road represented the promise of America as once envisioned by European immigrants; it was a way of keeping in touch with the pioneer enthusiasms of the past. As he was later to put it in *Big Sur*:

> The eyes of hope looking over the glare of the hood into the maw with its white line feeding in straight as an arrow, the lighting of fresh cigarettes, the buckling to lean forward in the next adventure something that's been going on in America ever since the covered wagon clocked the deserts in three months flat—

Whitman had announced that Americans should know "the universe itself as a road, as many roads, as roads for traveling souls." But for Whitman, the road was an opportunity for a perpetual journey of self-discovery, a search for a spiritual vision to illuminate the path one had chosen. Dean's hedonism, his speed itself, deprived Sal of any such possibility. Kerouac himself was to heed a different call which was voiced by Jaffe Ryder in *The Dharma Bums* who at one point exclaims that he had been reading Whitman, musing over the line "cheer up slaves, and horrify foreign despots" which Ryder

interprets as the keynote of Whitman's great independence, his
singular, stubborn refusal to follow any circumscribed path:

> . . . he means that's the attitude for the Bard, the Zen lunacy bard of old
> desert paths, see the whole thing is a world of rucksack wanderers,
> Dharma Bums refusing to subscribe to the general demand that they
> consume production and therefore have to work for the privilege of
> consuming, all that crap they didn't really want anyway such as
> refrigerators, TV sets, cars, at least new fancy cars, certain hair oils and
> deodorants and general junk you finally always see a week later in the
> garbage anyway, all of them imprisoned in a system of work, produce,
> consume, work, produce, consume, I see a vision of a great rucksack
> revolution thousands or even millions of young Americans wandering
> around with rucksacks, going up to mountains to pray, making children
> laugh and old men glad, making young girls happy and old girls happier,
> all of 'em Zen Lunatics who go about writing poems that happen to
> appear in their heads for no reason and also by being kind and also by
> strange unexpected acts keep giving visions of eternal freedom to
> everybody and to all living creatures . . .

Jaffe Ryder (in real life Gary Snyder) is a fulfilled version of Dean
Moriarty: both are remarkably energetic; both are irresistable to
women; both are close to the working class in origin and attitude.
But Ryder's energy is directed by a sense of purpose that Dean's
speeded lust for change cannot contain. Although they dress
similarly, Dean in his T-shirt and overalls, Jaffe in "rough workingman's clothes he'd bought secondhand in goodwill stores," and even
though they both manifest for Kerouac a similar hope and optimism,
Ryder is always constructive while Moriarty is destructive, Ryder
creates harmony in his environment while Moriarty thrives on
chaos. Dean expresses a thousand generous intentions in *On The
Road*, to read, to study, even to become a writer, but he is without
endurance or intellectual stamina, only full of zeal and the inventiveness of his next distraction. Ryder, instead of compulsively changing
the surface of his life with frequently alternating emotional entanglements, reforms its core through his study of Buddhism which acts as
a ground for his energetic capacities. Dean, working on railroads or

driving a car, is a projection of the rootless distemper of industrial America; Ryder, a wanderer among mountaintops, suggests a forecast of a postindustrial America that Kerouac envisaged in *Desolation Angels*: "presaging the ghostly day when industrial America shall be abandoned and left to rust in one long Sunday Afternoon of oblivion."

With his regular meditation and pursuit of oriental sources of wisdom like the *Book Of Changes*; his lack of inhibitions and the communal sex he encourages in his simple shack; his passion for the wilderness, for backpacking into the mountains to seek the purity of an unspoiled nature—Ryder is an avatar of a change in consciousness whose impact on American life would only be realized in the sixties. While Ryder shares Dean's carefree zest and gaiety, his insistence on freedom, Ryder's effect on Ray Smith, Kerouac's narrator in *The Dharma Bums*, is far less unsettling, always rejuvenating.

Kerouac wrote *The Dharma Bums* when Viking requested a sequel to *On The Road*. While he was pleased with the characterization of Ryder, he felt it was not as compelling as the picture of Dean, although he wrote Cowley that he thought the final section describing the exhilaration of living on Desolation Peak in Oregon as good as anything he had ever done. In *The Dharma Bums*, Kerouac's style is generally much calmer, simpler, more contained and less whimsically eccentric than in *On The Road*, almost reflecting the ineffable directness of Gary Snyder's own poems. Although the novel has its moments of power, like the description of Ryder and Smith dancing down the boulders of Mount Matterhorn in the California Sierras, or of Smith's night camping alone in the desert near El Paso, it suffers from a staged and contrived quality.

Kerouac's stress on the Buddhist notion of dharma, the ultimate law, the way to truth, creates an almost dogmatic insistence on Western inadequacies, and the lines of demarcation between illumination and enslavement to the material world become too programmatic. While the sections describing Jaffe Ryder have an entirely captivating authenticity—and the optimism behind the portrait is enough to win most readers—many of the incidents that occur to Ray Smith are engineered to further the distance between Ryder's kind of freedom and the rigidities of straight America. Such evidently novelistic ploys as the old lady Negro preacher who instructs Smith to expect a new field of vision, or the truckdriver who compares his bondage to his work to Smith's enjoyment of life as a wandering hobo, work against the illusion of spontaneity Kerouac sought to achieve. The novel is full of moments of flat indictment: after leaving the truckdriver, Smith notices the Monday-morning "eager young men in business suits going to work in insurance offices"; near the end of the novel he spreads his sleeping bag out in a dense thicket across from some suburban cottages whose occupants "wouldn't see me because they were all looking at television anyway." In other words, despite the philosophical charm of Ryder's message, the seams of fictional structure that Kerouac usually avoids are too apparent.

Gary Snyder wrote his friend Philip Whalen that he wished Kerouac had taken more trouble to smooth out dialogues and make transitions less abrupt, and he thought the descriptions of tantric sexuality in Ryder's cabin might cause censorship problems, but he admired the book. He told Whalen that Alan Watts was so impressed with the book that he planned to revise his "Beat Zen, Square Zen" essay, realizing because of *The Dharma Bums* that the Beats were serious, not hostile or irresponsible. *The Dharma Bums* is memorable because of the power of its characterizations. The life of the book was not, as it ordinarily was for Kerouac, in the mothswarm of detail, but in the depiction of characters like Henry Morley, an eccentric librarian who accompanies Smith and Ryder on the Matterhorn climb. Touchy and outspoken, Morley is one source of the comedy in the novel, and a sign of the individuality of Kerouac's characters. His own special surrealistic speech reflects this, as when he advises Smith:

> "Be sure not to roar at bees and don't hurt the cur and if the tennis party comes on with everybody shirtless don't make eyes at the searchlight or

the sun'll kick a girl's ass right back at you, cats and all and boxes of fruit and oranges thrown in"

At the end of *The Dharma Bums*, Ryder departs for Japan to study in a Zen monastery while Smith leaves for a job as a fire lookout in Oregon—an experience which is amplified in *Desolation Angels.*

In *Desolation Angels*, the meditative mood of *The Dharma Bums*—a Buddhist awareness of the unimportance of mundane matters in the light of what Kerouac called the Golden Eternity—is jeopardized by the excesses of Beat camaraderie: the drinking, drugs, frivolity, and Zen lunacies, the genuine loyalty and irascibilities of friendship.

The novel begins and ends with a period of intense confrontation of the self. The terror and beauty of utter solitude on Desolation Peak, sixty-three days of proximity to nature's powers: lightning storms, huge looming mountains, voids of gorges and canyons, brilliant sunsets "mad orange fools raging in the gloom," fog, silence, the loneliness of a "rugged faced man in a dirty ragged shirt," the daydreams, memories, boredom culminating in a lustful desire to return to the world as the adventure of isolation "finds me finding at the bottom of myself abysmal nothingness worse than that no illusions even—my mind's in rags—."

The same pattern was to be repeated later, in the experiences of *Big Sur* where Kerouac, alone with himself for three weeks in Ferlinghetti's cabin in Bixby Canyon, began to feel fearful anxieties, and had to return to San Francisco where he knew his energies would be depleted by friends who were excited into frenzied activity by his mere appearance. Paradoxically, in *Desolation Angels*, in San Francisco, Mexico, and Tangier, the figure who most typified the sense of exuberant release, of mad larks and rollicking good times, began to withdraw into a search for peace as a writer, becoming "a man of contemplations rather than too many actions, in the old Tao Chinese sense of 'Do Nothing' (Wu Wei) which is as a way of life in itself more beautiful than any, a kind of cloistral fervor in the midst of mad ranting action-seekers." This shift from the need to express self through adventure to an absorbing and contemplative adoration of nature is part of the general movement from beat to beatitude, and in Kerouac's work it is particularly present in a poem called "How To Meditate" where an instantaneous ecstasy is compared to a shot of heroin resulting in a trance that heals "all my sickness" and leaves mind "blank, serene, thoughtless." In *Desolation Angels*, the doctrine of "Do Nothing" receives final confirmation in Kerouac's mind after an opium overdose administered by Burroughs in Tangier.

Desolation Angels is much freer, looser, closer to Kerouac's ideal of spontaneity than *The Dharma Bums*, without the forced symbolism of the earlier book. Primarily descriptive, *Desolation Angels* is an account of Kerouac's daily life taken almost directly from his journals of the year before the appearance of *On The Road*. Despite Kerouac's fatigue at the enthusiastically importunate demands of his friends, their marvelous but taxing abilities to sustain wonder, to avoid the ordinary and exult in discovery, their frequent impetuosity and vociferous excitement, *Desolation Angels* is the best existing account of the lives of the Beats, and its influence on the "nonfiction" novel genre typified by Tom Wolfe's *The Electric Kool-Aid Acid Test* is clear. The book moves with a very natural flow, each section describing another journey, and it is full of the kind of stylistic animation that Kerouac achieved best when least pressured by editors to revise and excise. At one point, for example, as Cody Pomeray and Raphael Urso are engaged in a vigorous dispute, Duluoz interrupts with a private idiom: "The juicy Saviour that was manoralized and reputed on the gold hill." The Joycean potentials of Kerouac's language are often realized in *Desolation Angels*, as in the syllabic juxtaposition of "one unimaginable abominable snowman still squatted petrified on the ridge," or the lyrical memory of Maggie Cassidy, a Lowell sweetheart, rendered with rich rhythms, but not without a typical colloquial insouciance:

> I wake up in the middle of the night and remember Maggie Cassidy and how I might have married her and been old Finnegan to her Irish Lass Plurabelle, how I might have got a cottage, a little ramshackle Irish rose

cottage among the reeds and old trees on the banks of the Concord and woulda worked as a grim bejacketed gloved and bebaseballhatted brakeman in the cold New England night, for her and her Irish ivory thighs, her and her marshmallow lips, her and her brogue and "God's Green Earth" and her two daughters— How I would of laid her across the bed at night all mine and laborious sought her rose, her mine of a thing, that emerald dark and hero thing I want—remember her silk thighs in tight jeans, the way she folded back one thigh under her hands and sighed as we watched Television together—in her mother's parlor that last haunted 1954 trip I took to October Lowell— Ah, the rose vines, the river mud, the run of her, the eyes— A woman for old Duluoz? Unbelievable by my stove in desolation midnight that it should be true—Maggie Adventure—
   The claws of black trees by moonlit rosy dusk mayhap and by chance hold me much love too, and I can always leave them and roam along—but when I'm old by my final stove, and the bird fritters on his branch of dust in O Lowell, what'll I think, willow?—when winds creep inside my sack and give me bareback blues and I go bent about my meritorious duties in the sod-cover earth, what lovesongs then for old bedawdler bog bent foggy Jack O—?—no new poets will bring laurels like honey to my milk, sneers— Sneers of love woman were better I guess—I'd fall down ladders, brabac, and wash me river underwear—gossip me washlines—air me Mondays—fantasm me Africas of housewives— Lear me daughters—panhandle me marble heart—but it might have been better than what it may be, lonesome unkissed Duluoz lips surling in a tomb

   The Dharma Bums and *Desolation Angels* were written after the success of *On The Road*. Stylistically, they do not represent the essential Kerouac, his ideals of spontaneous composition, or his flaunting of conventional novelistic expectations. It is the books written before the appearance of *On The Road*, during Kerouac's years of Melvillean anonymity, the novels written with no real hope of publication from 1951 to 1956, that we must examine to discover Kerouac's real strengths as a novelist.
   By far the most important of these books—perhaps Kerouac's masterpiece—is *Visions of Cody*, a book that was only published in its entirety twenty years after being written. The book is the grand register of how Cassady affected the Beats with the kinesis of being

and an appreciation of the cataclysmic import of the here and now. Cassady was their contact to the backbone of America—the model of the common urge to communicate ordinary experience in a natural, unpretentious voice. When Kerouac was beginning *Visions of Cody*, he received a letter from Allen Ginsberg that stimulated the mythical potentials of his own quest:

> The point of your own soul begins in the racking life drenched struggle of joy to reveal further, prophecy, admit and comprehend and inscribe your final knowledges not of angels of mystery but of mortals of the heart. Find Neal's heart, not his gut or his cock or wig; stretch his heart out over America, crucify him in Texas, crown his head with thorns in Manhattan, pierce his side in Denver, moan for him in Mexico, tomb him in 1949 and resurrect his trembling eyes on the Pacific. Neal is Christ walking in the doubts of the Garden of Whores. Enough to make me weep.

Visions of Cody was inspired by Cassady's own racing letters as well, and Kerouac's excitement in the vagabond western outlaw sensibility that the letters revealed:

> I had been to Indianapolis for the 39 Auto classic and to South Bend to see Notre Dame and to Calif. to live in L.A. and all this hitchhiking on my own had made me see the wisdom of hiking in the day and stealing a car when nite fell to make good time. Well, when I returned to Denver this became a habit and every nite I'd sleep in some apt. house bathtub and get up and find some friends place to eat then steal a car to pick up girls at school when they got out. I might change cars in midafternoon, but at any rate I'd get some girl and spend the night in the mountains, returning at daybreak to my bathtub. I got tired of this and decided to go back to Calif. I knew a fellow named Bill Smith and he wanted to come along. One day in the spring of 41, I was just 15, we stole a Plymouth on Stout and 16th Sts. We ran out of gas just as we pulled into Colo. Springs. I walked a block or so and saw a 38 Buick at the curb, got in, picked up Bill on the corner and we were off again.
>   Passing thru Pueblo I saw a cop's car behind and suggested we cut and run, but Bill was adamant. Sure enough they stopped us, disbelieved our

story, and took us down. At the police station I found they had caught us so quickly because it happened I'd picked up the D.A.'s car. An hour later the C. Springs D.A. came to regain his car and take us back to be tried. They wouldn't believe Bill's name was really Bill Smith for it sounded so like an alias. They wouldn't believe he was a hitchhiker too, as I told them. I had some Vaseline for my chapped lips and the desk copper leered and asked if we punked each other. We were confined in the Springs County jail for thirty days, then taken to trial. Smith's father was there and got us off. Again I returned to Denver.

To plumb the dimensions of the Cassady legend, *Visions of Cody* became Kerouac's most elaborate literary enterprise, full of the gamy ploys and formal play usually deemphasized in his work. Nowhere else does Kerouac's own voracious reading make such an impact. The allusions—to the classics, the Bible, to *Huckleberry Finn*, to Blake's "The Sick Rose," to Yeats, Joyce, Faulkner— proliferate, almost as a paradoxical contrast to Cassady's natural- ness, but also as a way of measuring his potential. At one point near the end of the novel, for example, there is a passage with references to Melville and Thoreau that extends the naturalist's minute obser- vation of country beauty with a Joycean turn. Kerouac moves from the image of Moby Dick's white hump to the shape of lovers in the grass with a Lawrencian fusion of nature and sexuality, punning on the "hump," and presenting his transformation in a flowing Whit- manesque catalogue that is rhythmically contained by short bursts:

—while Melville made murky matter of the Battery, the Day Break Boys (busters of the river, raft bandits, hansom hustlers, still axing from the hills)—Handsome Herman, the Abyssinian King of Whorly Prints, the Assyrian busy beard, the Weaver of the Net, the Albatross, the Dung of the Albatross, the Calmer of Waves, Singer of Spars, Sitter of Stars, Maker of Sparks, Thinker of Helms, Rails, Bottles, Tubs, Creaks and Cringes of the Shroudy Gear; Seaman, Rower, Oarsman, Whaler, Whaler, Whaler . . . observer of rock formations in the Berkshires, dreamer of Pierres . . . O old Thoreau, hermit of the Woods, Spirit of the Morning Mist in Reedy Fields, Stalker of Serpentine Moonlights,

of Snowy Midnights, of Forests in Winter, of Copses in May Morn, of October Rusted Grapes, of the Bushel Basket of Apples, of the Green Ones, the Fallen Green Apples Turning Brown in the Wet Grass in the Morning; the dam, Beaver Brook, the Sudden Mill Dye, the pure Snow Creek in the Upper Land, the Dell of Flowers, the Warm Scent of Flowery Fields in August, Homer and the Woodchips, Koran and the Axe, the Hot Pinch of Grasshoppers, Hay, Hot Rock, the Whiff of the Country World, the Sand Road, the Wall of Stone, the Snow, the Star Shining on the Glaze of the Snow in March, the Barndoor Slamming Across the Snowy Woods and Fields, the Moon on the Pine Cone Glaze, the Cobweb in the Summer, the Waters Lapping, the Night, the Wind at Night and Lips Clinging in the Fields at Night, the Hump of the Meadow at Night, the Milky Hump of Lovers in the Grass, Me and She, Humping in the Grass, Under the Apple Tree, under Clouds Racing over the Moon, in the Broad World, the Moist Star of Her Cunt, the Universe Melting Down the Sides of the Sky, the Warm Feel of It, the Moist Star between her Thighs, the Warm Pull in There, the Action on the Grass, the Rubadub of Legs, the Hot Clothes, the Thirsting Mosquitos, the Tears, the Shuddering, the Bites, the Tonguings, and Twistings, the Moaning, the Moving, the Rocking, the Beating, the Coming, the Second Coming, the Third Coming—
The old void's still got it in him.

In *Visions of Cody*, Kerouac fashioned his most ebulliently lusty style as if intending to explore the full resources of Cassady's gusto and enthusiasm for living. Written with amazing inventiveness, stylistic freedom, and originality, *Visions of Cody* is Kerouac's most metaphorical book. Its texture is richer than any writing he ever conceived, an exultation of his best long-line sequences, passages combining the qualities of poetry (including several of his *Scattered Poems* run as prose) with the compressed intensity of haiku like the "dew shudder on the morning corn."

Cassady described his childhood in *The First Third*, but his labored accounts of life on the Denver skid row seem insipid when compared to Kerouac's more rhapsodic treatment of the same material. Kerouac renames Cassady Cody Pomeray and attemps to tell the whole story of his life from an internal perspective. *Visions of*

Cody suggests a level of despair and struggle that Cassady's optimism excludes, as when Kerouac describes an attempted sexual assault on young Cody by the legless beggar who shared his sleeping space. Kerouac's magic emerges as he evokes elegiac memories of popular culture as a backdrop by which to measure the Cassady legend: radio and "The Shadow," comics and the Katzenjammer Kids, movies and The Three Stooges, burlesque shows and boxing matches—all forces to which Cassady's imagination responded, but which serve as well to connect Kerouac as a writer to an audience that can savor and identify with such simple pleasures. An illustration of Kerouac's greater mastery of Cassady's material is the episode in which Cody accompanies his father and a friend, Bull Balloon, to sell flyswatters in Nebraska. The story is told in a tone of warm and often hilarious comedy, but the portrait of Old Bull becomes one of the many "unspeakable visions" that recur as an ominous motif of failure in American life:

> Old Bull Balloon who usually went around wearing a poker-wrinkled but respectable suit with a watch chain, straw hat, Racing Form, cigar and suppurated red nose (and of course the pint flask) and was now fallen so low, for you could never say that he could prosper while other men fell, that his usually supposititious half-clown appearance with the bulbous puff of beaten flesh for a face, and the twisted mouth, his utter lovelessness in the world among foolish people who didn't really see a soul in a man, hounded old reprobate clown and drunkard of eternity, was now deteriorated down to tragic realities and shabbiness in a bread line, all the rich history of his soul crunching underfoot among the forlorn pebbles.

This single winding sentence moans along with drawn-out open vowel sounds to create the feeling of Bull's suffering lostness, but the clown parallel offers a balancing fortitude and patience that redeem the passage from sentimentality. It is a typical illustration of Kerouac's success as a writer.

Kerouac's control is at its height in *Visions of Cody*, especially as he describes the vicissitudes of Cody's youth, his hunchbacked friend Tom Watson, the ambiance of the poolroom, the joy of Cody's first real suit, a fantastic Marx Brothers football scene where "Cody had actually gone chasing his own pass and was now in the road yurking with outstretched hands from the agony that he was barely going to miss, himself sprawling as terrorstricken motorists swerved and screeched on all sides"; Cody recovering to tackle an antagonist "with an unspeakable mute prophesied and profound humility like that of a head-down Christ shot out of a cannon for nothing, agonized," the whole scene ending with the naturalistic omen of a miscarriage found among the refuse and weeds of the football field.

Visions of Cody begins with an especially tight structure, as if to set a firm base for a book of marvelous flights from the limits of plot and fictional congruity. Its first section, however, is a fugal anticipation of the novel's motifs—sex, detailed views of the bums on the New York Bowery, the railroad (using the old Third Avenue elevated), parties and suppressed excitement, reflections on the differences between paranoia and psychosis, followed by dreams of Cody and a lengthy letter to him. These views of Times Square cafeterias, of a grimy weathered bathroom in the elevated, of the "bottom of the world" which is the Bowery, all described with astounding intricacy of detail, create a very vivid yet deliberate contrast to the disgressive exfoliation of the rest of the book. A teasing and paradoxical tautness of several lines in the opening section like "Everything belongs to me because I am poor" or "All you do is head straight for the grave, a face just covers a skull awhile. Stretch that skull-cover and smile" serve to imply the metaphysical direction that Kerouac intends to take, and also the vision of "dark laughter" that mediates between his tones of celebration and elegy. In *Visions of Cody*, while the overtones of Whitmanesque affirmation are still present, they are constantly accompanied by undertones reminiscent of Céline: images of crippled, stunted figures, Depression disasters, beaten bums, Cody's vicious angers, grinding despair and grimness, the miscarriage in the football field. The tension sustained throughout the book is analagous only to the "Nighttown" section of *Ulysses*.

Visions of Cody is the best example of how Kerouac's receptivity to jazz improvisation affected his sense of rhythm and structure as he approaches the Cassady legend: "like bop, we're getting to it indirectly and too late but completely from every angle." Using an involuted and deliberately archaic syntax, and a language that is especially free and often private, Kerouac's style is whimsically supple and playful. At times, it seems even eccentric, peculiar: "snaveled clouds across the glary pale above," or "drugging flies." Frequently, as with the word "crack" in the following passage, Kerouac's word play encourages the repetition of a phrase in the manner of a jazz musician who obsessively returns to a chord:

> On the vaudeville stage stood two little comedians; in the front row sat a blond; look at 'er, said the first comic; I'm 'avin her now, I'm 'aivin no I'm 'avin 'er now, that is it, with the britishaccent, I have it, yes, that's right, go ahead and forget what you were saying, if you can't remember, crack, go ahead, head, creak, crack, crack your head, head; go crack your head in a crack; go crack your head in a craggy rack; go crack your head in the bone yard rack; go crack your head in the wild blue rack; ah ha, go and crack in your heed; go keed, find your head, crack it, it is found, now listen, kiddies, go crack your head I say in the mailhouse rack, oh yes, zoom, go crack your head in the hailstorm black, the maelstrom sack; go crack, go crack, the shroudy stranger is my brother, he's the one who reached out his black hand in the dark and stole my roach pipe.

Sometimes, Kerouac will attempt an alliterative adjectival stream, as when describing Moe, leader of The Three Stooges, who is "mopish, mowbry, mope-mouthed, mealy, mad, hanking, making the others quake." More often, he skillfully arranges sounds to create poetic effects: "So they sell corn in dusty side streets; the paisans sink in the purple ground, the sun is the color of wine, the goats whine, the bellies fatten, the kern and the herd and the isle in the reeds and the paddles of day, all recline, in kind; and eventide is come upon old Mexico." Occasionally, the punning is used to exaggerate the garish vulgarity of Cody's sexual insatiability, as when he sees a beautiful woman entering a bus while he is working on a parking-lot: "Yow!—there . . . she . . . goes . . . now! The cunt of them all, the legs a mile wide, I mean long; ah, well, the bus swallered her whole, hole, her whole hole from sight of my eyeballs as I lean in this gastrous doorway all disastered and torn to die for love of Milady."

With rambling Melvillean sentences, stream-of-consciousness passages, with a digressive crowding of impressions, anecdotes, cons and tall tales, drawings and letters, imitations of Tom Sawyer and Bloom's trial in *Ulysses*, superbly rendered discontinuities and drug fantasies, the novel's Shandyean profusion leaves the reader giddy and unbalanced, prepared to accept Kerouac's series of visions, epiphanies of Cody walking down the street with the lurching stagger of The Three Stooges or driving an old jalopy along a rutted Mexican road. To control the increasing sense of disorder and diffusion, Kerouac repeats words like "unspeakable," entire passages in some cases, and crucial images like the recurrent juxtaposition of redbrick (suggesting stolid endurance of the working classes) to red neon (the excitement of cities, but also the externality of "desperately advertised life"). But like Gatsby, Cody is the kind of primal force for whom a neon sign might represent hope and accomplishment instead of vulgar change.

In stark stylistic contrast, almost as relief from the complexities of his most experimental book—"are we still supposed to communicate?" Kerouac queries—stands the famous tape, a series of conversations between Kerouac and Cassady while inhaling Benzedrine, smoking marijuana, and drinking quantities of alcohol. The tape is invaluable as a record of how the Beats sustained their friendships on the axes of drugs, sex, and jazz. The hipster scene is detailed: the Times Square underground, the Lower East Side flat on Henry Street that Burroughs once maintained and Huncke occupied as a place of sinister rendezvous. Cassady gives his account of the visit to New Waverly in 1947, stopping at a crossroads with Ginsberg to swear an oath of eternal love; he tells of Huncke's construction of a "love-bed" and of how Huncke, on Nembutals, would listen to Billie Holiday while Burroughs complained that he wished to hear

Viennese waltzes; he relates the highlights of how he drove the jeep full of marijuana back to New York with Burroughs and Huncke as passengers. Cassady conjectures on how Burroughs shot Joan Adams in Mexico. Kerouac, in turn, tells of how he found Edie Parker living with Joan Adams on 118th Street near Columbia University when he returned from his merchant-marine trip to Greenland, how Burroughs visited to learn about shipping out, how Kerouac became involved in Lucien Carr's murder of Dave Kammarer. These events and others (including some remarkable stories about Cassady in Denver) are told in a manner anticipating Pop realism, with the graphic and relentlessly obsessive concentration on the ordinary that is seen in Warhol's movies. The catalyzing principle is Rimbaud's aim of *dérèglement des tous les sens*. When Kerouac passes out near the end of the tape, the indefatigable Cassady continues like an overflowing dam, a model of the blocked writer with a story to tell and the ability to recall it, but lacking the patient fortitude to set it down.

Cassady's premise is that a story can be told only once to achieve its fullest impact (like Coleridge's belief that the original inspiration was closest to truth), and this may be one source of Kerouac's bias against revision, a reminder of how close the Beats are to oral tradition and the improvisatory spirit of jazz. But the real impunity of the tape follows from Cassady's premise of immediacy, as it tries to violate the barriers between art and life. Kerouac, of course, depending on "sketching" and relying extensively on journal notes in his own work, was evidently intent on dramatizing a very fine line between actual reality as transcribed by the tape recorder, and the text that reflects the natural skills of the writer. Ironically, the tape itself becomes the justification of literary enterprise, revealing the inadequacies of natural speech when juxtaposed to the more poetic resources of the writer, suggesting also in the boring bareness and rambling monotony of its antistyle that the genuinely "unspeakable visions of the individual" are realized most fully when rendered by an artist. Despite the stimulation of drugs, the talk is grounded in inhibition, never soaring or even searing, without the Zen zaniness of Kerouac's own more scintillating imitations of the tape where again craft courts the illusion of spontaneity with greater grace and fluidity than the actual can provide.

Kerouac presents Cassady in perpetual motion, like a man riding a wheel, impatiently intense, overspilling nervous anxiety, a torrent of words in a cage of restlessness. His conception of Cody is a masculine version of Molly Bloom's affirmation, a paean to vitality and passion:

> While eating supper he continually nudges his wife's thigh and sucks juices from her lips and pats her kindly on the head and slaps applesauce out of a can into his children's (his daughters') plates, drinks milk out of the bottle, won't hardly allow me a glass, himself doles out the Nescafé in cups, runs bread in hand and his bread always is wrapped in a sandwich around the evening meat to the stove, handles precarious cast-iron covers of old stove with teetering jumps and balances and Whoops like W. C. Fields, "Lookout there! lookout! lookout! yeaaah!" Everybody got excited this year about Marlon Brando in *Streetcar Named Desire*; why Cody has a thinner waist and bigger arms, personally knew Abner Yokum in the Ozarks (Marlon Brando is really Al Capp), has probably bigger bats and catchers mitts, wears week-old T-shirts covered with baby puke, is like a machine in the night, masturbates five or six times a day when his wife is sick (in fact all the time), has private secret rags all over the house (that I have seen), writes with severe and stately dignity under after supper lamps with muscular bended neck three or four times the half, can run the 100 in less than 10 flat, pass 70 yards, broad jump 23 feet, standing broad jump 11 feet, throw a 12-pound shot 49 feet, throw a 150-pound tire up on a 6-foot rack with just one arm and his knee, plays pinochle at night with the boys in the caboose, wears a slouched black hat sometimes, was walking champ in the Oklahoma State Joint Reformatory, cuts and switches poetic old dirty boxcars from the Main hills and Arkansas, holds his footing when a 100-car freight slams along in a jawbreaking daisy chain roar to him, drives a '32 Pontiac clunker (the Green Hornet) as well as a '50 Chevy station wagon sharp and fast (I see his head bobbing into sight from the sea of heads in cars on Market Street, girls throng at the bell and the greenlight walk among clerks and Bartlebies and Pulham Esquires and Victor Matures of California, Chinese girls, luscious office

girls with tight skirts Chineesing at their knee-sides and the juice drippin down their legs) (why I could tell you stories make your cock stand) and "Wow", "Yes!" Look at *that* one!"

This is the Cody of immediate action without judgment or reflection, the daredevil who once stopped a runaway freight train with his foot, or practically fell out of a car while doing a driving trick (to Kerouac's consternation) and reentered the car without losing control. Cody, whose first speeches were to a judge while pleading for his vagrant father, who dreamed in reform school that reading might save him from his father's dissolution, the speed freak painfully digesting all of Proust, the obsessive designer of schedules, a reminder of how deeply the Horatio Alger myth of self-improvement is embedded in the American national consciousness:

At fifteen this child had the regimen of his life worked out in a confused and still and all pathetically practical way. He rose at 7 A.M. from Old Bull Balloon's rolltop desk (his current bed); if the office was filled with poker players he slept in the bathtub of the Greeley or other hotels. At 7:15 he rushed downtown, washed at barbershop sink, if it was not available he used the YMCA sink. Then he delivered his paper route. Around nine he went to the Smith residence, where he knew a near-idiot maid that he made love to on the cellar cot, after which she always fed him a big meal. If this friendship with idiot maid sometimes failed he ran to Big Cherry Lucy's at the Texas Lunch (ever since thirteen Cody was able to handle any woman and in fact had pushed his drunken father off Cherry Lucy Halloween night 1939 and taken over so much that they fist fought like rivals and Cody ran away with the five dollar stake). At ten he rushed to the library for the grand opening, read Schopenhauer and magazines (sometimes when he wasn't reading funnies as a child he'd get a real book off the old Greeley Hotel shelf and read down over the first words of every line Chinese style in childly thought, which is early philosophizing). At eleven o'clock he asked to wash cars and sometimes asked to park cars at the Rocky Mountain Garage (already he could drive better than any attendant in Denver and in fact had stolen several other cars to try his skill since his time in the "joint" and parked them back on the same block intact except for change of position), noon hour he used a paper route friend's bike to ride five miles out to friends' families for big meals, then helped with chores till two. Back to library for afternoon reading, history, encyclopedias and the bloody sad amazing *Lives of the Saints*, and making use of the library toilet; four o'clock rest and meditation and connections in poolhall till closing time unless semipro twilight ballgame or other spectacles of interest sprung around town; eleven o'clock he stole nickels off newsstands for a Bowery beefstew and found the place to sleep.

Kerouac's Cody is strangely inhibited despite his extroversion, "neurotic, restless, too-intelligent, gone" way beyond the limitations of ordinary existence, yet somehow awesomely representative of the life of the average man, working as brakeman on the railroad, needing the established order of wife and children, with the "strength of the bourgeois and the lumpenproletariat all at once." At the same time this conundrum of contradiction approaches his work with a ferociously devouring ardor, finding it necessary to always be the best worker, just as it was "a matter of believing in his own soul; it's just a matter of loving your own life, loving the dreams in your sleep as parts of your life, as little children do and Cody did, loving the soul of man (which I have seen in the smoke)." But this was also the man who wrote to Kerouac once saying "I wound everyone I love." "I saw him as an angel, a god," Kerouac answers in *Visions of Cody*, and "I also saw him as a devil, an old witch." Cody is the supreme egotist, a great phallic con-man who lies effortlessly, especially to women whom he regards exclusively as sexual objects, a man "hankering, gross, mystical, nude" like the hero of Whitman's "Song of Myself":

> An American, one of the roughs, a kosmos,
> Disorderly fleshy and sensual . . . . eating drinking and breeding,
> No sentimentalist . . . . no stander above men and women or apart
>   from them . . . . no more modest than immodest.

"Trying desperately to be a great rememberer redeeming life from darkness" and devoting his most ambitious novel to an attempt to mythicize his friend, Kerouac became more interested in the affinities of relationship than in the actual man. Writing to Carl Solomon, encouraging him to consider what became Cassady's *The First Third* for Ace Books, Kerouac realized that *Visions of Cody* had suddenly and curiously become a book about himself. It stands as the realization of his most apt mode—a kind of free-form diary notation in which distinctions between fact and fancy, prose and poetry are deliberately blurred for the sake of imaginative recall.

Visions of Cody is Kerouac's most imaginative book. He also intended to write *Visions of Bill* about Burroughs, but *Doctor Sax* was as close as he would get. *Doctor Sax* was written during Kerouac's visit to Burroughs in Mexico City in 1952. In a letter to Ginsberg, Kerouac said that *Doctor Sax* was his indulgence in mystery, his *Pierre* (or *The Ambiguities* as Melville subtitled it), an attempt at a hallucinated, trancelike, and clairvoyant Yeatsian prose. Unlike any of Kerouac's other books, *Doctor Sax* continues the experimentalism of *Visions of Cody* with the baroque quality of its convoluted and deliberately archaic prose:

> I know there in the green opulence of dollars and in the grotto sorrow of rocks and plaster . . . gravel croaked and on-led for persetury inventigators in the wrong roil road to the flaminary immensities and up-fluge of the poor bedighted, be-knighted Crown and Clown of sorrowmary doom in This anyway-globe . . . .

Ostensibly the novel describes a flooding of the Merrimack River in Lowell in 1936 (the very flood which swamped Leo Kerouac's printing establishment). It is a Gothic fairy tale, the myth of puberty of an impressionable boy who fantasizes the presence of a mysterious alchemist named Doctor Sax, an embodiment of a recurrent nightmare Kerouac had as a child of a shrouded stranger (which Ginsberg used as the subject of the last poem in *Empty Mirror*) who represented death, and who was also partly a reflection of the mordant, brooding, and restless presence of Burroughs himself whom Kerouac was observing closely.

The figure of Doctor Sax is a presentiment of the death that Don
Juan, in Carlos Castaneda's *Journey To Ixtlan*, says is always behind
one's shoulder. When Kerouac wrote in *Doctor Sax* that "dreams are
where participants in a drama recognize one's death," he was not
only suggesting the subject of *Doctor Sax* but speaking in a language
Don Juan would have understood. The affinity is not surprising.
Kerouac was always speculating on the particular psychic or
mystical power of beings or inanimate objects, a propensity he may
have acquired from drugs like peyote or more directly from the
Indian culture he admired.

Doctor Sax, caped and hooded, has spent two decades planning a
special potion, an antidote to destroy the Cosmic Serpent. This
mythical beast figures in Hindu, Aztec, and earlier gnostic legend as
an apocalyptic power emerging from the earth to devour all living
creatures—an Indian version of the Last Judgment story. Actually,
Kerouac had first described the Satanic hundred-mile-long snake of
the underworld in *On The Road* in a dream which Sal relates:

> "A saint called Doctor Sax will destroy it with secret herbs which he is at
> this very moment cooking up in his underground shack somewhere in
> America. It may also be disclosed that the snake is just a husk of doves;
> when the snake dies great clouds of seminal-gray doves will flutter out and
> bring tidings of peace around the world."

In his conception of the great snake, Kerouac was being neither
perverse nor unnecessarily ambiguous. He had been introduced to
Gnostic texts by Raymond Weaver at Columbia, and he remembered the Gnostic tendency to reverse value systems of traditional
myth, to willfully subvert stereotyped allegorical interpretations of
reality by switching the roles of good and evil, the sublime and the
base, the blessed and the cursed to achieve the shock or reinterpreta-
tion of the most revered traditional religious elements. Thus, in
ophitic cults, the serpent in the Garden of Eden parable would be
seen as a catalyst of rebellion, awakening man from the binding
principles of the world to transcendence. Such views influenced

Milton in *Paradise Lost* as evidently as they did Burroughs in his concept of the Garden of Delights. The goal of the Gnostics was the release of inner man from the mundane prison of the material world in order to return to a realm of inner illumination. Gnostic lore appealed to Kerouac because it condemned the world absolutely. According to the Gnostics, since the world is a prison, its laws and conditions are unjust, and the illuminated—those sharing the spark of God-light—cannot be held accountable by society.

In Kerouac's novel, the snake is nurtured in an abandoned castle and tended by Count Condu, a vampirish relative of better-known but equally sanguine Transylvanian aristocrats (Kerouac knew a great deal about horror films as anyone can see after reading his essay on F. W. Murnau's movie, *Nosferatu*). The novel, however, is not nearly as sinister as it is lugubriously droll. Its more macabre aspects do resemble the fictions of William Burroughs (although the influence is from Kerouac to Burroughs since Burroughs had only written *Junkie* by 1952), as when Sax transports little Jack Duluoz to Snake Hill Castle on the night of the flood, and they see a giant scorpion accompanied by gnomish men, and a Wizard whose neck is twisted and strung with bits of tortured, dead flesh. Jack learns of Giant Insect Men and kidnapped boys paralyzed with a freezing drug that turns them into puppet dolls. Doctor Sax, green-faced and leering with a maniacal, hollow laugh, is a Faust-figure obsessed with the relation of knowledge to evil. His highly mannered speech and grandiloquent gestures, his almost delirious incoherence and murkily ominous prophetic tones recall Djuna Barnes' nocturnal doctor in *Nightwood*, Dr. Matthew Mighty O'Connor:

> "Anoint thee, son—" he hallooed in the mud cellar—"we're going into Homeric battles of the morn—over the dew tops of every one of your favorite pines of Dracut Tigers slants the far red sun that's just now rising from a bed of night-blue to a day of bluebells in the crime—the shores of oceans will crash, in Southern Latitude climes, and the bark will plow thru hoary antique sea with a vast funebreal consonant splowsh of bow-foams—you're in on no mean squabble the butcher's devil."

Kerouac had sent *Doctor Sax* to Mark Van Doren, the Columbia professor who had recommended publishing *The Town and the City* to Robert Giroux, but Van Doren could not understand the book, finding it dull and boring. This was a bitter surprise for Kerouac as he regarded Van Doren with an almost filial admiration, seeing him as a man of genuine humility, without pretensions. In all fairness to Van Doren, the novel is the most anomalous and expressionistic of Kerouac's books. Its aesthetic depends on a Proustian formula, the mixing of memory and dream, as for instance when Doctor Sax inherits the weird laugh of "The Shadow," the radio serial Kerouac listened to so faithfully as a boy in Lowell. The terrors of Count Condu and Doctor Sax are incongruously contrasted to such familiar objects as his mother's brown bathrobe, the wrinkly tar doorway to the tenement building in which Duluoz lives. The gothic potentials of the novel are tempered by such recollections of Kerouac's own childhood: the baseball games he invents for his own innocent amusement, the private occupations of a child immersed in comic books and radio, the hockey games he played with his friends, and the poolhalls they frequented. As Barry Gifford notes in *Kerouac's Town*, a memoir of Lowell two years after Kerouac's death, the town's adult chill could only have been enlivened by the fantasy of the child's eye.

This perspective of the child, and the shifting from the comforts of secure realities to the phantasmagoria of Sax and Condu, create the same alternating tension that Kerouac perfected in his other novel about childhood, *Visions of Gerard*. Told from the viewpoint of an admiring, younger, four-year-old brother, the book relates how Gerard died at the age of nine. The terrors in *Visions of Gerard*, however, are not the fears of death—always a desired release for Kerouac—but of bondage to pain. The novel, with its sweet reserve of implacable resignation, is the most charming of Kerouac's books. What is most remarkable about it is how the trauma that Kerouac felt as a child is ameliorated and softened as the novel's aura becomes a distant religious haze.

If *Doctor Sax* viewed Lowell through the mixed filters of childhood recollection and nightmare, *Maggie Cassidy* caught the town from the more nostalgic perspective of twilight. Set in Lowell in 1939, the novel describes the unfulfilled early yearnings of sixteen-year-old Jack Duluoz for his high-school love, Maggie, a girl only one year his senior but far more mature and sexually aware. The conflict is between the ideal of conventional domesticity—the small cottage with red windows near the railroad that would provide employment—and the goads of career and fortune.

Maggie Cassidy explores a familiar subject in American fiction, life in a small town, but significantly without the drabness, oppressive boredom, and colorless routine depicted by Sinclair Lewis, or the eccentricity and pathetic claustrophobia of Anderson's Winesburg. For Kerouac, Lowell was a place where one could still manage a perspective on changing America, and a view of the simple orders it once contained:

> We join the flow of the sidewalks leading downtown—to the Lobster Cot—Merrimack Street—the Strand—the whole dense almost riotous inwards of the city aglow for the Saturday night in that time only fifteen years ago when not everybody had cars and people walked to shop and from buses to shows, not everything was locked-in strange behind tin walls with anxious eyes looking out to deserted sidewalks of modern America now—

Kerouac begins by deliberately recording the adolescent awkwardness of Duluoz and his friends, examining the uninhibited relationships among the French-Canadian families of his boyhood. The ring of actual heard speech gives the novel its authenticity: the high-school classroom, boys playing and talking, track meets and a school prom, bread-and-butter sandwiches for lunch or hot date pie with whipped cream after school, all detailed exactly, vividly, creating a realistic base for a romantic framework. The most compelling feature of the prose descriptions of these ordinary activities is Kerouac's characteristic movement and rhythm—even idle conversations are full of impact and momentum as the characters speak about baseball, friendly boxing bouts, the pursuit of girls. Instead of football, Jack Duluoz excels in track, and the description of a track event at which Duluoz defeats a Negro runner for Worcester is taut, generating tension and excitement. But even as he examines the runners, Kerouac makes the black racer illustrate a vanguard, the omen of the new lifestyle he himself would disseminate to a wider audience:

> To my utter amazement I saw out of the corner of my eye the colored boy laid out almost flat on the floor in a low slung fantastic starting position, something impossibly modern and submarining and subterranean like bop, like the new gesture of a generation . . . . Later on in life I'd see American Negro boys imitating Charlie Parker and calling themselves Bird on street corners and it would be the same thing, and son to, this gesture of the early bop generation as I immeasurably understood it seeing it for the first time.

The track victories, even more than the accomplished football runs of *The Town and the City*, ignite Duluoz with a heroic awareness, the recognition of his own potential: "They'd put a poet in my craw." So he leaves Lowell and Maggie for Horace Mann and Columbia. Before departing, his family surprises him with a birthday party which occurs during an unexpected blizzard, and which expresses the good fellowship, vitality, and raucously boisterous hilarity of the French-Canadian community that Kerouac was later to miss in New York, and which he sought in the companionship of other writers and in the hip scene generally. In "The Origins of the Beat Generation," Kerouac asserted that the characteristic principle of the Beat movement was its intentness on joy, and he recalled "the wild parties my father used to let me have at home in the 1920's and 1930's in New England that were so fantastically loud nobody could sleep for blocks around." (It was this euphoria to which Kerouac responded in Cassady.) The party is held at the home of Jimmy Bissonette, known for his "mad maniac laugh," and despite such tame kissing games as spin-the-bottle, the gathering builds to the celebratory fury of some of the routs in *On The Road* or *Desolation Angels*:

> I see Iddyboy trying to be social like in movies the cake in his big paw laughing with Martha Alberge his girl and he lets out a big explosive Phnu! of laughter that kicks in his big battering-ram belly and blasts up his throat and out comes spewing a streamer of snivel all over the cake—nobody sees, he falls, kneels on the floor, holds his belly laughing—His fantastic brother Jimmy is screaming excitedly some dirty joke, my father is doing the same thing near the stove, the house-top shivers maniacally in the great now-howling swept over blizzard, heat beats at the windows, I grab Maggie by the waist, I yell—Door opens, fresh arrivers—red shouting faces turn to it as new people fall in. Roars of approval, applauses, raisings of bottles—

The party overflows with the "shining and spilling molten gold of real life" with revels of food, drink, song, and laughter.

Maggie Cassidy is a book of seething vitalities, unfulfilled turbulence, and much sadness caused by the relationship of Duluoz and Maggie. His first view of her is at a dance where Maggie appears forlorn, dissatisfied, dark, unpleasantly strange. Maggie has a curious affinity for disaster and she often compulsively relates news of some death or misfortune, once even in the middle of an embrace. Her gloominess, however, is balanced by a series of lyrical descriptive passages (the novel was originally to be called *Springtime Mary*) that powerfully animate the style:

> Fluting spring was racing through the corridors and ritual alleys of my sacred brain in holy life and making me wake and resurge to the business of being and becoming a man. I drew deep breaths . . . this I could smell in spring tonights coming back from Maggie, spring'd send the stale fender with its sweet rot swills caked underneath and I'd know—this

would be mixed with sweet breath river's voice Awing at me over the lake of the bend—From Lakeview clear I could literally smell the pinecones getting ready for gladsummers on the ground, the azaleas were ballooning again.

Maggie provokes Duluoz into the spring of his manhood, spurring his jealousy, then demonstrating her own possessiveness. Toward the end of the novel, she shows less and less interest, intuitively aware of how her very basic needs would only interfere with Duluoz's new goals.

But Jack Duluoz cannot so easily relinquish the romantic premise of his quest for Maggie—"That the only love can only be the first love." Very inappropriately, after his year at Horace Mann, he invites Maggie to New York for the spring prom. The result is disaster: Maggie's rude pastoral charms conflict with the sophistication of Duluoz's new friends. Maggie makes a final, passionate appeal to Duluoz to abandon the false chic and hollow glamour of the city where he can only "lose yourself from yourself" to return to the more reliable pleasures of life in Lowell, "the porch of the river," "walking across the top of America with your lantern." In this passage, Kerouac used Maggie to voice his own sentiments.

In *Visions of Cody*, he complained of what he called "Newyorkitis," a compound of incessant drinking, talk, exhibitionism, and narcissism. In many ways, Kerouac's years at Columbia, where he boasted that he set a record for cutting classes, developed in him the saddening awareness that he could never return to Lowell, to his own youth or to the uncomplicated lures of Maggie. In *Visions of Cody* he equated college with the idea of "prosperity just around the corner." But it was a false promise, he asserts. Instead, he was drawn to all the "mad elements of life," the sensibilities, books, and arts that make it impossible "to learn the simple tricks of how to earn a living" and deprived him of exactly what he admired in Cassady, an "innocent belief in my own thoughts that used to make me handle my own destiny." The result was a festering sophistication that led only to excess and "makes me lie around like a bum all day long and stay up all night long goofing"—that is, writing his stories!

Maggie returns to Lowell where Duluoz reappears three years later for a brief but brutal aftermath. His romantic illusions betrayed by time and experience, he attempts to gratify his pent desire for Maggie by assaulting her in the back of a car. Practical Maggie, a woman of the old order, has the foresight to wear a rubber girdle; she fights him off and laughs. This ironic parody of sex in prewar America, complete with its allusion to Maggie's impenetrable chastity belt, checks the euphemistic tenor of Duluoz's appreciation, and heightens the novel's undertone of despairing frustration. This final scene is as carefully detailed and finely etched as the track meet, the birthday party, the several dances; but more compact, condensed, and dynamic. The novel's power is a function of such scenes, volatile, charged with repressed energy, an excitement that finds no healthy outlet and sours to brooding internalized anger and the sense of turmoil that is so often felt just under the surface of Kerouac's fiction.

In *Maggie Cassidy*, Kerouac revealed an essential division in his own sensibility: the need for the familiar comforts that Maggie could provide (like the child's view of the protective mother in *Doctor Sax*), and the contrary need for the city, despite its potentially debilitating dangers and anonymity. Kerouac's view of the small town involved a romantic nostalgia, perhaps a sentimental distortion from a child's perspective of the attributes of such an existence. Kerouac could afford to idealize it because he left at seventeen; his own more adult awareness of the lack of freedom and variety afforded by such an environment kept him in the city. Kerouac's split loyalties are captured in two photographs taken at the birthday party at Jimmy Bissonette's in *Maggie Cassidy*: in the first, he is seen unsmiling, looking like a "moronic boy with a strange pinched drawn goofy peaky witless face," an "unnamably abnormal beast of a boy"—that is, the inarticulate country lout, the pastoral swineherd with his rustic contentments; the second picture presents a grave, vain, musing "Greek athletic hero with curly black locks, ivory white face," clear eyes, a strong neck, and powerful hands. While in the first photograph Kerouac sees himself as sad-faced and droopy, surrounded by festivity and the happiness of his friends, the second picture is joyless, stern, resolute. *Maggie Cassidy* marks the transition from romantic swain to worldly quester. But it was a transition that Kerouac was to manage better in his books than in his life.

The difference is seen in another love story, this one an affair of the city called *The Subterraneans* which describes a passionate two-month relationship between Leo Percepied and Mardou Fox. Mardou is lovely, thin, black, with a slurring sensuality in her voice, and she resembles Terry, Sal's Mexican mistress in *On The Road*. Mardou's mother died in childbirth; her father was a part Negro, part Cherokee hobo.

The first half of the novel relies on the close purgative intensities of an I/thou confrontation (Kerouac was thinking of *Notes From Underground* as he worked on *The Subterraneans*) as Kerouac explores the roots of Mardou's blackness, her weird estrangements and afflicted attraction to addicts. With a kind of profuse Faulknerian rambling narrative, Mardou compulsively relates her story and Kerouac surmises the rest with elaborate crisscrossing convolutions and associations of thought. Kerouac, far more literary than his popular reputation acknowledges, even signals his debt to Faulkner's labyrinthine methods by having his narrator read *Spotted Horses*. Mardou tells Leo Percepied how after months of losing herself in the bohemian recesses of San Francisco, she had suddenly broken loose, impulsively fleeing a lover to hide naked in an alley. Borrowing some clothing from a sympathetic neighbor, Mardou, the cool outsider, winds her way through the city and feels an ecstatic union with everyone she meets, an almost Buddhist awareness of the interpenetration of all sentient beings that becomes especially pronounced, as in a Joycean epiphany, when she hears some jazz:

she stood in drowsy sun suddenly listening to bop as if for the first time as it poured out, the intention of the musicians and of the horns and instruments suddenly a mystical unity expressing itself in waves like sinister and again electricity but screaming with palpable aliveness the direct *word* from the vibration, the interchanges of statement, the levels of waving intimation, the smile in sound, the same living insinuation . . .

In all of his novels, Kerouac is usually hard on his persona, almost always making him a projection of a failure he felt in his own life. Here, he demonstrates the shallowness of Percepied's feeling for Mardou by poignantly interweaving her affectionate letter of complaint through the history of their love. The character of Percepied adds to the brutal confessional dimension of the work. Early in the tale he admits to a self-hatred which he releases in bouts of drunken, foolish talk. He is always deserting Mardou after their love, to return home to the asexuality of his writing which is itself about the kind of life Mardou leads. Kerouac portrays Percepied in terms of deeply rooted middle-class attitudes toward order, cleanliness, terror of squalor and unwashed sheets or dirty dishes, fears of how his family would accept Mardou's blackness; he shows him participating in the vicarious rationalizations of an intellectual elite that actually aspires to a "lecherous lustful materialism" despite the ability to read and experiment with such theoreticians of the future as Wilhelm Reich. Percepied even admits the tyrannical sway of his mother. His suspicious doubting, his false testing of Mardou, become a cruel parody of the faith to which Kerouac aspires in his other books. Indeed, the portrait of Percepied is almost an anticipation of Kerouac's own growing ambivalence about his role in the generation to which he had given voice, about the future direction of his country and his own developing chauvinistic attitudes and hatred of communism that became so much more pronounced in his last years. In short, the split in *Maggie Cassidy* between town and city had now taken a more political and social direction as if Kerouac was using his own fiction to prepare himself for a withdrawal from the free spirit of the artistic community to a more private and bitter citadel of despair.

The great virtue of *The Subterraneans* is its manner, its style. *On The Road*, despite editorial castration, had tremendous rhythmic surge and volume and passages of dazzling beauty. It also had the animation of Kerouac's endemic colloquialism, a kind of hip argot that had Dean "balling" cars, or "lamming" from Hoboken. But at that point, editors were still not permitting Kerouac to indulge in the slangy homespun earthiness of "yestiddy," or the deliberately impudent syntax of "gloves from the ground pickied." There was no question of allowing him to use his own mischievously invented words like "furyiating" or "birl" (in *The Subterraneans*, a girl with pants), or "sloosesucking sweaters," or the portmanteau combinations of *Doctor Sax* like "respectaburban," "flambastic," or "fryalitatating."

In *The Subterraneans*, the accumulating energies of the Whitmanesque catalogues and long-line sequences, define Kerouac's strength as a writer. There is one section in particular, a single sentence comprising three pages of text, too long to quote fully. The scene is a jazz club called the Red Drum where Charlie Parker is playing:

> up on the stand Bird Parker with solemn eyes who'd been busted fairly recently and had now returned to a kind of bop dead Frisco but had just discovered or been told about the Red Drum, the great new generation gang wailing and gathering there, so here he was on the stand, examining them with his eyes as he blew his now-settled-down-into regulated-design 'crazy' notes—the booming drums, the high ceiling. . . . returning to the Red Drum for sets, to hear Bird, whom I saw distinctly digging Mardou several times also myself directly into my eye looking to search if really I was that great writer I thought myself to be as if he knew my thoughts and ambitions or remembered me from other night clubs and other coasts, other Chicagos—not a challenging look but the king and founder of the bop generation at least the sound of it digging his audience digging the eyes, the secret eyes him-watching, as he just pursed his lips and let great lungs and immortal fingers work, his eyes separate and interested and

humane, the kindest jazz musician there could be while being and therefore naturally the greatest—watching Mardou and me in the infancy of our love, and probably wondering why, or knowing it wouldn't last, or seeing who it was would be hurt, as now, obviously, but not quite yet, it was Mardou whose eyes were shining in my direction . . . .

The entire passage is overwhelming in its syncopated insistence on recording all the emotional and philosophical variables. Musically, the passage builds on improvised digressions as jazz does, using what blues players call "landmarks," repeated images that help to unify, and "scat calling," using the voice as an instrument. The passage approaches Kerouac's own ideal of the jazz saxophonist, avidly pursuing the ineluctably ultimate note, always progressively furthering his sound with another association, reaching for and extending an oceanic continuum as if secretly knowing that to cease means to die.

As Kerouac wrote in *Desolation Angels*, "music blends with the heartbreak universe and we forget the brain beat." The rhythms of jazz music, as he commented in his *Paris Review* interview, explained his prosody:

> Yes, jazz and bop, in the sense of a, say, a tenor man drawing a breath and blowing a phrase on his saxophone, till he runs out of breath, and when he does, his sentence, his statement's been made . . . that's how I therefore separate my sentences, as breath separations of the mind . . . I formulated the theory of breath as measure, in prose and verse, never mind what Olson, Charles Olson says, I formulated that theory in 1953 at the request of Burroughs and Ginsberg. Then there's the raciness and freedom and humor of jazz instead of all that dreary analysis . . . .

It was indeed a spontaneous bop prosody intended to be read aloud, as Allen Ginsberg has observed, to realize how the motion of the sentence corresponds to the actual excitement in the event or conversation. The passage quoted above from *The Subterraneans* is full of oddly personal leaps, associations that defy the tedium of ordinary description and the rational logic of conventional prose. The innovation of the line is the approximation of the thought process as it occurs, without literary simulation or fabrication. The best account of the impact of such a prose is by Henry Miller, who wrote a preface to *The Subterraneans:*

> Everything Kerouac writes about—those weird, hauntingly ubiquitous characters whose names may be read backwards or upside down, those lovely, nostalgic, intimate-grandiose stereopticon views of America, those nightmarish, ventilated joy-rides in gondolas and hot rods—plus the language he uses (à la Gautier in reverse) to describe his "earthly-heavenly visions," surely even the readers of Time and Life, of the Digests and the Comics, cannot fail to discern the rapport between these hypergonic extravaganzas and such perennial blooms as the *Golden Ass*, the *Satyricon*, and *Pantagruel*.
>
> The good poet, or in this case the "spontaneous Bop prosodist," is always alive to the idiomatic lingo of his time—the swing, the beat, the disjunctive metaphoric rhythm which comes so fast, so wild, so scrimmaged, so unbelievably albeit delectably mad, that when transmitted to paper no one recognizes it. None but the poets, that is. He "invented it," people will say. Insinuating that it was souped up. What they should say is: "He *got* it." He got it, he dug it, he put it down. ("You pick it up, Nazz!")

The signal triumph of *The Subterraneans* is Kerouac's ability to capture Mardou's voice, her special dialectical intonations and verbal inflections. It is an attribute of his ear and his spontaneous method. Allen Ginsberg, writing to his father, commented that he knew the woman Kerouac was describing:

> that was the way she spoke, the syntax even, her style of speaking—a very common style—he's caught her very well—and if you add his interpolations and private thoughts which he records semi-simultaneously with her monologues, and their conversation—you have a very complicated but real structure of events to try and get down on paper. Hemingway tried simplification and reduction (and was attacked for being too inhumanly

stripped down)—Jack trying (as Proust & Celine) to include all the little private thoughts you normally wouldn't mention—so he arrives at a complicated sentence structure. It's not trying to be English sentence structure. It's trying be American speech—and thought—reproduction. So it shouldn't be judged by the standards of a high school or college grammar course. It's not meant to be grammatical *that* way, it's meant to be right *another* way. Nor can one say that standard English syntax is the fixed and only way of transcribing human thought . . . . English grammar is only the formal way tied to fixed habits of feeling & communication—Jack, broken free of these fixed habits of thought, has to think and write in his own way . . . . The ideal is for me a sensitive prose or poetry syntax that is practical & follows the changes actually going on in the process of thinking or writing . . . . Language is to use not dictate our thoughts. But so much of our lives & feelings are tied down to the limitations of what we're taught—this is the importance of striking out into variation & experiment—this is not nihilism but courage—not really that—joy!

Much of the thematic material Kerouac began to explore in *The Subterraneans* is continued and clarified in *Tristessa*, another love story which Kerouac told Malcolm Cowley he wrote in a stone hovel by candlelight in Mexico City in 1955. It is the cult novel for Kerouac's admirers, virtually unobtainable as it was published exclusively in a cheap paper edition. Kerouac was living on the roof above Bill Garver whose morphine connection was a woman named Esperanza Villanueva, an addict since the age of sixteen. Kerouac called her Tristessa, sadness, partly because of her melancholy voice, partly because he saw in the affliction of her drug use an illustration of the Buddhist principle that all life is suffering, and also because she was the object of an impossible love. Always sick and high, her small thin body and radiant eyes, her black Indian hair in pigtails, she appealed to Kerouac because of the carefree quality of her life, despite its squalor and deprivation.

Even though the action is rather limited, *Tristessa* is remarkably rich, the result of Kerouac's receptivity to the exoticism and strangeness of Mexico City. For Kerouac, Mexico was a romantic place full of the danger and excitement of the old American West. In the story "Mexico Fellaheen," for example, he records a newspaper headline describing a gunfight between a police chief and a town mayor with all the enthusiasm of Stephen Crane in "Five White Mice" or "The Bride Came to Yellow Sky." Kerouac carefully depicts a visit to Tristessa's slum dwelling where she lives with an older sister, Cruz, in rooms filled with animals: a rooster under her bed, a dove cooing and flapping its wings on a mantel, a hen, a chihuahua howling in heat, a kitten; and El Indio, allegedly a vendor of curios but actually a thief and morphine dealer—all of them chattering, screaming, disputing in the littered disarray of the cluttered rooms, Cruz vomiting, Tristessa's huge icon of the Virgin Mary in a corner near her bed a silent witness to the addict's ritual of tying the arm, boiling the morphine in a spoon, and plunging the needle into the flesh. The novel is almost all observation. Kerouac leaves at 2 A.M. and walks for several miles through Mexico City's crowds, pushing and dodging "through moils of activity with whores by the hundreds lined up along the walks of Panama Street," and the loitering men, the assembled gangs, people eating at food stands, the streets lit phantasmagorically by candles, dim bulbs, lanterns. The sentences are much shorter than in *The Subterraneans* with a greater emphasis on omitted articles, prepositions, and connectives ("Reason I bring whiskey" or "At same time a comedian") in order to capture the feeling of Tristessa's own clipped and quaint English—"It got soch prurtyeyes." Kerouac noticed the change in style, and in a letter to Ginsberg he commented on its terse choppiness, its pointed humor, and its total elimination of the more euphuistic and flowery qualities of *The Subterraneans*.

The second half of *Tristessa* was written a year later, after Kerouac had spent the summer on Desolation Peak as a fire watcher, and after he had declared his love for Tristessa in letters. The tone is more sinister, hopeless, and resigned, style itself muted by the picture of Tristessa succumbed, virtually destroyed, more ill than ever because of an unregulated use of Seconals (goofballs). There is another scene reminiscent of Stephen Crane's short stories as Kerouac parties with a group of Mexican men who steal his money and his notebook, followed by a graphic visit to a house where a dozen people are injecting heroin, but on the whole there is an unassimilated and unfulfilled quality to the material, very much like the way Kerouac describes the impossible partiality of communication with Tristessa: "I feel we are two empty phantoms of light or like ghosts in old haunted house stories diaphanous and precious and white and not-there—"

Tristessa explores the holiness of the ugly and disaffiliated, and is punctuated by references to Catholic ritual and Hindu myth. Yet the novel seems an expression of an even deeper, more personal meaning, especially if Tristessa is compared to Terry, the Mexican girl in *On The Road* or to Mardou Fox. All three are black-haired women of another racial type; with each, the narrator fantasizes an idyllic vision of escape into a more primitive existence where material possessions are meaningless and undesired, the kind of world Melville envisaged in his first novels of the South Pacific. With Terry, the narrator succeeds for a time when they live in a tent and pick cotton. With Mardou, he plans a trip to Mexico which never occurs. Tristessa's crowded living space with its animals represents another projected escape from Western notions of cleanliness and propriety. Then, with each woman, Kerouac imagines paranoid possibilities: they are seen as thieving whores who will betray him. It becomes necessary in each case to smash the romantic pedestal by mistreatment of the woman he has placed upon it. As he writes in *Doctor Sax* from the adolescent viewpoint of Ti-Jean and friends, "the women of this world were only made to bang." In his *Paris Review* interview, Kerouac tells of how he finally "nailed" Tristessa when she was in a helpless swoon, an account which he wisely omitted from the narrative. With Mardou, he is most explicit about a gnawing fear he associates with the idea of sex with a black woman, a terror of a contraction of the womb, and of being sucked into it, "the pull and force of the muscles being so powerful she

unknowing often vice-like closes over and makes a damup and hurt."
At the end of *The Subterraneans*, when he realizes that he has finally
lost Mardou, Percepied cries in a railroad yard thinking of her and
sees a vision of his mother in the sky who tells him how she will
succor and protect him:

> I saw bending over me the visage of my mother, with impenetrable eyes
> and moveless lips and round cheekbones and glasses that glinted and hid
> the major part of her expression which at first I thought was a vision of
> horror that I might shudder at, but it didn't make me shudder—

In *Tristessa*, also at the end of the story, when Kerouac invites her up
to his rooms promising not to molest her—she has fallen on her head
and is bandaged—he reflects that:

> I've screwed everything up with the mama again, Oedipus Rex, I'll tear
> out my eyes in the morning—San Francisco, New York, Padici, Medu,
> Mantua or anywhere, I'm always the King sucker who was made out to be
> the positional son in woman and man relationships, Ahh-gaaaaa—(Indian
> howl in the night, to campo-country sweet musica)—'King, bing, I'm
> always in the way for momma and poppa—When am I gonna be poppa?'

That a writer's sexual condition is as important an aspect of his
vision and sensibility as his social or theistic views is a post-Freudian
commonplace. These instances with black or "Fellaheen" lovers
reveal an ambivalence toward sexuality that links Kerouac with
Ginsberg's fear of women and Burroughs' outright declaration of
hatred for them. Indeed, the general attitude to women in Kerouac's
books is a reminder of the homosexual orientation of the Beats. In
Desolation Angels, Kerouac wrote a sharp vignette of Bull Hubbard
(Burroughs) lifting a rock to show a female scorpion that had
devoured her mate, and then crushing the scorpion with the rock.
The scene, with its use of the scorpion which is one of Burroughs'
favorite images, may be more symbolic than actual, but is therefore

all the more revealing. While the Beats despised the bourgeois housewife, they did little to imagine or project her more-liberated sisters. Burroughs has been an extremely harsh misogynist: he has called love "a fraud perpetrated by the female sex" in *The Job*, and has advocated the complete separation of the sexes.

There are no women as fully realized characters in Kerouac's best books, *On The Road* and *Visions of Cody*. Terry, Mardou, Tristessa, all imply for Kerouac a primitive sexuality while evoking castration anxieties. In each case, the cultural remove of the woman leads to a loss of inhibition and reminds Kerouac of his dependence on his mother. This is sometimes accompanied by a fear of being returned to the womb which might represent either an emotional paralysis or a withdrawal from the world. In *Doctor Sax*, Kerouac recalls a boyhood hike to New Hampshire where "I judged I was being torn from my mother's womb with each step from Home Lowell into the Unknown . . . a serious lostness that has never repaired itself in my shattered flesh dumb-hanging for the light—" Ultimately, all Kerouac's adventures followed this pattern, all abortive, failed attempts to withstand the magnetic appeal of the maternal hearth. While the lifestyle he was to picture in his fiction was supremely masculine, even allowing for his great tender moments, there was always an emasculating latent threat that would compromise and somehow confuse the action with an unwanted anger, usually self-directed. In each of Kerouac's novels, the pervasive feeling of gloom, despair, and the pain of living dominates the more hopeful enthusiasms, and at times the forced cheer of the characters. Behind this contradiction is an Oedipal fear of being assimilated into the womb—meaning the end of creativity for Kerouac—and it is complemented by an unconscious urge for confrontation with the protective sanctuary of birthplace.

The resolution in Kerouac's work, as in Burroughs' and less obviously in Ginsberg's, is a drive for annihilation and death where the traumatic ecstasies of birth will be finally recreated. "Aging is ecstasy," Kerouac wrote in his poem "Lucien Midnight," and few

American writers have expressed as pronounced and eager a welcome for the ultimate release of death as Kerouac. He concluded another poem, "Hymn," with an appeal to God:

> So whatever plan you have for me
> Splitter of majesty
> Make it short
>   brief
> Make it snappy
>   bring me home to the Eternal Mother
>   today
> At your service anyway,
>   (and until)

Just as Kerouac's writing projected his deepest concerns, those who knew him well felt his closeness to death. As John Clellon Holmes put it in "The Great Rememberer": "And suddenly I felt, with a shiver, that Kerouac would not live much beyond forty. Such voracious appetites, such psychic vulnerability, such singleness of purpose, must ream a man out at the end, and the Kerouac I knew was as incapable of turning away from his own consuming consciousness, as he was of living for long once he had been burned out by it."

"I'm writing this book because we're all going to die," Kerouac advised in *Visions of Cody*. In *Big Sur*, one of his last novels, Duluoz—in the spirit of Norman O. Brown in *Life Against Death*—proclaims:

> 'O the sad music of it all, I've done it all, seen it all, done everything with everybody' I say phone in hand 'the whole world's coming on like a high school sophomore eager to learn what he calls New things, mind you the same old sing-song sad song truth of death . . . because the reason I yell death so much is because I'm really yelling life, because you can't have death without life . . . . '

Big Sur is Kerouac's novel of breakdown, disintegration, the actual fulfillment of the "everything is collapsing" refrain of *On The Road*. The novel is a strong and detailed record of physical illness, paranoia, and the total failure of spirit and body Fitzgerald described in *The Crack Up*. *Big Sur* begins with an attempt at rejuvenation from the three-year hangover of hopelessness after the publication of *On The Road*—such repercussions of notoriety as the people who haunted his home in Northport, Long Island, expecting to meet Dean Moriarty. Retreating to Lawrence Ferlinghetti's isolated cabin by the ocean in Bixby Canyon, fourteen miles from Monterey, California, Kerouac is able to evoke moments of the idyllic lyricism of *The Dharma Bums*. But just as solitude in nature proved unendurable on Desolation Peak, Duluoz craves the excitement of San Francisco. Quoting Emerson several times, he dramatizes the romantic thesis of Emerson's first major essay, "Nature," that the external world's appearance is a projection of our inner consciousness. Duluoz is desperate, He sees himself as a "trudging humpbacked monster" facing the "ponderous groaning unheaval" of the ocean. He presents himself as an infernal Sisyphus, "a bentback madman monster groaning underground in hot steaming mud pulling a long hot burden nowhere." Each night he sits by the Pacific to work on his poem on the sounds of the sea, afflicted by the "bleak awful roaring is olateness" of the scene.

Hitchhiking back to Monterey on his way back to San Francisco after three weeks alone in the fog, he is forced to walk with his pack almost the entire route. He despairs at the antiseptic families bypassing him in their sleek station wagons, and realizes the extent to which the West Coast has become a tentacled megalopolis. After carousing in the San Francisco area with Cody Pomeray (Neal Cassady) and others, he returns to Bixby Canyon with a group of friends, and from this point on painfully begins to reject the enthusiasm for life that his own prose had suggested to so many others. *Big Sur* anticipates the confused angry bitterness of the syndicated "I'm a Bippie in the Middle" article that he published shortly before he died in 1969. Soured by his own alcoholic excesses, the "soul groans" of delirium tremens, he begins a withdrawal into a prison of the self that becomes a negative extension of his own "Do Nothing" version of Buddhism, and an ironic final rejoinder to Jaffe Ryder's engaged commitment in *The Dharma Bums*.

The novel culminates with a thrashing affair with Billie Dabney, one of Cody's mistresses, and the mother of a precociously inquisitive son. Together with another couple, they drive down to Bixby Canyon planning to remain for a week. But Duluoz, his nerves frayed by wine, is tortured by a series of venomous fantasies bordering on psychosis: Billie is deliberately depleting his spinal powers through sex; the others are communists poisoning his food because he is Catholic. Duluoz, caught in the spinning torments of anxiety, persuades the group to return to San Francisco, and the action ends flatly, followed by the abstraction of the poem to the ocean.

Although *Big Sur* is written with a control and descriptive excitement that is entirely absent from the two novels that followed, *Satori in Paris* and *Vanity of Duluoz*, it registers the difficulty Kerouac was having with writing. The novel is riddled with sentimental references to dead animals—an unconvincing symbolism, and its flatness of expression is an inadequate vehicle for conveying the hysteria and madness which is its subject. However, the book furthers the confessional mode of *The Subterraneans*, and it correctly predicted the sorrow of his last years.

The last novels reveal the strain of fatigued imagination, the fact that the discipline of writing had become almost intolerable. *Satori in Paris*, more an anecdotal sketch than a developed fiction, describes a trip to Paris to discover the genealogy of the Kerouac name. The sense of detail, the memory for the minute and particular that distinguished his best efforts had now faded, and this is especially evident in the labored description of Paris. *Vanity of Duluoz* is even less convincing, suffering from a failure of tone, rhythm, and the cadenced power of his earlier efforts. The novel is a return to the experiences previously described in *The Town and the City*, football

at Columbia, the merchant marine during the war, but retold with
such bland neutrality and patronizing diffidence as to sound **boring**.
Kerouac had always substituted feeling for the ironic mode that
dominated the writing of his era, and that was his strength. But here
his scorn for the changes in American life that he despises is not
rendered with the bitter anguish of *Big Sur*. Writing with regular
punctuation for the "new illiterate generation," he seems unhappy
with his own literary reputation and his affiliation with youth
culture. Vainly, in a letter, he called the book his Mozart shot:
Mozart writing a symphony while creditors bang on the door, his
wife has a baby, and he is coughing his life away. But the
comparison does not stand. The book is proof of Cassady's conten-
tion in *Visions of Cody* that a story can only be told once before an
audience to achieve its fullest effect, that spontaneity is lost in the
retelling.

Kerouac's insights were the releases of a man who knew words so
well that he did not have to pause to shape the flow. His prose,
always devoted to moving some emotion, person, idea, or object
along a descriptive continuum, may be effectively appreciated by
comparison to the work of Jackson Pollock. Their art and aesthetic
are strikingly reciprocal: Kerouac's eulogy of the "Fellaheen" has its
parallel in Pollock's use of the totemic imagery of Mexican and
Amerindian ceremonial masks; Pollock, too, eschewed revision, and
his drip technique was an equivalent of automatic writing; his
concept of unframed space arose from an impulse similar to
Kerouac's desire to tell it all as it occurred. Both men used their
talents as a mode of catharsis, a way to discover hidden recesses of
personality. One might compare the torrential cascades of Kerouac's
prose to Pollock's sweeping brush strokes and surging rhythms.
Pollock used his body as an instrument, bending, pouring, throwing
paint on the floor where his canvas lay; Kerouac, concerned with the
flow of his thought and feeling, created an action painting of the
word. Curiously, there are parallels as well in the lives of both

artists: both were provincials attracted to New York City who loved jazz and alcohol; both searched for a new spontaneity; both personalities were fusions of outward tenderness and inner raging despair; both received enormous publicity too late in their careers and both reacted hypersensitively to the exposure.

Kerouac was always the artist of contradictions: zest for experience and withdrawal, excess and meditation, the pursuit of love and the feeling of betrayal. The balancing factor for him was that his sensibility was essentially devotional. His was virtually the only novelistic voice that could naïvely exult in the life of the spirit in a materialistic era: as he proclaims in *Visions of Cody*, "My heart broke in the general despair and opened up inwards to the Lord." Kerouac continuously recognized the powers of deity and appreciated the examples of Christ and Buddha in a time when intellectuals had agreed that God was dead.

Reading and writing were his sustenance, his solace and joy. He existed primarily for the time he described in *The Subterraneans* "when visions of great words in rhythmic order all in one great archangel book go roaring through my brain." Kerouac's particular genius was a use of sound that created wells of feeling without sentimentality. The sounds he actually heard, the various voices he could imagine, were almost always combined with a perfect touch of antithesis, a balance of tenderness and toughness that rendered feeling with passion. "That crazy feeling in America when the sun is hot on the streets and music comes out of the jukebox or from a nearby funeral" Kerouac wrote, describing the quality of Robert Frank's photographs in *The Americans*, and the line itself is so characteristic of just this dexterity of antithesis, the fact that joy in sound can emanate from dance or from death, the jukebox of popular culture or the coffin that carries us all in the end.

As Norman Mailer once observed, "When you write about something the way Kerouac writes about hipsters, it's never the same afterwards. Instead of the actual thing becoming the model, the writing becomes the model." Ironically, the writer who had popularized the dynamics of hip, who had reveled in Cassady's wild exaltations, turned himself to a more quietistic retreat, advancing far beyond rebellion to reach a more profound understanding of the American psyche. It was this transformation that gave Kerouac his following.

ALLEN GINSBERG
AND
THE MESSIANIC TRADITION

The *only* way out that they generally now prescribe, generally in India at the moment, is through bhakti yoga, which is Faith-Hope-Adoration-Worship, or like probably the equivalent of the Christian Sacred Heart, which I find a very lovely doctrine—that is to say, pure delight, the only way you can be saved is to sing. In other words, the only way to drag up, from the depths of this depression, to drag up your soul to its proper bliss, and understanding, is to give yourself, completely, to your heart's desire. The image will be determined by the heart's compass, by the compass of what the heart moves toward and desires. And then you get on your knees or on your lap or on your head and you sing and chant prayers and mantras, till you reach a state of ecstasy and understanding, and the bliss overflows out of your body. They say intellect, like Saint Thomas Aquinas, will never do it, because it's just like getting all hung up on whether I could remember what happened before I was born—I mean you could get lost there very easily, and it has no relevance *anyway*, to the existent flower. Blake says something similar, like Energy, and Excess . . . leads to the palace of wisdom. The Hindu bhakti is like excess of devotion; you just, you know, give yourself all out to devotion.

—Allen Ginsberg
Paris Review interview

"I would call that man poet," Henry Miller once wrote, "who is capable of profoundly altering the world": "Howl" and "Kaddish" are two examples of a body of poetry that has had a tremendous impact on the values of a generation. Ginsberg has focused his vision on the forces depleting the life spirit of the West. While his inspiration has been apocalyptic, he offers us compelling alternatives to the general disaster he sees.

Allen Ginsberg comes to his readings with an implicit faith in the holiness of personal impulse. There is no holding back, no repression because of time or circumstance, no polite restraint or euphemism. "Go fuck yourself with your atom bomb," he exclaims in a poem called "America"—a line that has excited many audiences while making countless critics cringe. And Ginsberg is feared in America just as Whitman was feared: to believe in democracy is the first step toward making it possible, and such seriousness is dangerous. It has been difficult for some to understand the quality of this seriousness because of the necessity Ginsberg feels to become part of the absurdity he perceives. This was his message when, for example, during his testimony at the Chicago Seven trial he stated that the radicals' purpose had been to transmit joyous feelings of delight despite the horror of the 1968 Democratic political convention and Mayor Daley's army. For Ginsberg, integrating the absurd into the imagination is a process that violates the artist's sense of his own superiority, and leaves him more vulnerable to the wisdom of everyday experience.

Ginsberg's poetry is an expression of the simultaneity of what he has termed an "undifferentiated consciousness." In *Axel's Castle*, Edmund Wilson observed that the energy of poetry had been appropriated by novelists after World War I as writers like Joyce and Virginia Woolf fashioned a prose style of such imagistic intensity and linguistic density as to end all distinctions in English between prose and poetry. These writers, Joyce in particular, created an inner perspective that perceived like the unspeaking mind, that encountered reality through the full play of the senses rather than through the intellect as in omniscient fictions. This unconscious, or at least unarticulated flow that surrounds our being, that constitutes most of what we call sensibility, even as we are but dimly aware of its potential in our daily lives, is the source Ginsberg draws on for his poems.

His original intention as a poet was to achieve an emotional breakthrough of individual, subjective feeling and values as a way of overcoming the Kafkian intimidation of the fifties. Relying on natural speech and spontaneous transcription, Ginsberg sought a nonliterary poetry based on the facts of daily existence. Jazz, abstract painting, Zen and haiku, writers like William Carlos Williams and Kerouac, Apollinaire and Artaud, Lorca and Neruda, were to influence his development of a new measure that corresponded more closely to the body's breath than to the artifice of iambics. The result for Ginsberg, as it had been for Gertrude Stein earlier in the century, was composition as creation, that is, the act of writing itself leading to a pursuit of the unknown rather than to a recovery of the already revealed. As with Burroughs and Kerouac, form would not be predetermined, but would follow the sequence of perception in the course of the writing, even if the route became as irrational, intuitive, and discontinuous as the shape of the mind itself. Syntax, therefore, would not accord with the imposed logic of grammar, but would correspond to the essentially nonsequential flow of the mind. As the mind does not perceive in the orderly arrangement of expository prose, it becomes almost a pretentious fiction to write a poem or a story as if it did.

In an unpublished piece called "A Few Notes On Method," Ginsberg argued that since Imagism, the movement initiated by Pound before World War I, there had been no "crystalization of real grief" in poetry, nor had poets attempted to explore "superhuman" or eternal verities. Imagism, while perfecting the poetic medium, removed from the poem a whole world of subject matter and the kind of "concretion of personal experience" that interested Ginsberg. Influenced by Burroughs' theory of factualism, Ginsberg proposed a juxtaposition of his imaginative interpretation of actual data within a narrative system that eliminated rational connectives. Ginsberg called this "ellipsis," a way of presenting images as they flashed through the mind. It was the equivalent of removing the voice of the omniscient narrator in Burroughs' work, for example. In a letter to Kerouac, Ginsberg described a dream he had about Joan Adams Burroughs which was the occasion of a theory of how the sublime could be invoked and excited in his poems by creating several "image points in time separated by a wide gap showing the distance between them, the jump, or interval, or ellipsis of consciousness actually attaining an inner secret time shock, a sort of mystical eclipse of time." Ginsberg compared his method to Cezanne's theory of *petites sensations* of experience, which his teacher, the art historian Meyer Shapiro, had explained as an attempt to delineate through color, perspective, and brushstroke every detail in the flux of experience, sensation, and time. Ginsberg studied the Cezanne paintings in the Museum of Modern Art while on marijuana, and realized how the painter manipulated space by the alternation of hot and cold colors so that the result was a kind of "space pun," as he told Kerouac, of coexisting planes that would separate mysteriously as the light source was indeterminate and shifting. Ginsberg compared this principle of "spacetimejump" to the telescoping of time in Eliot. Ellipsis applied to both narrative and syntax—the sacrifice of what Ginsberg called "syntactical sawdust," articles, prepositions, and connectives that impeded the flow and did not actually occur in the mind. The result was a richer texture and greater density of language .The prose base of Ginsberg's unusually long line (the length Whitman used to explode all metrical confinements, and which was later sustained in American poetry only by Vachel Lindsay and Robinson Jeffers) is deliberately distorted by condensation or dislocation, a form of compression of basically imagistic notations into surrealistic or cubistic phrasing like the "hydrogen jukeboxes" of "Howl." The key is a rhythmic shift or acceleration like the staccato abruptness of the primitively naïve grammar of "America"—a kind of mock American Indian dialect used ironically—which distinguishes between the flow of a mind's perceptions and less intuitively sponsored flights.

In both his rhythm and his use of the long line, Ginsberg has acknowledged Kerouac's influence, and the following passage from *Visions of Cody*, rearranged as poetry, may indicate what Ginsberg learned:

> I've pressed up girls in Ashville saloons, danced with them
>   in roadhouses where mad heroes stomp one another to death
>   in tragic driveways by the moon:
> I've laid whores on the strip of grass runs along a cornfield
>   outside Durham, North Carolina, and applied bay rum
>   in the highway lights;
> I've thrown empty whiskeybottles clear over the trees in
>   Maryland copses on soft nights when Roosevelt was President;
> I've knocked down fifths in trans-state trucks as the Wyo. road
>   unreeled;
> I've jammed home shots of whiskey on Sixth Avenue, in Frisco,
>   in the Londons of the prime, in Florida, in L.A.
> I've made soup my chaser in forty-seven states;
> I've passed off the back of cabooses, Mexican buses and
>   bows of ships in midwinter tempests (piss to you);
> I've laid women in coalpiles, in the snow, on fences, in beds
>   and up against suburban garage walls from Massachusetts
>   to the tip of San Joaquin.
> Cody me no Codys about America,
> I've drunk with his brother in a thousand bars,
> I've had hangovers with old sewing machine whores that were
>   twice his mother twelve years ago when his heart was dewy.
> I learned how to smoke cigars in madhouses; and hopped boxcars in
>   New Orleans;
> I've driven on Sunday afternoon across the lemon fields with
>   Indians and their sisters;
> and I sat at the inauguration of.
> Tennessee me no Tennessees, Memphis; aim me no Montanas, Three
>   Forks;
> I'll still sock me a North Atlantic Territory in the free.

That's how I feel.
I've heard guitars tinkling sadly across hillbilly hollows
  in the mist of the Great Smokies of night long ago . . . .

The passage suggests a momentum that Ginsberg was to reproduce
and extend in "Howl" several years later, a force that depended on
the personal, the confessional, the excessive and volatile, and a
rhythm that accumulates power through repetition. Kerouac sought
new speech rhythms, the patterns of blacks, rednecks, westerners,
hearing in them a return to the nonliterary origins of an oral
tradition. He also wanted to capture the rapid, excited current of
American speech, and this, too, influenced Ginsberg. Actually, each
writer benefited from the other's freedom, from mutual departures
from conventional approaches to literature—as when Kerouac, in a
letter, advised Ginsberg to change the phrase "startle the fox" to
"star the fox," or when Kerouac sat Ginsberg at his typewriter and
urged him to type whatever came into his mind and accept it as a
poem. It took Ginsberg several years to assimilate such lessons, and
the first realization of Kerouac's mode of composition occurred with
"Howl." In August of 1955, Ginsberg wrote Kerouac to acknowl-
edge his debt:

> The pages I sent you of "Howl" (right title) are the first pages put
> down, as is. I recopied them and sent you the 100% original draft. There
> is no preexistent version. I typed it up as I went along, that's why it's so
> messy. What I have here is all copies cleaned & extended. What you have
> *is* what you want.
> I realize how right you are, that was the first time I sat down to *blow*, it
> came out in *your method*, sounding like you, an imitation practically. How
> far advanced you are on this. I don't know what I'm doing with poetry. I
> need years years of isolation and constant everyday writing to attain your
> volume of freedom & knowledge of the form. . . .

Ginsberg was not always able to sustain the intensity necessary for
Kerouac's spontaneity, and later admitted to Kerouac that even
"Kaddish" needed revision to avoid "wearisome repetition & draggy

self-pity fatigue vagueness." Still, the essential discovery that he could release secrets of memory, free of rational restrictions since consciousness itself was without limitations, was learned from Kerouac who had derived his new rhythms from hearing jazz musicians in places like Minton's in Harlem during the war. But Ginsberg was an adept student: in *Desolation Angels*, while describing a historic visit to William Carlos Williams (then seventy-two), Kerouac compared Ginsberg to Dizzy Gillespie on trumpet because each "comes on in *waves* of thought, not in phrases." The comparison seems all the more prescient in the light of Ginsberg's recent attempts to allow blues to influence his work. The long line offered Ginsberg the necessary dimension to re-create the process of thought which occurs in visual images as well as words, taking the course of endlessly digressive associations and ramifications and confusions for there is no logic to thought (except when arbitrarily applied). As Ginsberg put it in a letter to John Hollander: "I want to get a wild page, as wild and as clear (really clear) as the mind—no forcing the thoughts into straightjacket—sort of a search for the rhythm of the thoughts & their natural occurences & spacings & notational paradigms."

This search for a form to articulate what Kerouac called "the unspeakable visions of the individual" represented a fundamentally new direction for poetry, although Pound began forging that way in *The Cantos*, and other poets like Charles Olson, Robert Creeley, and John Ashbery were on a similar journey. Ginsberg's critics, however, have failed to see the nature and intention of this voyage within. Unfortunately, most academicians are more comfortable with what might be called the confined—as opposed to the open— poem, and so Ginsberg's critics tend to admire the early work in *Empty Mirror* because they can cope with experiences that have recognizable formal contours like the sonnet, the dramatic monologue, or the brief lyric. But Ginsberg will not focus on a situation in the manner of Wallace Stevens or Robert Lowell, poets who will employ such familiar rhetorical devices as ironic contrast to locate a centering point. Instead, he directs his considerable energies to the hundreds of points constituting the perimeter of the experience, and then plunges beyond expansively, illogically, tumultuously encouraging digression just as the mind in the natural flow of its bewilderment does. Ginsberg argued in *Indian Journals* that "We don't think in the dialectical rigid pattern of quatrain or synthetic pattern of sonnet: we think in blocks of sensations & images." As Emerson advised in "The Poet," "It is not metres, but a metre-making argument that makes a poem—a thought so passionate and alive that like the spirit of a plant or an animal it has an architecture of its own, and adorns nature with a new thing."

Thomas Merrill, who wrote a book on Ginsberg for the Twayne American writers series, believes that Ginsberg's poetry is merely a means to an end, a way of delivering apocalyptic prophecy or encouraging religious awakening. Merrill subscribes to Allen Watts' denigrating idea that Ginsberg's poetry is primarily therapy, rather than art. A similar argument might be applied to Wordsworth, to Matthew Arnold's "Dover Beach," to Eliot's "The Waste Land," which was, after all, written in a Swiss sanitarium while Eliot was recovering from a nervous breakdown. Of course, this list might be extended infinitely, but the point is that Watts' distinction between art and therapy is false and misleading. Watts and Merrill seem to suspect Ginsberg all the more, however, because he seeks some integration, some useful resolution of madness, so they claim he is more concerned with healing himself than offering himself (as Edmund Wilson suggested in "The Wound and the Bow") as a totemistic scapegoat for our general illness. Theodore Roszak, in *The Making of a Counter Culture*, offers a similarly uncharitable view of Ginsberg's poetry, finding it "a subsidiary way of publicizing the new consciousness." Roszak gratuitously and foolishly suggests that Ginsberg need only appear at his readings without bothering to read the poetry at all, but simply demonstrating his person to achieve the desired effect. Merrill is forever accusing Ginsberg of "exploiting" this or that device, and finds it difficult to "digest" Ginsberg's excesses. Merrill's strangest proposal is that "Howl" is not an

original departure, that its accomplishments were somehow anticipated by the short lines and imagistic notations of *Empty Mirror*.
Roszak, also, prefers *Empty Mirror* to Ginsberg's later poetry, and so
did John Hollander in his angry review of "Howl." The real
problem for Ginsberg's critics has been that they have been unable
to respond to a living example of Romanticism (besides the fact that
they find his sexual references obscene and distasteful), and so they
have tried to deny him his point of departure.

The reviews of *Howl* document Ginsberg's position in American
letters through the sixties. John Hollander, poet and professor,
writing in a spirit of evident distrust for what he felt was a modish
façade of avant-garde posturing, deplored in *Partisan Review* the
"utter lack of decorum of any kind in his dreadful little volume."
James Dickey, in *Sewanee Review*, established Ginsberg as the very
citadel of modern Babel, and found the poem full of meaningless
utterances. Dickey, at least, had the grace to allow that Ginsberg
was capable of "a confused but believable passion for values." Even
Michael Rumaker, reviewing *Howl* for the *Black Mountain Review*,
certainly a friendly organ, had few words of praise. Rumaker
perversely read Ginsberg according to the expectations of New
Criticism (exactly what Ginsberg was reacting against!) and found
only imprecision everywhere. For Rumaker, the title poem especially was corrupted by "sentimentality, bathos, Buddha and hollow
talk of eternity." The poem was uncontained, its language cumber-
some and hysterical, but its most unforgivable quality was that it
tried to use art to induce spiritual values.

Ginsberg's critics have been completely unresponsive to the oral
tradition in poetry, and even seem to hold his marvelous abilities as a
reader against him—which they never did in the case of Dylan
Thomas. The fact that the eye simply cannot contain the poem on a
page, the expansive scope and surreal leaps of Ginsberg's poetry
have all contributed to preventing the critics from inventing the
necessary categories through which to view his work.

Ginsberg has provided numerous clues to his own method in
several interviews, and in a diary he kept while traveling in India

from March 1962 to May 1963. In *Indian Journals* he includes some revealing notes for a lecture delivered to a Marxist literary conference in Benares that comment on his prosody. His reason for the change from the terse line of *Empty Mirror*, influenced mainly by William Carlos Williams, to the longer line of the subsequent work was an increased depth of perception on a nonverbal and conceptual level. Motivating the change as well was Kerouac's ideal of spontaneity, and the impact of his own visionary experiences. The models for the change were jazz ecstasy, mantra chanting, drug experiences, and Zen meditation. The resulting notation of simultaneous perception was an attempt to "capture the whole mind of the Poet," the process of thought occuring without any censoring factors. Ginsberg's means were the swift "jump of perception from one thing to another," like Olson's composition by field theory, which in Ginsberg's hands was to lead to a surrealistic violation of the old narrative order.

It seems clear that Ginsberg, like Blake, is seeking to purge language of stultifying formalisms. In the pure simplicity of rhythm and diction in *Songs of Innocence*, Blake reacted to the intricate rhetorical and metrical complexity of eighteenth-century verse. He needed a new language because he was to deny the emphasis of his day on the verifiable, the familiar and general, and to devote himself to the numinous mysteries anticipating the Romantic movement, and to the very real social concerns of poems like "London." It was Samuel Johnson who praised the "grandeur of generality," and who sonorously asserted that "nothing can please many and please long, but just representations of general nature." To this smugly congealing view Blake might well have retorted—"To generalize is to be an Idiot. To particularize alone is the Distinction of Merit." Instead of the generality of the commonplace, the regular and expectable (all reflected in the eighteenth-century insistence on heroic couplet as perfect form), Blake studied hermetic medieval manuscripts, and read Thomas Taylor's translations of the Gnostic texts (which Coleridge and Shelley later read, and which Bronson Alcott brought to Emerson). Blake, also, began the romantic reaction against reason and deductions resulting from observations of the senses. Such deductions, as Yeats was later to argue in *Ideas of Good and Evil*, only bind men to mortality as the senses become the exclusive means of perceiving the world; reliance on the senses, Yeats added, would also divide men from each other by revealing their clashing interests. Blake preferred relying on the imagination, Yeats asserted, because it bound men together by "opening the secret doors of all hearts."

Ginsberg's most significant relationship to Blake has been ideological—a sympathy with social concerns, a desire to transform consciousness, to use poetry as an instrument of power or as sacramental invocation. Ginsberg also shares Blake's attitude to the child in man: "Better murder an infant in its cradle than nurse unwanted desires," Blake wrote, and behind the extravagance of the remark is the idea that maturity implies the abandonment of natural spontaneity. Since Freud, we have been taught that the condition of the child is suspect and fallen. But Blake believed that man had lost the intuitive harmonies inherent in childhood. So if for modern Freudians infantile childishness is a term of condemnation, for Blake the child's delight in his surroundings, his curious whimsy, were exactly the attributes that prepared for mature judgment.

In technique, Ginsberg has maintained his link to Blake in various ways: through his musical settings of Blake's *Songs of Innocence and Experience*, and the imitations in *Gates of Wrath*, a collection of very early and uneven work. In "September On Jessore Road," the last poem in *The Fall Of America*, Ginsberg employs Blake's early metrical devices with great exactness. An even more pervasive influence is felt in poems like "The Lion For Real" or "Sunflower Sutra."

The latter poem is an elegy of glorious optimism for a dead sunflower, a refutation of its "corolla of bleary spikes pushed down and broken like a battered crown" among the "gnarled steel roots of machinery" on a railroad dock overlooking the San Francisco Bay. Blake's sunflower, too, represented mutability, the transience of the living and the inevitability of death. But Ginsberg, in a letter to

Kerouac, described the sunflower he saw as the flower of industry, tough-spiked and ugly, "the flower of the world, worn, brittle, dry yellow—miracle of gravel life spring (ing to) the bud." Experimenting with rhythmic buildup without relying on a repetitive base (like the use of the pronoun *who* in "Howl") to sustain its powerfully increasing tempo, Ginsberg offers us a paean to the life-force within the heart of the wasteland, the sordid details of junk, treadless tires, used condoms, and abandoned tin cans and industrial grime, enveloping the dessicated sunflower in which Ginsberg chooses to believe, vigorously asserting his belief by seizing the skeleton stalk and holding it at his side like a scepter:

> —We're not our skin of grime, we're not our dread bleak dusty imageless locomotive, we're all beautiful golden sunflowers inside, we're blessed by our own seed & golden hairy naked accomplishment-bodies growing into mad black formal sunflowers in the sunset, spied on by our eyes under the shadow of the mad locomotive riverbank sunset Frisco hilly tincan evening sitdown vision.

The verse paragraph ending "Sunflower Sutra" recalls Walt Whitman, another seminal influence on Ginsberg, and a key figure in the visionary tradition. Malcolm Cowley has observed Whitman's close resemblance in *Leaves of Grass* to works which he could not have or probably did not read like the *Bhagavad-Gita* or *The Upanishads*. Cowley claimed that Whitman's sources were internal, the larger consciousness in which he participated being occasioned by a mystical experience that Dr. Richard Maurice Bucke—one of Whitman's disciples and author of a book called *Cosmic Consciousness*—dates around 1853–54. Whitman's experience, like Ginsberg's with Blake, resulted in an ecstatic sense of ineffable joy, a knowledge of the unity of the universe, of the bonds existing between men and all living things. In Whitman's poetry, these feelings emerged as an unprecedented celebration of his fellow men, an effusive outpouring of pity, affectionate sympathy, and love so genuinely sincere that it could only be called sentimental by cynics.

"In me the caresser of life wherever moving," Whitman wrote in "Song of Myself"; "to me all the converging objects of the universe perpetually flow." The close connection between Whitman and Ginsberg may be measured by Whitman's expectation of the poet, as he characterized it in the preface to *Leaves of Grass*—a document which along with Emerson's essay "The Poet" constitutes the first signs of a native American poetic, standing among the most significant utterances on the poetic process in any era. As the poet sees the farthest, Whitman argues, "he has the most faith. His thoughts are the hymns of the praise of things." In the following statement, Whitman could almost be predicting Ginsberg's future appearance:

> This is what you shall do: Love the earth and sun and animals, despise riches, give alms to every one that asks, stand up for the stupid and crazy, devote your income and labor to others, hate tyrants, argue not concerning God, have patience and indulgence toward the people, take off your hat to nothing known or unknown or to any man or number of men, go freely with powerful uneducated persons and with the mothers of families, read these leaves in the open air every season of every year of your life, re-examine all you have been told at school or church or in any book, dismiss whatever insults your own soul, and your very flesh shall be a great poem and have the richest fluency not only in its words but in the silent lines of its lips and face and between the lashes of your eyes and in every motion and joint of your body.

Whitman goes on to address himself to what Bucke called cosmic consciousness: "From the eyesight proceeds another eyesight and from the hearing proceeds another hearing and from the voice proceeds another voice eternally curious of the harmony of things with man." Whitman declared that this inspiration of the inner eye would lead to a new order of poets who would replace religion. This new poet, now "priest of man," would "not deign to defend immortality or God or the perfection of things or liberty or the exquisite beauty and reality of the soul. They shall arise in America and be responded to from the remainder of the earth."

A number of American writers have struggled with Whitman's example. William Carlos Williams recognized him as the poet who "broke through the deadness of copied forms which keep shouting above everything that wants to get said today drowning out one man with the accumulated weight of a thousand tyrannies of the past, the very tyrannies we are seeking to diminish. The structure of the old is active, it says no! to everything in propaganda and poetry that wants to say yes. Whitman broke through that. That was very basic and good." But this Emersonian view of the writer was not shared by many modern American authors. Henry James later regretted his criticism of Whitman's Civil War book, *Drumtaps*, and atoned by reciting Whitman's poetry to friends visiting him at Lamb House in Rye. Pound wrote several attacks on Whitman, the most notorious of which appeared in an essay on Villon where he complained of "the horrible air of rectitude with which Whitman rejoices in being Whitman," and claimed that Whitman pretended to be "conferring a philanthropic benefit on the race by recording his own self-complacency." Pound's rage was at something he sought to release in himself, without quite knowing how. In "A Pact" he offered amends:

> I am old enough now to make friends.
> It was you that broke the new wood,
> Now is a time for carving.
> We have one sap and one root—
> Let there be commerce between us.

Whitman smashed the containing forms of nineteenth-century metrical structure in the manner that Blake began to in the *Prophetic Books*. Whitman composed, properly speaking, with no logical structure, creating, as Cowley suggested, the equivalent of an oneiric, waking dream. The wavelike flow of his music was like a rhapsodic tone poem, as he released prolonged bursts of inspiration. His expansive amplitude became a kind of euphoria, a way in which, as Waldo Frank once put it in *Our America*, "We go forth all to seek

America. And in the seeking we create her." This, in particular, is Allen Ginsberg's point of departure as a poet.

Ginsberg has acknowledged the formative influence for him of Whitman's concept of "adhesiveness," his feeling of kinship with all classes and kinds of people. "Who need be afraid of the merge?" Whitman proclaimed in "Song of Myself" as he lists the thief, the venereally diseased prostitute, the slave, the workingman, and the businessman in his egalitarian audience. This must have been one of the generous qualities of heart that appealed to Emerson, and which caused his famous praise of *Leaves of Grass*, for the sage of Concord himself had announced in "The American Scholar" essay that "I embrace the common. I explore and sit at the feet of the familiar, the low." It was inevitable that once such sentiments were to be taken seriously by our poets, a new and broader concept of what constituted the poetic vernacular would develop. To be sure, the idiom of the common man was the language that Wordsworth intended to recreate, but never really managed. "Language is fossil poetry," Emerson jubilantly offered in one of his disassociated exclamations in "The Poet," but no nineteenth-century ear was tuned to such a key. Even Whitman's language was often too rotund and inflated, not quite as pretty as Tennyson's or Swinburne's, but also not fully in touch with the rhythms of the ordinary ear. And Whitman, in his later years in Camden, New Jersey, became less and less receptive to the familial harmonies of familiar tongues and the louder vitalities of street speech. It was another New Jersey poet, William Carlos Williams, who discovered how to hear, as Ginsberg once put it, with "raw ears."

Blake, Whitman, and Williams are the figures who have most inspired Ginsberg, but an equally significant, if less finitely measurable, source has been Surrealist poetry and painting. Blake permitted entry into the prophetic tradition; Whitman offered the infusion of democratic optimism; Williams inspired a new diction; but Surrealism suggested the state of mind that proved liberating enough for Ginsberg to see the political realities of his day with passionate clarity.

In a poem called "At Apollinaire's Grave," Ginsberg was to voice his appreciation for the insights learned from the French Surrealist poets:

> I've eaten the blue carrots you sent out of the grave and Van
> Gogh's ear and maniac peyote of Artaud
> And will walk down the streets of New York in the black cloak of
> French poetry
> Improvising our conversation in Paris at Père Lachaise
> and the future poem that takes its inspiration from the light
> bleeding into your grave

Surrealism was very much a part of the *Zeitgeist* surrounding Ginsberg in his youth. During the war, a number of the key Surrealist painters had settled in America, and by 1942 Ernst, Masson, and Tanguy were living in New York City, as well as André Breton, one of the theoreticians of the movement. Breton's belief that subconscious irrationality could provide the basis for a positive social program separated the Surrealists from the Dadaists, their more nihilistic forebears. Breton's manifestoes contain arguments that anticipate the inner flow of experience Ginsberg was to express so powerfully in his poetry. Breton sought a "monologue spoken as rapidly as possible without any interruption on the part of the cerebral faculties, a monologue consequently unencumbered by the slightest inhibition and which was as closely as possible akin to spoken thought." This "psychic automatism" proposed to express the mind's actual functioning in the absence of controls like reason, or any superimposed moral or aesthetic concern. If Ginsberg was to remain in touch with Blake's tradition of magic prophecy, he would have to find ways to release that vision without unnecessarily tampering, interfering, or distorting, and the Surrealist bias against revision that Kerouac maintained prevented the danger of any fatal loss of impetus.

The Surrealists in France had distinguished between literature as a craft or talent exercised within certain traditional and prescriptive formal limitations and poetry as a mode of visionary discovery. To induce revelation, they pursued their dreams, finding in them a route to the unconscious, and a way of capturing the uncensored maturity of Rimbaud's child-man. Like Blake's idealization of the child, the Surrealists sought a model for wonder, spontaneity, and destructiveness—which, by the way, they interpreted as the end of adult self-control and obedience to conditioning. So Breton began attending with fascination to phrases running through his mind as he fell asleep, just as Williams in *Kora In Hell* was to improvise disconnected passages composed just prior to sleep. Related to such experiments was the Surrealists' interest in Charcot's *Studies In Hysteria* and Robert Desnos' self-induced trances. As Alfred Jarry urged, true hallucination is the sustained waking dream, and this becomes the premise of much of Ginsberg's poetry as he applies the phantasmagoria of dream to everyday reality. As Breton formulated it in his *Second Manifesto*:

> Surrealism aims quite simply at the total recovery of our psychic force by a means which is nothing other than the dizzying descent into ourselves, the systematic illumination of hidden places and the progressive darkening of other places, the perpetual excursion into the midst of forbidden territory. . . .

It is quite clear that this consciousness was present in Ginsberg's earliest poems. In "Psalm I," the second poem in *Empty Mirror*, Ginsberg refers to his poems as the product of a "vision haunted mind," and writes of "majestic flaws of mind which have left my brain open to hallucination." In the initial poem of the volume, the marvelously understated "I feel as if I were at a dead end," Ginsberg describes a state of psychic and moral impotence whose metaphor is the head severed from the body. This impotence expresses itself as a terrible inability to act in the face of a paralyzing absurdity which stalks through the poems; hallucination, visionary messages from the unconscious, serve to fuse head and body, to reconnect intellect and feeling. A number of the best poems in the collection are called dreams, like the Kafkian "A Meaningless Institution" where Ginsberg invents an enormous ward filled with "hundreds of weeping/ decaying men and women." Everyone in the poem is impassive; everything in it is static; there is no interrelationship anywhere—and in the end the observer wanders futilely "down empty corridors/ in search of a toilet." The view of the world implied by such a poem is dismal, a miasma of quiescent disappointment and stagnant despair, a pervasive mood in the book appearing with special poignance in "Sunset," "A Ghost May Come," "A Desolation," "The Blue Angel," and "Walking Home At Night." These poems reflect terrible entrapment in mechanical situations revealing men devoid of humanity, like those "cowering in unshaven rooms in underwear" in "Howl." Occasionally, the depression is alleviated by childish rage, as in one of the best poems in *Empty Mirror*, "In Society":

> I walked into the cocktail party
> room and found three or four queers
> talking together in queertalk.
> I tried to be friendly but heard
> myself talking to one in hiptalk.
> "I'm glad to see you," he said, and
> looked away. "Hmn," I mused. The room
> was small and had a double-decker
> bed in it, and cooking apparatus:
> icebox, cabinet, toasters, stove;
> the hosts seemed to live with room
> enough for only cooking and sleeping.
> My remark on this score was under-
> stood but not appreciated. I was
> offered refreshments, which I accepted.
> I ate a sandwich of pure meat; an
> enormous sandwich of human flesh,
> I noticed, while I was chewing on it,
> it also included a dirty asshole.

More company came, including a
fluffy female who looked like
a princess. She glared at me and
said immediately: "I don't like you,"
turned her head away, and refused
to be introduced. I said, "What!"
in outrage. "Why you shit-faced fool!"
This got everybody's attention.
"Why you narcissistic bitch! How
can you decide when you don't even
know me," I continued in a violent
and messianic voice, inspired at
last, dominating the whole room.

The periodic ending of the poem is a Kafkian delusion, like Joseph K
criticizing court practices in *The Trial* only to learn later that he had
been haranguing his judges instead of visitors to the court. The
aggressively explosive tirade of "Why you shit-faced fool!" is the
culmination of a series of four utterly absurdist enclosures like the
room without room to live, all beautifully emphasized by the short,
abruptly declarative lines. Behind the subject of the poem is
Ginsberg's discomfort with his own homosexuality, and its most
compelling image is the sandwich of human flesh containing the
dirty asshole. Like the talking asshole in Burroughs' *Naked Lunch*,
Ginsberg's image provides an apt illustration of what Lautreamont
thought of as systematic bewildering—the beauty of the "fortuitous
meeting of a sewing machine and an umbrella on an operating
table." The image of the dirty asshole returns the reader to the
uneasiness with the homosexual condition that the poem dramatizes, starting with the shift from queertalk to hiptalk. Calling the
fluffy female "shit-faced" creates a continuity of image, just as the
emphasis on the hosts' kitchen and cooking apparatus prepares the
reader for the dirty asshole. While the continuity from eating food to
defecating on those about you does unify the poem, it is by no means
an apparent motif, and the categories of kitchen, asshole, and
"shit-faced fool" exist like realities on different planes. The asshole

image can be taken as an example of what Breton called incandescent flashes linking those different elements of reality together with a vital metaphor, even though those elements seem so far removed that reason alone could never connect them. The impact of the poem, the depth of the anxiety betrayed by its central image, defies a realistic mode. The poem, culminating as it does with a view of messianic anger "dominating the whole room," shares the qualities of self-revelation and honest exposure associated with Robert Lowell's *Life Studies*. As Ginsberg has written in a poem "On Burroughs' Work":

> A naked lunch is natural to us,
>   we eat reality sandwiches.
> But allegories are so much lettuce.
> Don't hide the madness.

A similar strength occurs in a number of the poems in *Empty Mirror*—little wonder that Ginsberg's critics like the volume—especially in "A Crazy Spiritual," another one of the dream poems that anticipates the bizarrely driving absurdity and fulminating ironies of the songs on Bob Dylan's *Bringing It All Back Home* album ("Maggie's Farm" and "Bob Dylan's 115th Dream" in particular).

The poems in *Empty Mirror* employ short lines predominantly, stripping "yakking down to modern bones" Ginsberg wrote to Cassady, and at one point Ginsberg expresses metaphorical dissatisfaction with Yeatsian terseness:

> I attempted to concentrate
> the total sun's rays in
> each poem as through a glass,
> but such magnification
> did not set the page afire.

He begins to move in the direction of his long-line experiments in "Hymn," a series of five verse paragraphs (animated by such antiprose and surreal formulations as "clock of meat"), or

"Paterson," a poem no one seems to have noticed even though it anticipates the rhythmic power of the later poetry as well as the thematic rejection of American materialism. Rather than live in rooms "papered with visions of money," rather than cut his hair, dress properly, bathe, and work steadily for the "dead prick of commonplace obsession," the hero of "Paterson," a Beat code figure, would choose madness:

> . . . gone down the dark road to
>   Mexico, heroin dripping in my veins,
> eyes and ears full of marijuana,
> eating the god Peyote on the floor of a mudhut on the
>   border
> or laying in a hotel room over the body of some suffering
>   man or woman;

The hero prefers to "jar" his "body down the road" of dissipation rather than conform to the conventions of the everyday, and he lists a series of ecstatic excesses, culminating in a screaming dance of praise to an eternity that annihilates reality as in a Dionysian frenzy he impales himself in nature, "leaving my flesh and bones hanging on the trees." "Paterson" is a psychological fulcrum for Ginsberg's early poetry, charging the sense of heavy doldrum and ennui, the sentimentality of his earliest Columbia College verse, with a quality of scatological hysteria he may have learned from Céline. Actually, in a review of Céline's *Death On The Installment Plan* that Ginsberg wrote in his last year at Columbia, he recognized the persona he was later to assume in "Paterson":

> The mad author has taken the weird mask of an aggressive character, self-sufficient, skeptical, sentimental, self-disgusted, self-protecting, all because he is convinced of the dangerousness of modern life, and has passed it [the mask] off as a natural, "just" development of mind.

"Paterson" is a poem of excess, an early sign of Ginsberg's surrealism. Breton noted that surrealism acts on the mind very much like drugs, creating a need for the mysterious effects and special pleasures of an artificial paradise, but at the same time pushing men to frightful revolts as that paradise seems unattainable. Like opium-induced images, surrealistic images seem to occur spontaneously, or despotically as Baudelaire once claimed, ringing with unpremeditated juxtaposition. Apollinaire, in *Le poète assassiné*, glorified physical disequilibrium as divine, and Rimbaud, earlier, had called for a violent derangement of the senses.

Ginsberg has heeded this imperative, risking his sensibility to widen the area of his consciousness with drugs. As Coleridge claimed to have composed "Kubla Khan" during an opium reverie, Ginsberg has admitted to writing a number of poems while using marijuana or the stronger hallucinogens like peyote, LSD-25, mescaline, and ayahuasca (yage, the drug for which Burroughs traveled to South America to find the "final fix"). The experiences described in these poems, often titled by the name of the drug employed, are very similar to the effects in Burroughs' fiction: déjà vu, death hysteria, extreme paranoia, disembodied awareness of a decomposing body, demonic mind-monsters, loss of identity as in "The Reply" where the "universe turns inside out to devour me," and only occasionally a sense of ecstatic, spiraling energy. The greatest concentration of drug poems is in *Kaddish*, but they are clearly the weakest part of the volume. Oddly enough, Ginsberg is unable to suggest a convincing state of transport in these poems, and they seem grounded compared to a natural high like the one Emerson described in his first essay, "Nature":

> Standing on the bare ground—my head bathed by the blithe air and uplifted into infinite space—all mean egotism vanishes. I become a transparent eyeball; I am nothing; I see all; the currents of the Universal Being circulate through me; I am part or parcel of God.

Ironically, in the *Kaddish* drug poems, just where a reader might expect a sacrifice of intellect and a total involvement with the senses, the intrusion of the poet's questioning mind misdirects the tensions.

Ginsberg seems almost aware of this, as when in "Aether" he mentions "the threat to magic by writing while high." "Aether," the last poem in *Reality Sandwiches*, comes closest to fulfilling Ginsberg's ideal of the poem as notation of undifferentiated consciousness (drugs theoretically assisting in such an effort by deemphasizing mind), a quality felt in the poem's movement toward new line arrangements and visual impact.

Over the years, Ginsberg has defended the legalization of marijuana and spoken of his experiences with hallucinogens without proselytizing for them. He regards these drugs as the American and South American Indians have traditionally used them, as potent medicines with ritual significance. When he advocates their use, it is less for pleasure than for the sake of increased consciousness—the necessity of transcending normative behavior, "getting out of one's head" so as to view ordinary realities from an entirely different perspective. On June 14, 1966, Ginsberg testified before a special Senate subcommittee on his own drug experiences. He stated that drugs had helped him overcome stereotypes of habit by releasing inner and latent resources of feeling for other human beings, especially women, and for nature, that had been stymied and almost conditioned out of existence by the mechanization of modern culture with its emphasis on muting the senses, reducing language and thought to uniform patterns, slogans without character, monopolizing attention with packaged news and stale imagery that failed to satisfy his own need for communication. The psychedelics in particular, Ginsberg advised, had helped end the atmosphere of fear and repression induced by Cold War politics, causing a breakthrough to common sympathy:

> Now so many people have experienced some new sense of openness, and lessening of prejudice and hostility to new experience through LSD, that I think we may expect the new generation to push for an environment less rigid, mechanical, less dominated by cold-war habits. A new kind of light has rayed through our society—despite all the anxiety it has caused— maybe these hearings are a manifestation of that slightly changed

awareness. I would not have thought it possible to speak like this a year ago. That we are more open to hear each other is the new consciousness itself.

Although for some hallucinogens telescope madness, they can prove—for those able to handle the situation, Ginsberg warns—therapeutically restoring. Ginsberg himself has not always been able to contain his drug experiences, and on his trip to India in 1962 he reached an apex with morphine injections and opium that produced a recurrence of the death-terror he felt in 1948 when he tried to deliberately induce the spirit of Blake. Generally, Ginsberg has used drugs as an aid to releasing blocked aspects of his consciousness which are expressed in his poetry, like the Moloch vision in "Howl" which was induced by peyote, or "Kaddish," written while using amphetamines.

"Kaddish" is an elegy to the suffering madness of Ginsberg's mother, Naomi. It testifies to Ginsberg's capacity for involvement with another human in torment, for the acceptance of another's weirdness. While successfully capturing the historical ambiance of the thirties—socialist idealism, communist factionalism, martyrdom, and the reflexive paranoia of fascism—the poem is most memorable as a torrential and cathartic release of Ginsberg's complex relationship to his mad mother, at times compassionately tender, full of sweet regrets and losses, at times full of the frustration, rage, and anger that poor Naomi, locked into her tormented self, provoked. The racing, breathless pace of the poem reflects its manner of composition—the stimulation of morphine mixed with meta-amphetamine (then new to Ginsberg, and a conflicting combination as well since morphine slows time while amphetamine speeds it up) as Ginsberg sat at his desk from six in the morning and wrote until ten the following night, leaving the poem only for coffee, the bathroom, and several doses of Dexedrine. While the poem was written in a very brief period of time, Ginsberg had been thinking and writing about the subject for years—as early as

1957, in a letter from France, he told his father that he was working on a requiem for Naomi. Ginsberg's intention was to purge his consciousness of his "whole secret family-self tale—my own one-and-only eternal child-youth memories which no one else could know," as he claimed in "How Kaddish Happened."

The narrative, part purgation, part reconciliation and acceptance, relates a story that contains more sheer feeling than any poem of its time: Naomi was a Russian Jewess raised on the Lower East Side, who became a teacher of retarded children ("morons with dreamy lips"). After marrying Louis Ginsberg, poet and teacher, she became involved in socialist and communist circles:

> with the YPSL's hitch-hiking through Pennsylvania, in black baggy
> gym skirts pants, photograph of 4 girls holding each other
> round the waste, and laughing eye, too coy, virginal
> solitude of 1920

Such details are interwoven with the story of how Allen, at the age of twelve, elected to accompany his mother on a six-hour trip from Paterson to the Greyhound bus depot on Times Square to a rest home in Lakewood, New Jersey, while she was in the process of a nervous breakdown. The lyrical poignance of the memories of Naomi's past, her physical beauty, her mandolin, the left-wing summer camps and songs of revolution are juxtaposed with the sordid presence of her horrible suspicions—that her mother-in-law is trying to poison her, that Roosevelt himself has wired her room to spy on her. Naomi's anguished hysteria—demanding blood transfusions, demanding assistance from strangers on the street, demanding release from asylums—combined with the reach of Ginsberg's grief (assuming a less strident, more mournful tone in accord with the Hebrew prayer for the dead from which he quotes), allows the poem an almost unbearable threshold of pain. Naomi's intensity is like Medea's, a quality that made Ginsberg's adaptation of his poem for the stage unforgettable as theater.

The poem suggests a vast range of feelings by constantly propos-
ing such shocking contrasts as the fifteen-year-old Allen lying in bed
with his mother just after she has returned from a three-year stay in
a New Jersey mental institution, proffering and imploring love, and
a few lines later:

> One night, sudden attack—her noise in the bathroom—
> like croaking up her soul—convulsions and red vomit coming
> out of her mouth—diarrhea water exploding from her behind—
> on all fours in front of the toilet—urine running between
> her legs—left retching on the tile floor smeared with her black
> feces—unfainted—
> At forty, varicosed, nude, fat, doomed, hiding outside the
> apartment door near the elevator calling Police, yelling for her
> girl-friend Rose to help—

The contrasts proliferate throughout the poem with details like
Naomi's insulin, Metrasol, electric-shock, lobotomy treatments, and
her insistence, when living with her sister Eleanor in the Bronx after
separating from Louis that, "I will think nothing but beautiful
thoughts." And after the joy of her struggles to regain a semblance of
sanity, working for a doctor, taking painting lessons, relating to
Allen a dream of feeding God a Jewish meal, the final vision of
Naomi utterly broken, again in the sanitarium:

> Too thin, shrunk on her bones—age come to Naomi—
> now broken, into white hair—loose dress on her skeleton—
> face sunk, old! withered—cheek of crone—
> One hand stiff—heavyness of forties & menopause
> reduced by one heart stroke, lame now—wrinkles—a scar on
> her head, the lobotomy—ruin, the hand dipping downwards to
> death—

The language of the poem comes closer to prose syntax than most of
Ginsberg's work, but the lines often become fragmentary and

discontinuous, suggesting that certain perceptions are too intolerable to be fully developed. Ginsberg has commented on his own unease in wrestling with form through such long notations, but the result is another new direction for poetry. "Make it new," Pound said; "Invention," Williams declared—and "Kaddish" is a major formal departure from our expectation of what poetry should look like on the page, just as thematically the elegy departs from tradition by refusing eulogy, developing a heroic resistance by revealing Naomi's negative qualities. The moods of the poem vary widely from imprecation and curse to sympathy and physical desire (at one point, Naomi makes sexual advances to her son while dancing before a mirror), and ultimately, at the end of the poem, a ghostly disassociation as Naomi fails to recognize Allen on his last visit to her. And even that mood changes as he receives her letter of prophetic instruction just before hearing of her death: "The key is in the window, the key is in the sunlight in the window—I have the key—Get married Allen, don't take drugs—the key is in the sunlight in the window." The letter, which Ginsberg rewrote himself, revives the spirit of millenarian optimism that Naomi epitomizes throughout the poem, a pathetically disoriented yet actively striving figure.

The four final sections, each very short, relieve and disperse some of the intensities developed in the narrative, as if the momentum could not be suddenly released, but needed to be gently assuaged. The "caw caw caw" section, for example, soothes like a resolving fugue with its two parts, one representing the realistic bleakness of materialism and pain, the second a source of mystical aspiration, both harmonized by the last line with its collocation of "Lord" and "caw." Even these last sections, however, contain signs of the poem's tremendously successful excessiveness, especially a litany which brutally and without explanations lists the horrible shocks of Naomi's life.

Judging from their correspondence, the poem had a complex affect on Louis Ginsberg. While he found it on the whole "heart-wrenching" and "magnificent," he was disturbed by the implicit sexuality of the poem, finding his son's references to homosexuality, incestuous yearnings, and the allusion to Louis' affair with another woman embarrassing. He felt his son was reaching for a sensationalism that was irrelevant to the poem's literary merit, and he specifically requested the deletion of the "long black beard around the vagina" as vulgarly obscene. It was a classic illustration of generational difference. In the margin of his father's letter, Allen wrote a large NO! in red, and then answered in a separate letter:

> The line about the "beard around the vagina" is probably a sort of very common experience and image that children have who see their parents naked and it is an archtypal experience and nothing to be ashamed of—it looks from the outside, objectively, probably much less shocking than it appears to you. I think it's a universal experience which almost everyone has had though not many poets have referred to it.

The original draft of the poem, as Ginsberg told Kerouac, was changed significantly. Lawrence Ferlinghetti advised the elimination of several repetitions, urging Ginsberg to seek greater density and concentration while clarifying his narrative sequence. Ginsberg responded to these suggestions rather than to his father's more personal requests.

The overall effect of the final version of "Kaddish" is unlike that of any other modern poem, even "Howl." The reader is left in a state of utter exhaustion, the feeling one often has after a particularly harrowing dream. The aesthetic paradox of "Kaddish" is that despite all its terror and the shockingly relentless and obsessive manner in which Ginsberg pursues his mother's haunted memory, the result is a poetry of the sublime, the rare kind of exalted rejoicing in being that occurs in the poetry of Christopher Smart, in Richard Crashaw's description of his love for God, or Francis Thompson's "The Hound of Heaven."

The crucial question for any poet capable of creating poems like "Howl" or "Kaddish" is whether that imaginative energy can be sustained. There are those who have wondered whether Ginsberg is the agent or the vessel of his poetic inspiration, whether he is the author of his poems or whether, like Burroughs, he may be the telepathic register of some otherly source. In this connection, it is useful to remember that the poets we most admire in any age manage to leave us with only a few major poems: indeed, it would be difficult to measure the greatness of the best of Dryden, Pope, Wordsworth, Coleridge, Browning, or Tennyson without the light of their total efforts. *Empty Mirror, Howl*, and *Kaddish* are all exceptional volumes, but the beginning, not the high point, of a continuing productivity, a steady stream of poems that achieve different kinds of power and insight.

The collection after *Kaddish* was *Reality Sandwiches*, and except for "Siesta in Xbalba" (written in 1954, one year before "Howl," and Ginsberg's first major formal innovation) and "Love Poem on Theme By Whitman," it was definitely less effective than any previous book, and as such caused suspicions that Ginsberg's talents had been depleted by his other activities. A poem like "Sather Gate Illumination" stands for the weaknesses of the book. The poem is about self-worth as a function of love, "broken minds in beautiful bodies unable to receive love because not knowing the self as lovely." Although like "Sunflower Sutra" the subject is as central to Ginsberg's poetry as to Whitman's, the poem lacks imaginative tensions, and its relaxation is reflected in lines that approach prose without the surreal jumps and syntactical excitements animating Ginsberg's usual flow. Near the beginning of the poem, as Ginsberg walks through the Berkeley campus, a crippled French teacher is explaining some grammatical point to her class:

> Regarder is to look—
> the whole French language looks on the trees on the campus.

There is a certain intrusive and staged obviousness about using French, the traditional language of love, and a teacher who stresses the act of looking in a poem that observes instances of failed love. Making that teacher a cripple and a woman who later saunters through the poem's center "with loping fuck gestures of her hips askew" creates a rhetoric of construction that is just too apparent in a poem that encourages love of body despite external defects. The result is obviousness rather than directness, the single dimension of allegorical lettuce. The poem becomes too dogmatic in its very structure, too insistent on a generous theme that needed more deftness, delicacy, and freedom than Ginsberg could manage at the moment.

These very qualities are all present in "Love Poem on Theme By Whitman," a poem that improvises on lines in one of Whitman's more mysterious poems, "The Sleepers."

I'll go into the bedroom silently and lie down between the
    bridegroom and the bride,
those bodies fallen from heaven stretched out waiting naked and
    restless,
arms resting over their eyes in the darkness,
bury my face in their shoulders and breasts, breathing their skin
and stroke and kiss neck and mouth and make back be open
    and known,
legs raised up crook'd to receive, cock in the darkness driven
    tormented and attacking
roused up from hole to itching head,
bodies locked shuddering naked, hot lips and buttocks screwed
    into each other
and eyes, eyes glinting and charming, widening into looks and
    abandon,
and moans of movement, voices, hands in air, hands between
    thighs,
hands in moisture on softened hips, throbbing contraction of
    bellies
till the white come flow in the swirling sheets,
and the bride cry for forgiveness, and the groom be covered with
    tears of passion and compassion,

and I rise up from the bed replenished with last intimate gestures
    and kisses of farewell—
all before the mind wakes, behind shades and closed doors in a
    darkened house
where the inhabitants roam unsatisfied in the night,
nude ghosts seeking each other out in the silence.

Early in "Song of Myself" Whitman imagines God as a loving bedfellow, the "noble bridegroom" of religious love poetry whose nocturnal visit causes the poet to "scream at my eyes" in the plenitude of received energy. Several times in "Song of Myself" Whitman alludes to the bride and her groom; once he turns the groom out of bed to "tighten" with the bride all night. Among those whom Whitman visits in "The Sleepers" is a calmly reclining married couple, each with a palm on the other's hip. In an image embodying Emerson's concept of the "oversoul," Whitman dreams "all the dreams of the other dreamers" and becomes the other dreamers. Ginsberg begins at this point of intense identification (a contemporary "caresser of life"), breathing into his lovers, actually Neal and Carolyn Cassady, the divinely creative power of sexual energy that is expressed as a rhythmic whirlwind of physical passion and ecstatic release, a paean of one long and continuous line that so brilliantly renews the excitement and beauty that Whitman conveys, and whose rhythms simulate as well the overtures, passion, and climax of actual intercourse. While the poem's fierce rotation is about the body's axis, there is none of Iago's "beast with two backs" view of bestial lust in love; we are left uplifted by the poem, perhaps because of the skillful manner in which Ginsberg mixes tender images like "moans of movement" and "moisture on softened lips" with his lovers' contracting, pounding bodies.

    Ginsberg has commented on the tradition he sought to continue in "Love Poem on Theme By Whitman" in, of all places, his testimony before Judge Hoffman at the Chicago Seven trial. Ginsberg, along with Burroughs and Jean Genêt, had attended the Democratic presidential convention in Chicago in the summer of

1968. As journalists, they were allowed entry to the convention area
where they witnessed the excessively rigorous security precautions
and controls, even extended to the delegates themselves, which
created a suffocating and regimented atmosphere hardly conducive
to political process. Ginsberg spent most of his time outside the
convention hall in support of the vociferous and militant group of
young dissenters who were protesting the fiasco inside. Terror and
latent violence suffused the air as the threats of tear gas and more
aggressive police measures were realized in vicious attacks. Ginsberg
exerted an enormously calming presence, chanting mantras to
relieve tensions, meditating and counseling in the midst of the
turmoil and uncertainty. At the trial, however, prosecutor Foran
hounded him for his views on sex with all the vulgar zeal of lawyer
Carson grilling Oscar Wilde on *The Picture of Dorian Gray*. Ginsberg's reply to Foran's rude query on the religious significance of the
poem is a definition of what Whitman meant by "adhesiveness," as
well as an explanation of his own frequently candid use of sexuality:

> Whitman said that unless there were an infusion of feeling, of tenderness,
> of fearlessness, of spirituality, of natural sexuality, of natural delight in
> each other's bodies, into the hardened materialistic, cynical, life denying,
> clearly competitive, afraid, scared, armored bodies, there would be no
> chance for spiritual democracy to take root in America—and he defined
> that tenderness between the citizens as, in his words, an "Adhesiveness,"
> a natural tenderness, flowing between all citizens, not only men and
> women but also a tenderness between men and men as part of our
> democratic heritage, part of the Adhesiveness which would make the
> democracy function: that men could work together not as competitive
> beasts but as tender lovers and fellows. So he projected from his own
> desire and from his own unconscious a sexual urge which he felt was
> normal to the unconscious of most people, though forbidden for the most
> part.

In an earlier poem, "A Supermarket In California," addressed to
Whitman "lonely old courage-teacher," Ginsberg wondered whether they could ever "stroll dreaming of the lost America of love?" In

Planet News this question is reiterated with a graphic insistence, as at the end of "Journal Night Thoughts":

> I come in the ass of my beloved, I lay back
> with my cock in the air to be kissed—
> I prostrate my sphincter with my eyes in
> the pillow, my legs are thrown up
> over your shoulder,
> I feel your buttocks with my hand
> a cock throbs I lay still my
> mouth in my ass—
> I kiss the hidden mouth, I have a third eye
> I paint the pupils on my palm, and an
> eyelash that winks—

Ginsberg has been progressing steadily in the tradition of Henry Miller toward a description of particulars that once would have been regarded as obscene or scatological ("How big is the prick of the President?" he humorously queries in "Wichita Vortex Sutra"), but which Ginsberg sees as natural speech. Whitman had proclaimed that copulation was no more rank than death, that both had aspects of holiness, and in "Song of Myself" there are several descriptions of mystical ecstasy that are rendered with the metaphor of masturbation (recalling Ginsberg's Blake visitation). Whitman's "prurient provokers" and "red marauders," as well as his *Calamus* poems, suggested a potential for American letters (which few except Henry Miller have had the courage or the folly to fulfill) that leads to poems like "This form of Life needs Sex" in *Planet News*. Sexuality, both as release and as a trigger for latent psychic energies and realizations, in short as a vehicle for awareness and liberated consciousness, has been an object of repression for a long time in America and Ginsberg has taken many public risks to widen those particular perceptual gates.

In "Please Master" (which appears in *The Fall Of America* as a part of a series of elegies to Neal Cassady), Ginsberg writes one of his most memorable poems, perhaps the finest attempt by an American poet to describe physical love between two men. The refrain of the title suggests Ginsberg's obeisance, his desire to accept both the rough and gentle pleasures of anal sex. Though the poem is exceptionately graphic, it never loses its undertones of warmth:

Please master can I lick your groin curled with blond soft fur
Please master can I touch my tongue to your rosy asshole

The poem's movement is from the initial disrobing, to courtly preliminaries, to easing entry and more lunging, ravishing penetration. Despite its violence, it sustains its tone of tender supplication, fusing the phallicism with receptivity of love. "Please Master" is characteristic of the Beats' frankness, their lack of shame or guilt, their openness to new subject matter.

As far as obscenity is concerned, there is an interesting and revealing difference between Burroughs and Ginsberg that is analogous to the pessimism of the Dadaists and Breton's belief that Surrealism could lead to a general revolutionary awakening. While both Burroughs and Ginsberg deny ordinary guilt and shame, Burroughs employs sex viciously to create the consciousness of suffering; Ginsberg is always endearing, "charming" is the word he used before Judge Hoffman, always in accord with Blake's "naked human form divine" and Whitman's "I keep as delicate around the bowels as around the head and heart." The Beats, as Michael McClure argues in *Meat Science Essays*, intended to free the word *fuck* from its chains: "The obscenity barrier is raised by censorship and fear. It is built by a fear of the natural and the idea that nature is obscene." Ginsberg has always reveled in the divinity of his own sexuality, his homosexuality, adoring his own physical propensities and urging the life of the body on his readers.

Planet News, Ginsberg's poems of the sixties, marked a sharp resurgence of power, containing at least six splendid poems: "Television was a Baby Crawling Toward that Deathchamber," "The Change," "Kral Majales," "Who Be Kind To," "Wichita

Vortex Sutra," and "Wales Visitation." In *Planet News*, the demands of the self so insistently pronounced in the earlier poetry are modulated to harmonize with the larger concerns of the earth, and the poet's role in dramatizing those concerns. The first and last poems in the collection, both on the dangers inherent in the American military system, form an envelope for inner unities. No one seems to have noticed the way in which so many of the poems lead into each other and relate organically (as earlier *Kaddish* consisted of a number of elegies). In *Planet News* these interconnections—"Lost in Calcutta" pointing directly to "The Change"—are part of a grand network of the poet's awareness of the planet as he travels through India, Japan, California, New York, Havana, Warsaw, Prague, and London. Ginsberg is essentially a city man writing about city life with a gregarious impulse to engage and contend with cosmopolitan energy centers.

What is most impressive about *Planet News* is Ginsberg's sense of himself and his place in the general order of things. He acknowledges an obligatory role as the prophetic witness of American imperialism—kind of a Rudyard Kipling in reverse—in "Television was a Baby Crawling Toward that Deathchamber," a lengthy and innovative poem about technological control over consciousness that is reminiscent of Burroughs:

> Screech out over the radio that Standard Oil is a bunch of
> spying Businessmen intent on building one Standard Oil in
> the whole universe like an egotistical cancer
> and yell on Television to England to watch out for United Fruits
> they got Central America by the balls
> nobody but them can talk San Salvador, they run big Guatemala
> puppet armies, gas Dictators, they're the Crown of Thorns
> upon the Consciousness of poor Christ-indian Central America
> and the Pharisees are US Congress & Publicans is the
> American People

The poem, dense with associations that create a labored, staccato rhythm, builds to a point approaching hysteria as Ginsberg denounces the "Six billionaires that control America" and focuses on historic Paterson which he imagines (as Burroughs once saw Times Square crawling with centipedes) as devoid of human life. Ginsberg feels all the more impelled to address "all these lacklove/ suffering the Hate" who have been conditioned by the forces of those six unnamed controllers:

> all day I walk in the wilderness over white carpets of City, we
>   are redeeming ourself, I am born,
> the Messiah woke in the Universe, I announce the New Nation,
>   in every mind, take power over the dead creation,

"Television was a Baby . . . " is a continuous cadenza, practically one long obsessive sentence of locomotive propulsion. Its spurting, trumpeting, ranting tone of indictment might be too much to bear were it not for Ginsberg's characteristic humor, his sense of the bizarrely comic absurdity of things, carrying "subversive salami" in his ragged briefcase as he put it in *Reality Sandwiches.*

The sense of speaking directly to a "new nation" (the notion of a constituency emerging from the radical activities of the sixties) with a messianic message of salvation is continued in "Kral Majales," a poem about the enthusiastic reception of Ginsberg by Prague students under the hostile surveillance of the Czechoslovakian police and secret agents who followed Ginsberg everywhere. The poem is a denial of the conspiratorial military-police closure on consciousness—communist and capitalist—and a joyous recognition of the Dionysian "King of May" spirit which, as Plato warned, has always been the great catalyst for change:

> And I am the King of May, that I may be expelled from my
>   Kingdom with honor, as of old,
> To shew the difference between Caesar's kingdom and the
>   Kingdom of the May of Man—

The poem depends on a sense of Blakean antithesis, the heavy industry and heavy heart of communism and the "shutdowns" of

national statism in Cuba, America, or Czechoslovakia, dominating
the first half of the poem, then with a sudden violence, an utter lack
of any transition, changing into an ebullient and soaring celebration
of the May Day festivities—ironically appropriated by world communism, but actually, as Ginsberg implies, belonging to the "new
nation" of freed spirits who accept the hegemony of man over state.

In "Wichita Vortex Sutra," a ritual declaration of the end of the
Vietnam War, part of a longer project called "These States,"
Ginsberg offers a view and a prayer for that "new nation":

> No more fear of tenderness, much delight in weeping, ecstasy
>   in singing, laughter rises that confounds
>   staring Idiot mayors
>   and stony politicians eyeing
>   Thy breast,
>   O Man of America, be born!

This is a potential that Ginsberg first commemorated in *Kaddish*'s
"Ignu," an "angel in comical form" that attends to life with
passionate intensity, with the social concerns of Blake and Whitman,
with the abandon of Rimbaud, and the native American surrealistic
antics and anarchistic tactics exemplified by the Marx Brothers (as in
Kerouac's poem, "To Harpo Marx" where Harpo steals the silver-
ware at a party and sprays the guests with insect repellent). For
Ginsberg, as for Kerouac, fools, idiots, hobos, and social pariahs like
the retarded Iddyboy in *Doctor Sax* serve to extend our general
notion of what it means to be human, and often represent potentials
of almost saintly purity because they are uncontaminated by the
social games and lures that so easily corrupt the rest of us.

In "Who Be Kind To," as in "The Change," Ginsberg suggests
that it is now time to turn from Rimbaud's hedonistic and socially
irresponsible escape into adventurous sensations to face the problems of this world, the looming dangers of planetary biocide. "The
Change: Kyoto-Tokyo Express" describes Ginsberg's own evolution
from a destructively obsessive refusal to deal with the social realities
of the West (by traveling in India and taking drugs) to a desire to

"open the portals to what Is." The poem virtually declares that the despair of the time of "Howl" is no longer justified as an end, that it was only the beginning of consciousness but not a program:

> Come, sweet lonely Spirit, back
> to your bodies, come great God
> back to your only image, come
> to your many eyes & breasts,
> come thru thought and
> motion up all your
> arms the great gesture of
> Peace & acceptance Abhya
> Mudra Mudra of fearlessness
> Mudra of Elephant calmed &
> war-fear ended forever!

"The Change" also signals a return for Ginsberg to the tensions of a tightly involuted line, still dependent on surreal dislocations of image, and rhythmic power of voice, but for the moment more compactly self-contained than even the *Empty Mirror* poems. As in "Journal Night Thoughts" or "Wichita Vortex Sutra," Ginsberg reveals an encouraging curiosity about new modes of presentation and formal arrangement.

"Who Be Kind To" is both an advisory and a benediction to the radical spirit in our time, urging the discoveries of "The Change" on a wider audience while wishing for its preservation and continuity: "Be kind to yourself, because the bliss of your own/ kindness will flood the police tomorrow." Ginsberg exhorts:

> For this is the joy to be born, the kindness
> received through strange eyeglasses on
> a bus through Kensington,
> the finger touch of the Londoner on your thumb,
> that borrows light from your cigarette,
> the morning smile at Newcastle Central
> station, when longhair Tom blond husband
> greets the bearded stranger of telephones—

The poems ends with another vision of the "new man" that reappears throughout *Planet News*:

> That a new kind of man has come to his bliss
> to end the cold war he has borne
> against his own kind flesh
> since the days of the snake.

Planet News is imbued with the vatic sense of the seer one finds in the best of romantic poetry, and the authenticity one feels after speaking with someone who has undertaken a long hazardous journey and returned with informing insights. Perhaps the most beautiful poem in the volume, certainly in the Wordsworthian spirit of communion with nature and the transport this can impart, is "Wales Visitation," a poem written while taking LSD that successfully captures the sense of energy flow animating all living things that the drug seems to enhance. The poem flows musically with what Pound called the tone leading of vowels, and succeeds particularly in eliminating all sense of self. Instead of a human center, it lavishly records the flux of phenomena:

> Out, out on the hillside, into the ocean sound, into delicate
>   gusts of wet air,
> Fall on the ground, O great Wetness, O Mother, No harm on
>   thy body!
> Stare close, no imperfection in the grass,
>   each flower Buddha-eye, repeating the story,
>   the myriad formed soul
> Kneel before the foxglove raising green buds, mauve bells drooped
>   doubled down the stem with trembling antennae,
> & look in the eyes of the branded lambs that stare
>   breathing stockstill under dripping hawthorn—
> I lay down mixing my beard with the wet hair of the mountainside
>   smelling the brown vagina-moist ground, harmless
>   tasting the violet thistle-hair, sweetness—
> One being so balanced, so vast, that its softest breath
>   moves every floweret on the stillness on the valley floor,
>   trembles lamb-hair hung gossamer rain-beaded in the grass,

lifts trees on their roots, birds in the great draught
hiding their strength in the rain, bearing same weight

In Ginsberg's most recent work, *The Fall of America*, long series of
poems on the spiritual condition of "these States" during the sixties,
the idea of the "fall" develops out of "Howl." In a notebook dating
back to 1957, Ginsberg wrote:

> Therefore I prophecy the Fall of America
> Bitter, bitter tongue to tell

The Fall of America shows Ginsberg moving closer to Kerouac's
conception of the writer as memoirist: much of the book is drawn
from journal transcriptions, or composed directly on the tape
recorder as Ginsberg traveled about the country by car, plane, and
train. The book records a cumulative pain, the anguish of Vietnam
all the more wrenching because of the lies of "progress" as the nation
Ginsberg observes suffers its most intense self-confrontation since
the decade of abolitionist fury before the Civil War. More than *Howl*
or *Kaddish*, this is Ginsberg's most despairing and least affirming
book, haunted as it is by a constant sense of doom. Instead of the
ecstatic resources of drugs or mysticism, the only relief Ginsberg
projects—like Burroughs in *The Wild Boys*—is an apocalypse of
self-destruction. Perhaps this new irredeemable despair is responsible for the purgatorial tone of the collection. In *Planet News*, travel,
movement in space and time, was treated adventurously, euphoric-
ally, expectantly. But in *The Fall of America*, the motion is burdened, deliberate, weighted with sorrow and seriousness, unallevi-
ated by new impressions or expectations, restricted somehow to the
boundaries of a country in its saddest hour.

The basis of *The Fall of America* is an Emersonian correspondence:
the violence of Vietnam is reflected in an inner violence, the
destruction of foreign war is complemented by the devastation of
our own natural environment. Ginsberg sees the external misadven-
ture and the internal blindness of what we have done to our own

land as organically related—like the Buddhist notion of karma that promises that any present action will affect future incarnations, or the biblical maxim on sowing and reaping. Ironically, the poem is dedicated to Whitman and prefaced by the selection from *Democratic Vistas* on adhesiveness, the sense of male comradship that Whitman supposed would spiritually leaven American materialism. But Ginsberg's own tone is uninspired by Whitman's cheer. With brutal relentlessness, in poem after poem, Ginsberg's eye fixes on the pocks of industrial spoilage scarring the face of the land.

In *The Fall of America*, the Moloch of "Howl" has finally consumed our youthful hope, transforming any Jeffersonian aspirations of a society whose real strength was rooted in the back country to an infernal view of belching smokestacks, Poe's red death pervading the acrid atmosphere. Ginsberg, in his half-century on the planet, has been a Tiresian witness to this harrowing change:

```
I was born there in Newark
     Public Service sign of the 'Twenties
          visible miles away through smoke
               grey night over electric fields
My aunts and uncles died in hospitals,
          are buried in graves surrounded by Railroad Tracks,
               tombed near Winking 3 Ring Ballantine Ale's home
                    where Western Electric has a Cosmic plant,
     Pitt-Consoles breathes forth fumes
               acrid above Flying Service tanks
          Where superhighway rises over Monsanto
                    metal structures moonlit
          Pulaski Skyway hanging airy black
                         in heaven my childhood
          neighbored with gigantic harbor stacks,
                         steam everywhere
     Blue Star buses skimming skyroads
          beside th' antennae mazes
               brilliant by Canalside—
```

Everywhere, the horror is the city's filth spilling over into the countryside, festering contamination and scourge, the land blighted, wasted and prone to plague like Thebes before the exorcism of Oedipus:

> Living like beasts,
> befouling our own nests,
> Smoke & Steam, broken glass & beer cans,
> Auto exhaust—
> Civilization shit littering the streets,
> Fine black mist over apartments
> watercourses running with oil
> fish fellows dead—

Ginsberg extends the scope of the disaster with a pop mosaic of complicity, a collage of simultaneous data, actual sensory details and historical referents, mixing news of Vietnam atrocities and establishment apologies—like Ambassador Lodge's infamous Christmas Eve assertion that the United States was morally justified in its actions—with the new American landscape of hamburger advertisements, motels, automobile junkpiles:

> Car graveyard fills eyes
> iron glitters, chrome fenders
> rust—
> White crosses, Vietnam War Dead
> churchbells ring
> Cars, kids, hamburger stand
> open, barn-smile
> white eye, door mouth.

The technique is primarily juxtaposition—the smell of burning oil and an advertisement for mouthwash—and no overt comment is needed because of the graphic quality of the depiction. In "Friday The Thirteenth," the natural correspondence becomes more explicit:

Earth pollution identical with Mind pollution, conscious-
    ness Pollution identical with filthy sky,
dirty-thoughted Usury simultaneous with metal dust in wa-
    ter courses
murder of great & little fish same as self besmirchment
        short hair thought control
mace-repression of gnostic street boys identical with DDT
        extinction of Bald Eagle—
Mother's milk poisoned as fathers' thoughts, all greed-
        stained over the automobile-body designing table—

Ginsberg's bias is humanistic and international. The awful power of American industry with its iron landscape of "Triple towers smokestacking steaming," of open-hearth furnaces and the smells of creosote and butane replacing alfalfa and wheat, seems to Ginsberg to be designed to burden the rest of the world, to kill peasants in South America or Asia. In a sense Ginsberg has turned a full circle, returning to the damned terrain of Eliot's wasteland, but now without the remotest flicker of hope. The agonized cry in "Northwest Passage" of "Wallula Polluted! Wallula Polluted! Wallula Polluted!" recalls the mounting wail of despair which Eliot expresses in "The Fire Sermon":

        Weialala leia
        Wallala leialala

The vision of a new nation, and a resurgence of life-forces that Ginsberg envisaged in *Planet News* has been blurred by fire and smoke, but is not yet extinguished despite the politics of repression. Ginsberg vaunts his fury with a Blakean sense of purpose, lashing his own resolve to "haunt these States" in "A Vow":

Common Sense, Common law, common tenderness
        & common tranquillity
our means in America to control the money munching
        war machine, bright lit industry
everywhere digesting forests & excreting soft pyramids
    of newsprint . . . .

With the ferocity and anger of Ezra Pound, Ginsberg threatens in "War Profit Litany" to list the names of the companies who have profited through the war in Vietnam, their corporate directors and major stockholders, the banks and investment houses that support them. In "Returning North of Vortex," Ginsberg startlingly (in 1967) appeals for an American military defeat in Vietnam, prophesying that we will lose our will. Ginsberg's passion reaches an apex here, a point of crisis which diminishes, or changes course, with a group of elegies to Neal Cassady.

The vision then shifts from the city to his own farm in the country. Living without electricity, surrounded by animals rather than the carrion of stripped cars in the city, this more pastoral dimension functions ironically in the book, as a backdrop by which to measure the ruination of the land. There are very few lyrical moments in the book (as in "Easter Sunday") which are not used to contrast some discordantly jarring industrial rapacity. The finest poem in the volume is a vision of this unsettled pastoral, "Ecologue," a long account of winter preparations on the farm that is impinged upon by the consciousness of Vietnam, of the incipient fascism Ginsberg feels in his country, of "millions of bodies in pain." The poem pivots on omens of disaster, and uses the picture of the farm as a microcosm of the larger breakdown of civilization.

Ginsberg himself becomes one of the correspondences in *The Fall of America*: his automobile accident near the end of 1968, and a fall on the ice several years later, are a synecdoche of the general collapse he sees about him. In his earlier work, no matter how dispiriting or anguished the degree of torment, the voice was always powerful enough to sustain the reader, to suggest that existence depends on resistance and active effort, on the definition of a direction whose goal might be pleasure or personal salvation, but whose purpose would be to free the individual from the Circe of materialism. In *The Fall of America*, however, Ginsberg seems temporarily disoriented, despite the power of his invective:

Now I don't know who I am—
    I wake up in the morning surrounded
                by meat and wires,
        pile drivers crashing thru the bedroom floor,
War images rayed thru Television apartments,
Machine chaos on Earth,
        Too many bodies, mouths bleeding on every
                                        Continent,

In "Death On All Fronts," a poem revealing the dominating
influence of Burroughs' vision in *The Fall of America*, Ginsberg
admits to being unable to find order or even solace in his own work.
In "Friday The Thirteenth" he wonders about the efficacy of poetry,
its ability to raise consciousness in the presence of the implacable
destructiveness in the world. These are very real questions for a poet
who has aspired to millennial prophecy, and who has exerted
himself so energetically in realizing a particular vision of the world.
Part of Ginsberg's gift as a poet has been his faith in vision that has
been characteristically American because of its bouyance, its ability
to return with hope despite disaster. Like the American transcen-
dentalists, that vision has been the fruit of wonder and a voyaging
imagination. To discover the new, one needs to have faith in old
tools. In *The Fall of America*, that faith seems to have been
profoundly shaken. Perhaps, too, this is why Ginsberg has temporarily shifted from bhakti yoga—delight in song—to long periods of
meditation, up to ten hours a day for weeks on end.

Allen Ginsberg's poetry is a record of surprising conversions—
from the tersely unfulfilled anguish of *Empty Mirror*, the rage of
"Howl," the mourning dirge of "Kaddish," the bare brutalities of
Reality Sandwiches, the celebratory incandescence of *Planet News*, the
apocalyptic terrors of *The Fall of America*. The poems exist not only
as a formidably substantial body of work, but as a demonstration
that poetry need not be disembodied, removed from a natural base
in chant and song. Rhythm, Ginsberg has shown his own generation, is less a matter of seeing the poem on the page than hearing it

sounded. As with Indian mantras or traditional religious meditation, the effect is to slow the consciousness flow, to change ordinary conditioning so that new perceptions can occur. The words repeated aloud assume a new transporting density, become a kind of magical incantatory vehicle for body and nonconceptual sensation as well as mind. The poems are made to be sung; the singer uses them to see what is there and what possibilities lie beyond. Ginsberg's most recent readings show that he is headed in a folk and blues direction enriched by the discipline of lengthy meditation and Eastern mantra. "Allen Ginsberg's naked dance" Gary Snyder called it years ago in a letter from Japan: it has been the bardic dance of our day, shocking the word from the security of the printed page and spinning it into our very midst.

Afterword

ULTIMATELY, *the significance of a literary movement may be measured by its vision of the world. The inflection of the Beat writers has been more political than that of most of their contemporaries. Hopeful questers in an era of gutted national ideals, they have been even more perplexed than the rest of us by irreconcilable interpretations of the American potential. The heritage of American transcendentalism had promised an amicable cooperation in a land populated by nationalities as heterogeneous as Melville's crew on the* Pequod, *but graced by a more trusting atmosphere, responsive to social experiment and vigilantly guaranteeing civil rights. While such an ideal resonates through American creative expression, it has been threatened since the end of the Second World War by the oppressive demands of a technocracy imposing the rhythm of the machine and the idea of military enclave on the resources and spirit of a free society. This dialectic of the private and the monolithic has been the crucial political tension in our history.*

*"The attitude of great poets is to cheer up slaves and horrify despots," Walt Whitman once proclaimed, and the Beats have vigorously responded to this standard. Books that once seemed so anomalous—*Howl, On The Road, Naked Lunch—*can now be read as celebrations of both inextinguishable aspiration and terrible despair. Their cadence has been what Emerson called the "military attitude of the soul." While the humanitarian values of the Concord group were announced from a podium of respectable eminence, the*

Beats were regarded as brigands of the underground; they had to find new ways to remind their culture of the dignity of self-reliance and to provide an Emersonian awareness of the tyranny of institutions. Execrating the worldly, dreading the implications of control, they chose to consecrate the whims of the individual. Ecstatic iconoclasts, youthful seekers of what Kerouac called "potent and inconceivable radiances," they simultaneously heralded an impending apocalypse and dramatized the irrational, the oral, and the improvisatory to provoke the end of an omnipresent stupor. The Beats attempted to transform consciousness by merging the Symbolist stress on sensations with the Surrealist tactic of absurd encounter and in doing so found a new style.

As our last romantics in a time of muteness, their strategy was a philippic of excess. In the fifties, they were condemned as hysterics of hyperbole in the manner that Carlyle dismissed Rousseau's "delirations": "His Ideas possessed him like demons; hurried him about, drove him over steep places." Harried by a vision of the end of everything, the Beats were possessed by an Orphic song of alternatives. The "steep places" of complacent acquiescence to the comfortably acceptable in politics and prosody were overcome by a fever of engaged commitment.

"People wish to be settled," Emerson wrote. "Only as far as they are unsettled is there any hope for them." Emerson predicted the contest of the "genuine self against the whole world," and the Beat pendulum swung from delirium to clairvoyance, from an enthusiastic embrace of American energy to monastic seclusion in the work of the word. The velocity animating their style was based on intuition, an impulsive resistance to dogma that Emerson characterized as magnanimity: "Heroism feels and never reasons . . . . [It is] an obedience to a secret impulse of an individual's character." The Beats tested their private knowledge by redefining popular notions of sanity and extending the borders of social prudence. They earned their healing powers shamanistically, suffering personal psychological crises while articulating the "unspeakable visions of the individual."

Once the Beats were a few Lears raging in the storm, obscured by the vastness of the system. Their transformation of literary form and the informing power of what they had to say aroused mounting interest. A growing audience responded to their expression of libertarian values while recognizing them as prophets of the future. Perhaps the receptivity of that audience was inevitable, for sometimes—as Burroughs observed when comparing Kerouac to Fitzgerald—the effect produced by writers is immediate, as if a generation were waiting to be written.

Notes and Acknowledgments

THE MATERIAL in the first two sections of this book is largely based on the twenty boxes of letters in the Ginsberg Deposit at Columbia University which contains correspondence between Allen Ginsberg, Jack Kerouac, William Burroughs, and others who have figured in this study. The second major source is at the Humanities Research Center in Austin, Texas where there are many letters by Ginsberg, Kerouac, and Neal Cassady. I have also used a number of previously published interviews, and tape recorded my own with Allen Ginsberg, William Burroughs, Herbert Huncke, Carl Solomon, and John Clellon Holmes. I spoke with Lucien Carr and Lionel Trilling, and corresponded with numerous others who were intimates of the writers under discussion here.

THE BROKEN CIRCUIT:

The title for this section as well as some of its ideas were derived from my long interview with John Clellon Holmes that appeared in *The Beat Book*, edited and published by Arthur Winfield Knight and Glee Knight (P.O.Box 439, California, PA. 15419). The correspondence of 1957–65 relating to Buddhism between Gary Snyder and Philip Whalen (Reed College collection) and Snyder's essay, "Buddhism and the Coming Revolution," *Earth House Hold* (New York: New Directions, 1969) were invaluable. Other general sources were Jack Kerouac's "Origins of the Beat Generation,"

Playboy (June, 1959), Vol. 6, No. 6, John Clellon Holmes' "The Philosophy of the Beat Generation," in *The Beats*, ed. Seymour Krim (New York: Fawcett Publications, 1960), and Thomas Parkinson's *A Casebook On The Beat* (New York: Thomas Y. Crowell, 1961).

FIRST CONJUNCTIONS:

William Burroughs.

I interviewed Burroughs on March 24, 1974. The *Paris Review* interview by Conrad Knickerbocker is collected in *Writers At Work: The Paris Review Interviews*, Third Series, Introduced by Alfred Kazin (New York: Viking Press, 1967). Robert Palmer's interview of Burroughs appeared in *Rolling Stone* on May 11, 1972. Laurance Colinson and Roger Baker's interview with Burroughs appeared in *Gay Sunshine* (P.O.Box 40397, San Francisco, CA. 94140) in the spring of 1974. Two other helpful interviews were Winston Leyland's of Harold Norse in *Gay Sunshine* in June, 1973, and "Conversations in Morocco: An Interview with Paul Bowles," Michael Rodgers, *Rolling Stone*, May 23, 1974. Some of the details of the composition of *Naked Lunch* come from Paul Bowles' "Burroughs in Tangier," *Big Table* (Summer, 1959), Vol. 1, No. 2. Burroughs' South American travels are described in *The Yage Letters* (San Francisco: City Lights, 1963). Burroughs' life in Tangier is described by his son in *Kentucky Ham*, William Burroughs, Jr. (New York: Dutton, 1973). A number of fascinating details can be found in the *Catalogue of the William S. Burroughs Archives*, compiled by Miles Associates (London: Covent Garden Press, 1973). Many of Burroughs' letters and manuscripts are owned by the International Center of Art and Communication at Vaduz, Lichtenstein.

Jack Kerouac.

Ted Berrigan and Aram Saroyan interviewed Kerouac for the *Paris Review* (Summer, 1968), No.43. The best biographical treatment is by John Clellon Holmes in *Nothing More To Declare* (New York: Dutton, 1967). Holmes graciously allowed me to study his own unpublished journals from 1948 to

1951 and to read his large collection of letters from Jack Kerouac. I also studied the letters Kerouac wrote to Malcolm Cowley which are at the Newberry Library, and Joyce Glassman allowed me to read her letters from Kerouac. A necessary perspective was provided by Ann Charters' *Kerouac: A Biography* (San Francisco: Straight Arrow Books, 1973). Some of the material on Neal Cassady comes from his autobiography *The First Third* (San Francisco: City Lights, 1971). I am also indebted to Allen Ginsberg, John Clellon Holmes, and William Burroughs for their recollections.

Allen Ginsberg.

The *Paris Review* interview by Thomas Clark is collected in *Writers At Work: The Paris Review Interviews*, Third Series, Introduced by Alfred Kazin (New York: Viking Press, 1967). Paul Carroll interviewed Ginsberg for *Playboy* (April, 1969), Vol.16, No.4. Alison Colbert interviewed Ginsberg for *Partisan Review* (1971), Vol. 38, No.3, and my own "Conversation with Allen Ginsberg" appeared in *Partisan Review* (1974), Vol. 41, No.2. Perhaps the most revealing interview is by Allen Young, *Gay Sunshine Interview* (Bolinas: Grey Fox Press, 1974). The episode with Herbert Huncke that led to Ginsberg's period at Psychiatric Institute is detailed in an unpublished diary called "Journal of the Fall" in the Columbia Archives. My interview with Huncke appeared in *Unspeakable Visions of the Individual*, edited by Arthur Winfield Knight and Glee Knight, Vol. 3, No. 1. My interview with Carl Solomon appeared in *The Beat Book*. Diana Trilling's "The Other Night At Columbia," *Partisan Review*, (1959), Vol. 26; Jason Epstein's "The Chicago Conspiracy Trial: Allen Ginsberg On The Stand," *The New York Review of Books*, Febuary 12, 1970; and Jane Kramer's *Allen Ginsberg In America* (New York: Random House, 1968) were useful sources for this chapter.

THE BOOKS:

The Black Beauty of William Burroughs.

An excellent source for Burroughs' narrative theory is *The Job: Interviews with William S. Burroughs*, Daniel Odier (New York: Grove Press, 1969).

Minutes To Go, a collaboration by Sinclair Beiles, William Burroughs, Gregory Corso, and Brion Gysin (Paris: Two Cities Editions, 1960), provides an invaluable introduction to the cut-up. An unpublished essay called "The Future of the Novel" in the Columbia Archives is also an important document. The most perceptive criticism of Burroughs is found in Mary McCarthy's "Dejeuner Sur Herbes," which appeared in the first issue of *The New York Review of Books* in February, 1963, Tony Tanner's chapter on Burroughs in *City of Words* (New York: Harper & Row, 1971), Marshall McLuhan's "Notes on Burroughs," *The Nation*, Vol. 199, No. 21, and Eric Mottram's *The Algebra of Need* (Buffalo, N. Y.: Intrepid Press, 1970).

Jack Kerouac: Eulogist of Spontaneity.

Kerouac's publications are itemized in *A Bibliography of Works by Jack Kerouac*, compiled by Ann Charters (New York: Phoenix Book Shop, 1967). The theory of this chapter was outlined in my review of *Visions of Cody* that appeared in *Partisan Review* (1973), Vol. 40, No. 2. Kerouac's "The Essentials of Spontaneous Prose" appeared in *Evergreen Review* (Summer, 1958), Vol. 2, No. 5. "Belief and Technique For Modern Prose" appeared in *Evergreen Review* (Spring, 1959), Vol. 2, No. 8. "The Last Word," Kerouac's statement on sentence structure, originally appeared in a little magazine called *Escapade*, (Spring, 1959), Vol. 3, and was quoted in a review of *The Dharma Bums* in *The Saturday Review* on May 2, 1959. An important document is Allen Ginsberg's unpublished "Notes On Kerouac's Prose" in the Columbia Archives. Ginsberg's comments on the original manuscript of *On The Road* are from his review of *The Dharma Bums* which is reprinted in *The Village Voice Reader*, eds. Daniel Wolf and Edwin Fancher, (New York: Doubleday, 1962). Ginsberg's comments on Kerouac's style in *Allen Verbatim*, edited by Gordon Ball (New York: McGraw-Hill, 1974), and in the introduction to *Visions of Cody* are the best criticism of Kerouac's work. Another excellent essay is Seymour Krim's introduction to *Desolation Angels* (New York: Bantam Books, 1966).

Allen Ginsberg and the Messianic Tradition.

Ginsberg's books are listed in George Dowden's *A Bibliography of Works by Allen Ginsberg* (San Francisco: City Lights Books, 1971). Two important documents in the Columbia Archives, both undated, helped my understanding of Ginsberg's prosody: "14 Notes On the Development of Modern Poetry" and "A Few Notes On Method." Ginsberg also comments on his own techniques in *Indian Journals* (San Francisco: City Lights, 1970), in *Improvised Poetics* (San Francisco: Anonym Press, 1972), and in the interview collected by William Packard in *The Craft of Poetry* (New York: Doubleday, 1975). George Dardess transcribed Ginsberg's "Beat Poetry Seminar" at Tufts University, October 26, 1970.

I have been assisted by the generous cooperation of Allen Ginsberg, William Burroughs, John Clellon Holmes, Carl Solomon, Herbert Huncke, Lucien Carr, and Carolyn Cassady. I wish to also thank Malcolm Cowley, Lionel Trilling, Keith Jennison, John Montgomery, Arthur and Glee Knight, Rlene Dahlberg, Marshall Clements, Morris Dickstein, and Michael Timko. My mentor over the years, Leon Edel, was always encouraging. William Phillips, Barry Wallenstein, and Harold Jaffe read various parts of the manuscript and offered useful suggestions. George Dardess shared some of his research and helped me with several provocative letters and discussions. I am indebted to Kenneth Lohf of Columbia University Special Collections, to David Farmer of the Humanities Research Center at the University of Texas in Austin, to the Reed College Library, and the Newberry Library. I am also grateful to have been awarded a Fellowship from the National Endowment to the Humanities in 1974 which freed me from teaching so that I could complete this book. My greatest debt, however, is to my editor, Joyce Johnson, whose constructive criticism was most helpful in shaping this book.

Selected Bibliography

WILLIAM BURROUGHS

The Exterminator. New York: Viking Press, 1973.
Junkie. New York: Ace Books, 1953.
Naked Lunch. New York: Grove Press, 1959.
Nova Express. New York: Grove Press, 1964.
The Soft Machine. New York: Grove Press, 1966.
The Ticket That Exploded. New York: Grove Press, 1966.
The Wild Boys. New York: Grove Press, 1969.

JACK KEROUAC

Big Sur. New York: Farrar, Straus & Giroux, 1962.
Desolation Angels. New York: Coward-McCann, 1965.
The Dharma Bums. New York: Viking Press, 1958.
Doctor Sax. New York: Grove Press, 1959.
Lonesome Traveller. New York: McGraw-Hill Book Company, 1960.
Maggie Cassidy. New York: Avon Books, 1959.
On The Road. New York: Viking Press, 1957.
Scattered Poems. San Francisco: City Lights Press, 1971.
The Subterraneans. New York: Grove Press, 1958.
The Town and the City. New York: Harcourt, Brace, 1950.
Tristessa. New York: Avon Books, 1960.

Visions of Cody. New York: McGraw-Hill Book Company, 1972.
Visions of Gerard. New York: Farrar, Straus & Giroux, 1963.

ALLEN GINSBERG

Empty Mirror. New York: Corinth Books, 1961.
The Fall of America. San Francisco: City Lights Press, 1972.
Howl. San Francisco: City Lights Press, 1956.
Indian Journals. San Francisco: City Lights Press, 1970.
Kaddish. San Francisco: City Lights Press, 1961.
Planet News. San Francisco: City Lights Press, 1968.
Reality Sandwiches. San Francisco: City Lights Press, 1963.

INDEX

ABOUT THE AUTHOR

Born in Antwerp, Belgium, in 1939, John Tytell was educated in the New York City public school system. He attended the City College of New York, completed his doctoral dissertation on the fiction of Henry James at New York University in 1968, and in 1974 was awarded a Younger Humanist Fellowship from the National Endowment to the Humanities. He was the editor of *The American Experience: A Radical Reader,* and his articles have appeared in *Partisan Review, The American Scholar,* and *Commonweal,* among other publications. Since 1965 Dr. Tytell has taught at Queens College, where he is currently Associate Professor of English.